SACRED SUBDIVISIONS

Sacred Subdivisions

The Postsuburban Transformation of American Evangelicalism

Justin G. Wilford

NEW YORK UNIVERSITY PRESS
New York and London

NEW YORK UNIVERSITY PRESS
New York and London
www.nyupress.org

References to Internet websites (URLs) were accurate at the time of writing.
Neither the author nor New York University Press is responsible for URLs that
may have expired or changed since the manuscript was prepared.

LIBRARY OF CONGRESS CATALOGING-IN-PUBLICATION DATA
Wilford, Justin G.
Sacred subdivisions : the postsuburban transformation of American evangelicalism / Justin
G. Wilford.
p. cm.
Includes bibliographical references (p.   ) and index.
ISBN 978-0-8147-2535-1 (cl : alk. paper)
ISBN 978-0-8147-7093-1 (pb : alk. paper)
ISBN 978-0-8147-0830-9 (ebook)
ISBN 978-0-8147-0839-2 (ebook)
1. United States—Church history—21st century. 2. Church growth—United States—
History—21st century. 3. Evangelicalism—United States—History—21st century.
4. Saddleback Valley Community Church (Mission Viejo, Calif.) I. Title.
BR526.W533 2012
277.3'083—dc23   2012024951

New York University Press books are printed on acid-free paper,
and their binding materials are chosen for strength and durability.
We strive to use environmentally responsible suppliers and materials
to the greatest extent possible in publishing our books.

Manufactured in the United States of America
c 10 9 8 7 6 5 4 3 2 1
p 10 9 8 7 6 5 4 3 2 1

For Audra, Max, and Maesie

CONTENTS

LIST OF FIGURES

LIST OF TABLES

ACKNOWLEDGMENTS

This book would not have happened without the many different kinds of help I received. My wife, Audra, provided me encouragement, criticism, inspiration, and resources from the beginning to the end of this project. I could not have written this book without her. At the University of California–Los Angeles, Nick Entrikin, John Agnew, Nick Howe, and Tristan Sturm provided crucial insight and support all along the way. Also, Michael Curry, Denis Cosgrove, Pablo Fuentenebro, and Timur Hammond all read and gave valuable feedback on different chapters and versions of the manuscript.

I am indebted to Richard Flory and Donald E. Miller at the University of Southern California's Center for Religion and Civic Culture for listening, reading, responding, and encouraging at several crucial junctures. I would also like to thank the many individuals who have personally shaped my thinking on the variety of issues raised in this book: Richard Dagger, Jack Crittenden, Avital Simhony, Stefan Dolgert, Nan Ellin, and Allison Coudert during my time at Arizona State University; Setha Low, Marshall Berman, Mitchell Cohen, and Richard Wolin at the CUNY Graduate Center; and John Broughton at the Teachers College Columbia University. Even though we have never met, the scholarly work of Jeffrey Alexander, Robert Fishman, and Christian Smith has been absolutely crucial to this project. I also greatly appreciate the thoughtful comments of my editor at NYU Press, Jennifer Hammer, and the anonymous reviewers of the manuscript. This book is a better one because of them.

The several dozen congregants I came to know at Saddleback Church were unfailingly kind and generous. Many of the pastors were incredibly giving of their time and worked hard to help me understand what they do and how they do it. I am especially grateful to the Saddleback small group on that one cul-de-sac, in that one neighborhood. A more caring and committed group of individuals I have not met.

Finally, I thank my friends and family for emotional support. Greg and Terri Wilford, Ted DiPadova, Laurie DiPadova-Stocks, Hugh Stocks, and Anthony Skinner were all important participants in the creation of this book. In different ways, you all inspired me to work, think, and write better.

1

Introduction

Postdenominational Evangelicalism, Saddleback Church, and the Postsuburbs

Orange County, California, has a contradictory reputation. It is known simultaneously as the home of insular, conservative retirees (Richard Nixon being the most famous) and also as the setting for the shallow, plastic libertines of the reality television series *The Real Housewives of Orange County*. It is considered to be a high-tech hub for computers, military technology, and industrial design while also a center for major global surf and skate retailers. It is as straight-laced and traditional as it is laid-back and iconoclastic.

On many warm, sunny Sunday afternoons in south Orange County, this contradiction can be seen in the flesh when a heavyset, middle-aged man in a comfortable T-shirt and swim shorts wades into a fountain that would not be out of place in a new suburban, open-air mall. Surrounded by a crowd that sometimes numbers in the dozens and other times in the hundreds, he has an easy, jovial control over his audience. As the sun glistens off the water splashing around his considerable belly, others begin to line up near the edge of the fountain. On this Sunday, the first to join him is a ten-year-old named

Kyle. His parents and extended family, pushed now to the edge of the fountain, cheer as he wades close enough to the older man to hug him.

The man keeps his left arm snuggly around Kyle and raises his right as he speaks. The crowd immediately attunes to his words. In a friendly, comfortable manner, he tells them that this is his favorite activity because his father once did this to him. He tells them that this is a symbolic act not *the real act*. He tells them that they have already accomplished *the real act*, and now through this act they can tell the world about what has happened to them. He tells Kyle to cross his arms, and lean back. "I baptize Kyle in the name of the Father, the Son, and the Holy Spirit," he says gently as Kyle leans backwards, becoming fully immersed in the water. "As you are buried with Christ in death, you are raised to walk in the newness of life." The crowd cheers as if the boy had a hit a home run. And the next one in line wades over to the half-soaked, fully cheerful man in the fountain.

This man is Rick Warren, a multimillionaire, best-selling author, and megachurch pastor who gives away 90 percent of his income. The fountain, though indistinguishable from one in any contemporary mall or office park, is part of the 120-acre campus of Saddleback Valley Community Church, known more commonly as "Saddleback" to Orange County, California, residents. Baptism scenes like this take place dozens of times a year at Saddleback's main campus, usually after the largest weekend services. In what appears to be any place but a church, often dozens, sometimes hundreds, and, on rare occasions, thousands line up to be baptized "in the name of the Father, the Son, and the Holy Spirit." The sprawling campus blends seamlessly into the Orange County landscape of well-manicured office parks, oversized shopping and entertainment districts, high-end subdivisions and condominiums, and meticulously maintained freeways. A mundane space as this, so accommodating to the secular design aesthetics of newly sprouted sprawl, is a frontline in a battle for souls.

Saddleback Church is one of the largest and most influential evangelical megachurches in America. Its pastor, Rick Warren, is author of *The Purpose Driven Life*, a book that has sold more than 40 million copies, as well as *The Purpose Driven Church*, the best-selling church-growth manual in the history of the genre.[1] In fact, "purpose driven" has become a popular brand of its own in American evangelicalism. The term, Warren argues, denotes a set of key purposes that should be at the focus of every Christian and church community, but it more subtly implies an alliance with Warren's broader theology and church-growth strategies. There are now "purpose driven" spin-off books, websites, church conferences, business strategies, addiction recovery programs, self-help regimens, and even sports camps.

In 2011 Saddleback held its highest attended Easter service in its history, bringing in over 50,000 churchgoers through the course of Easter weekend. Just weeks before the holiday, this south Orange County megachurch baptized more than 1,000 people in an afternoon after its introductory membership class (in 2008, they baptized some 2,600 before Easter). In the previous three years it planted three new satellite campuses, each drawing hundreds in their first weeks and now growing rapidly. And in the midst of the worst national financial turmoil since the Great Depression, it increased its revenue and operating budget to an all-time high of $47.9 million.

All of this growth and burgeoning attendance has occurred despite that fact that contemporary America is seen by many to be a nation losing its religion.[2] In a series of recent polls on religious attitudes and behaviors in the United States, the American religious landscape is shown to be quite fluid and fragmented, far from one nation under God. One of these polls, conducted by the Pew Research Center, showed a near majority of respondents switching denominations or faith traditions throughout their lives. It also showed that a strong majority of religious adherents in the United States are quite tolerant of other faiths and thought that "many religions can lead to eternal life."[3] In early 2009, the American Religious Identification Survey (ARIS, a large national survey of religious attitudes conducted previously in 1990 and 2001) showed a historical decrease in religious adherence over the previous decade and a half.

Both the Pew and ARIS studies garnered quite a bit of attention. In the spring 2009 these surveys, alongside smaller post-election surveys, drove cover-page and above-the-fold headlines such as, "Losing Faith in Modern America," "More People Say They Have No Religion," "Almost All Denominations Losing Ground," and "The End of Christian America."[4] The president of the Southern Baptist Theological Seminary, R. Albert Mohler Jr., exclaimed, "The most basic contours of American culture have been radically altered. The so-called Judeo-Christian consensus of the last millennium has given way to a post-modern, post-Christian, post-Western cultural crisis which threatens the very heart of our culture."[5]

If America has entered a secular, post-Christian era, evangelical churches like Saddleback have found a winning counterstrategy. This book looks at the ways churches like Saddleback are growing in size and influence while older, mainline churches and denominations continue a decades-long decline in membership. However, while there are many excellent studies of thriving contemporary evangelicalism, this book examines the particularly geographical strategies these churches employ in their quest for growth and relevance. This requires looking at and listening to not only *what* they say and do but *where* they are saying and doing it. From this perspective, place (and other geographical concepts such as space, landscape, and scale) emerges not only as a setting or stage for religious action but as fundamentally integral to such action. The strategies that lead to Saddleback's growth and influence, then, are in part geographical. They are not just bound to their geographical settings, but they are also densely composed of geographical representations— of "the church," "the family," "the believer," "home," "the world," "the globe," and, most importantly, their postsuburban environment—the sprawling, freeway-laced landscape that is the setting for Saddleback and thousands of evangelical churches like it.

These geographical representations work within a set of cultural performances, acts that draws on deep cultural structures of meaning that bind or fuse individuals together in groups both small and large. This cursory definition relies on the recent work of the sociologist Jeffrey Alexander and others who argue that cultural action cannot be reduced to economic or political interests, and that effective cultural action "fuses" the elements of performance: actor, background culture, audience, setting, and structures of power are all seamlessly woven together in successful cultural acts, while they are "de-fused" or disconnected in unsuccessful ones. I explain in greater detail in chapter 3 that performance is a useful metaphor for cultural-geographical action because it alerts us to the ways such action, when it is successful, creates and is created by *place.*

The performances of Saddleback and churches like it work, in part, because they seamlessly incorporate everyday places into larger evangelical narratives, fusing them with deep religious themes and thereby transforming everyday places into religiously meaningful places. Through sermons, weekly small-group meetings in members' homes, monthly training classes on evangelism, religious service, and worship, and the more intimate exercise of prayer and fellowship, Saddleback members recast places in their lives as sites of spiritual self-transformation. The freeway, the office cubicle, the soccer field are no longer mundane locales; they are made holy by incorporating them into evangelical narratives of grace, salvation, and holiness, which are crafted within the organizational infrastructure of Saddleback Church. Far from withdrawing from these mundane and secular places, Saddleback draws them into webs of sacred significance that its pastors and members co-create. The church sanctuary at Saddleback, then, becomes but one religious island in a sea of religious potentiality. This is in sharp contrast to "traditional" religious performances that rely on strictly marking and separating secular and sacred place.[6] Sacred place achieves its power precisely because it is sharply bounded and removed from everyday life. But these new evangelical performances blend the sacred and secular so that the secular becomes only the *potential* for the sacred, not its opposite. From one perspective, the sacred in these performances invades every crevice of daily life, but it is this invasiveness that also makes them so fragile. The proximity of the secular and sacred in late modern societies means that invasion and corruption goes in both directions, with the sacred in peril as much as the secular. But more than this, what makes these performances precarious and unstable is the geographic paradox that lies at their core. The paradox is that these evangelical churches are aimed at, and must cohere within, an understanding community even as their location in postsuburban peripheries means that they lack such a community.

Overwhelmingly, the contemporary evangelical "local" is situated in what is often referred to as the suburban fringe, exurbia, sprawl, or postsuburbia. By any name, the most common site for large and growing evangelical congregations is on the multi-functional periphery of large metropolitan centers. Almost all of the largest and most influential evangelical churches are in such postsuburban locales as Bill Hybels's Willow Creek Community Church outside of the Chicago metropolitan area (23,500 weekly attendees), Kerry Shook's Fellowship of the Woodlands on the periphery of Houston (15,600 weekly attendees), or Andy Stanley's North Point Community Church on the edge of Atlanta (17,700 weekly attendees). Rick Warren's Saddleback Valley Community Church in postsuburban Orange County, California, with its 22,000 weekly attendees, is perhaps the most famous. Clearly, the metropolitan periphery is fertile ground for some of the largest, most innovative and influential evangelical churches in America. But is it the ground—the cultural geography, the built environment of postsuburbia—that is so fertile? It is not just the felicitous socio-spatial context of postsuburbia that allows these churches to grow to such sizes and exert such influence. Their success is rather the product of a very active but tenuous collaboration between church organizers, postsuburban constituents, and postsuburbia as a cultural and material place. In other words, successful evangelical churches are culturally responding to both their social and spatial environment.

To say that Saddleback's success is due to it responding to its environment is to restate a set of influential explanations of recent evangelical popularity that cohere around what is broadly conceived as the religious market model.[7] From this perspective, churches are firms that deal in supernatural goods, and they thrive in an open religious market so long as they respond effectively to the needs and desires of local communities as potential customers. As the sociologist of religion R. Stephen Warner puts it, "religious institutions flourish when they reflect, as well as engage, the cultures of the people who are their local constituents."[8] But what does it mean for postsuburban evangelical churches to respond to the cultures of local communities when the latter are newly formed, fragmented, dispersed, and transitory, as post-suburban communities typically are?

The evangelical church does not simply survive in its postsuburban environment, it thrives. This presents the religious market approach with two problems. First, the post–World War II American metropolitan periphery is socially and spatially fragmented with few homogenous communities expressing clearly delineated values, needs, and desires. The broad sea change in consumer preferences postulated by proponents of the religious market approach assumes a relatively coherent and homogenous group of churchgoers.[9] But this jibes neither with the socio-spatial environment of postsuburban evangelical churches nor with these churches' highly differentiated and dispersed organizational structures. The second but related problem is that the largest, most popular and influential churches reach well beyond a local area for constituents. Even if homogenous and coherent local communities exist in postsuburbia, the evangelical church's reach is so geographically vast that no single local community could be its sole target. In other words, what it would mean to "reflect, as well as engage, the cultures of . . . local constituents" in a postsuburban evangelical church is not immediately clear.

The religious market approach, though, has a larger and more general problem. It forestalls the question of meaning. If a church is a firm that deals in supernatural goods—goods that are inextricably connected to "existential" or "fundamental" meaning[10]—and its congregants are customers, we have explained very little by referring to the effective marketing campaigns of successful congregations.[11] The real question is how meaning is made, shared, and negotiated. The religious market approach, in essence, reinterprets the question of variation in religious popularity by re-envisioning the effects of pluralism; it does little to explain such popularity. To explain why churches, in this case, postsuburban megachurches, are successful, we must get to the heart of the matter: the socio-spatial work of making, sharing, and negotiating meaning.

By looking at such work as a set of *performances,* the postsuburban megachurch seems to reconfigure its local environment in ways that infuse the secular geographies of postsuburbia with spiritual significance. The mundane spaces of recreation, consumption, and labor become stages for spiritual self-transformation. A strictly critical approach to these socio-spatial performances would surely find them embodiments of false consciousness, enactments of self-delusion, self-grandeur, and self-therapy. While this project does not absolutely eschew such an approach, it is above all an effort to "give a brother's account of belief," in the words of the literary critic James Woods, rather than treating sincere religious action as "some unwanted impoverished relative."[12] This so-called brother's account is concerned with how practitioners of American evangelicalism use the spatiality and materiality of their postsuburban environment to make their lives meaningful. Such an account is based on the premise that every act of inhabiting, using, and thinking about a place is an act of meaning-making[13] and therefore open to the charges of false-consciousness, self-delusion, and so forth. To take such geographic meaning-making seriously is to focus on not only what is false about such acts but what is also, in the very same instance, true.

Megachurches, Evangelicalism, and Saddleback Valley Community Church

There is no more perfect expression of American evangelical vitality than the megachurch. While technically a century-old phenomenon (and by no means evangelical in origin), megachurches did not become identified with evangelicalism until their rapid proliferation in the 1970s and 1980s.[14] When they became popularly known in the 1980s and 1990s, especially through the soft-edged "seeker" megachurch, Chicago's Willow Creek Community Church, and the hard-edged, fundamentalism of Jerry and Jonathan Falwell's megachurch, Thomas Road Baptist Church in Lynchburg, Virginia, the many variations were quickly conflated in the popular imagination.[15] One reason for this is that the common definition of a megachurch is any congregation with more than 2,000 weekly attendees. Such a definition makes it easy to speak of megachurches as a unitary phenomenon. This is especially the case when the most prominent examples of megachurches, both within the United States and internationally, share many important characteristics. But it is important to note that there are significant differences.[16]

The most important differences are in aesthetic and organizational style. By contrast, the theological differences are minimal. Most megachurches can be considered nondenominational evangelical. The most recent and authoritative data on megachurches[17] shows that of the one hundred largest megachurches, only four have mainline denominational affiliations. An overwhelming majority (68) are either nondenominational or part of the loosely organized Southern Baptist Convention (SBC) or Calvary Chapel network (see the appendix for a detailed table). The former type is best exemplified in Willow Creek Community Church or Joel Osteen's Lakewood Community Church, and the latter two in Rick Warren's Saddleback Valley Community Church (SBC) and Chuck Smith's Calvary Chapel in Costa Mesa, California.

While these churches and the thousands of smaller counterparts are not connected by any formal structure (again, save for those connected with the loosely networked SBC and Calvary Chapel), they are strikingly similar. Donald E. Miller's characterization of the typical nondenominational evangelical church (in his words, "the new paradigm church") highlights several similarities:

> The typical new paradigm church meets in a converted warehouse, a rented school auditorium, or a leased space in a shopping mall. These meeting places boast no religious symbols, no stained glass, and no religious statuary. Folding chairs are more common than pews. At the front is a stage, often portable, which is bare except for sound equipment, a simple podium, and sometimes a few plants. People come to worship in casual clothes that they might wear to the mall or a movie. On a warm day, they might wear shorts and a polo shirt. The clergy are indistinguishable from the audience by dress.[18]

Behind these few stylistic accommodations to contemporary white, middle-class American tastes, lies an unwavering commitment to traditional evangelistic orthodoxy. From its inception, evangelicalism was a broad religious movement that nevertheless worked through the distinct ideology, symbolism, and materiality of the individual's relationship with God. Against religious formalism, early evangelicals like John Wesley, George Whitefield, and Jonathan Edwards advocated for a personal religious transformation through an intimate relationship with the spirit of Jesus Christ. The mass revivals in eighteenth-century England, Ireland, Scotland, and New England were backdrops to the accounts by these evangelicals of specific individual, spiritual awakenings.[19] Evangelicalism, from its beginning, has focused primarily on the individual *qua* individual. Its pietist origin, stressing above all an "inward spiritual renewal," is evident in the common defining elements of evangelicalism: "new birth" through the acceptance of "Christ's redeeming work on the cross" (conversion and crucicentrism), the ultimate authority of the Bible (biblicism), and an engaged sharing of one's faith with nonbelievers (activism).[20]

Contemporary American evangelicalism is a diverse movement containing countless refinements of each of these elements.[21] However, our focus here is not on American evangelicalism per se, but rather on one particular configuration that I call "postdenominational evangelicalism" (PDE). The overarching characteristic of PDE is its unbending concern with engaging contemporary secular life with the goal of converting the "unchurched" and retaining the already churched. Several other terms have been coined for this subset of evangelicals, such as "postdenominational confessionalism" "seeker," "neo-evangelical," and "new paradigm."[22] The problem with using these terms is that they are either too broad or too narrow. For example, "seeker" is a well-known and fairly precise term used to describe churches that are intensely concerned with reaching the "unchurched." However, it is sometimes used in contrast to other evangelical churches that are focused on pastor-centered, charismatic worship or on culturally contemporary churches interested in a more explicit devotion to doctrine.[23] Churches like Saddleback, Willow Creek, and North Point, however, are variegated institutions that include these other styles of evangelicalism. What is needed, then, is a term that captures the similarities between different large and influential postsuburban evangelical churches. Therefore, PDE is the term devised to categorize a subset of evangelical churches that share important religious, organizational, and geographic characteristics.[24] Among these are:

1. A loose denominational or nondenominational church structure[25]
2. An overarching and fundamentally guiding concern with evangelizing (spreading *evangelium*, the "good news") to the unchurched and underchurched (i.e., their growth is not meant to be at the expense of other churches)[26]
3. Weekend and weekday services that are produced in multiple contemporary idioms[27]
4. Services and programs that have a markedly therapeutic style and message[28]
5. Internal church structures that are highly segmented to accommodate smaller demographic niches within the church[29]
6. A highly conservative and traditionally evangelistic theology[30]
7. A location typically on the extreme periphery of large cities, what I will call postsuburbia[31]
8. A heavy reliance on small groups of members, no more than fifteen in each group, which meet in each other's homes—as opposed to a central church campus—at least once a week to share about their daily lives, pray together, and participate in Bible studies or prepared church programs.[32]

Saddleback Valley Community Church embodies each of these characteristics (see chap. 7, n. 37, for a full description of small groups). Planted in a far-flung postsuburban high school gymnasium on an Easter Sunday in 1980, Saddleback has pioneered or perfected over the years many of these postdenominational elements. After attending an SBC seminary in Texas in the mid-1970s, its pastor, Rick Warren, received various levels of support from SBC contacts in planting his new church (including help from the Southern Baptist Director of Missions in Orange County, California). However, the word "Baptist" would not be a part of the church's name nor would it be advertised at any of the weekend services. For Warren, the key goal was to grow a church by reaching those without a church, but denominational affiliation was not the way to do it. Warren spent his first three months in Orange County going door to door, surveying residents on their views of churches (expressly following the example of megachurch pioneer, Robert Schuller[33]). His respondents, according to Warren, found churches to be insular cliques unconcerned with their real-world, daily problems. Warren writes, "What seemed interesting to me about our survey was that none of the complaints from the unchurched in our area were theological. I didn't meet a single person who said, 'I don't go to church because I don't believe in God.'"[34] In this environment, denominational affiliation would do little to attract new churchgoers and could possibly repel them.

These marketing strategies—along with several others, such as delivering therapeutic and easily applicable sermons, producing high-quality, upbeat, and cutting-edge worship services, and promoting and maintaining small groups—have proved quite winning. With over 22,000 weekly attendees, an almost $50 million annual operating budget, and the cultural capital to have its church and pastor *invited* into American presidential politics, Saddleback is not only a prime example of the popularity and influence of PDE churches, it is also a leader of this movement. From 2005 to 2009 it held at least five international conferences a year on its main campus in which hundreds and sometimes thousands of pastors and staff from around the United States and the world would come to learn about the "purpose driven" methods of church planning and growth. Additionally, Warren claims that through these conferences, his pastoral resource website, and international consulting, Saddleback has led more than 500,000 pastors "in purpose driven training."[35] Saddleback, then, is not just a popular, influential church in south Orange County. Its influence is felt nationally and globally.

Secularization, Postsuburbia, and the
Flexibility of Religious Community

The success of Saddleback and PDE churches in general is notable not simply because their attendance numbers are large, local financial impacts significant, or cultural presence widely felt. Rather their success calls for closer examination because they are growing within a larger context of secularization. This does not mean that PDE churches are growing as *individuals* become more secular, although there is evidence for this. Instead, PDE churches are growing as their *socio-spatial context* becomes more secular. This assertion runs against the grain of the growing assumption of secularization theory's demise.[36] The most sophisticated renderings of secularization theory provide a useful foundation for understanding how PDE churches grow within a larger context of pluralism and differentiation (what I later refer to as cultural de-fusion). From this perspective, secularity (as opposed to secular*ism*, a particular historical ideology) is a macro-social situation in which explicitly religious practice becomes differentiated from secular spheres of action such as the market, state, and civil society. As religion is confined to its own sphere of action, no single religious group receives formal support from the state, and thus all religious groups are (theoretically) free to participate within this religious, differentiated sphere of action. Because this means that any incursions by religious groups into the market, state, and civil society can be seen as illegitimate, religious practice becomes an ultimately local phenomenon.[37] Therefore, the success of religious organizations is dependent on their appealing to local communities.

The socio-spatial situation of religious organizations in the United States is one of differentiation (of social spheres and functions), fragmentation, and diversity. This is even more true for PDE churches because of their spatial location in postsuburbia. Suburbia and postsuburbia can be seen as the spatial manifestation of the social differentiation at the core of secularization theory. Just as the specialization of different spheres of social action was integral to the emergence of the nation-state, techno-scientific bureaucracy, capitalism, and civil society, so it was integral to the specialization of space. For the present study, the most important specialized differentiation of space occurred between work-space and family-space because this separation is at the heart of suburban form and function.

The differentiation of work-space from family-space was conceived, perceived and lived as one of center and periphery.[38] This spatial binary was fused with cultural binaries so that the peripheral spatiality of the family, home, emotions, meaning, and spiritual life became opposed to the central spatiality of society, work, rationality, economic interest, and politics. However, these cultural binaries became blurred and reconfigured as the nature of suburban spatial differentiation changed. With the rise of the automobile, the socio-spatial experience of center and periphery was inverted so that the home came to be the center of everyday life and anything within reasonable driving distance was periphery.[39] This inversion of center and periphery is the apotheosis of the logic of spatial differentiation. The result is not only a spatial fragmentation of contemporary U.S. cities (evinced in such adjectives as "multi-nodal," "multi-polar," "satellite," and "edge"), but also a social fragmentation of daily life.

The most significant result of socio-spatial differentiation for explaining the success of postsuburban PDE churches is not anti-modernist withdrawal, white-flight revanchism, or consumerist decadence. It is the fragmentation of daily life, experienced in a variety of ways. Members of Saddleback in south Orange County related feelings of absence, loss, and emptiness in their stories ("testimonies" in evangelical parlance) about becoming Christians and members of Saddleback. Of course, these are old themes in Protestant narratives of salvation. But for Saddleback members these stories were experienced in terms of an absence not of salvation, grace, or God's love, but of social orientation. The terms "aimless," "lost," or "disconnected," and explanations like "I didn't know where I was going in life," and "I needed something to center my life on," were elaborations on one of Saddleback's signature themes: Purpose. Often these stories of salvation, or of simply deciding to attend Saddleback over another nearby church, were about the radically different and usually opposing demands of work-life and family- or personal-life that led to what was later interpreted as a fractured sense of purpose. What spoke to this work/family tension for many of these Saddleback members were (1) the sermons that related directly and easily to mundane but crucial problems in work and at home' (2) the diversity, accessibility, and flexibility of the numerous programs and events at the church; and, (3) later on, the communal intimacy of small home groups. The sermons, programs, and small groups came to serve as threads that sewed together the differentiated, fragmented aspects of these members' lives.

Or at least this is how many of the stories went. What I began to see over time at Saddleback, however, was how this megachurch was just as socially and spatially fragmented, and its membership just as dynamic and flexible, as its postsuburban environment. Despite the stories of Saddleback members that suggest communal reintegration (from socio-spatial differentiation) and the stated mission of Saddleback to continuously deepen the connection of its members to the "body of Christ" (i.e., the church), I saw members (both newer and older) take very fluid and variegated approaches to church belonging. Because sermons are streamed and archived online, a member could skip attending a week or several and still not miss a single message. Or if the amount of time it would take to stream a sermon is too much, the member could catch the highlights in a Tuesday night small group. If, alas, Tuesday night won't work, this week or the next, someone from small group will email or post a message on a Facebook page, just checking in. In all likelihood, this member will be back at small group next week, sincerely thankful for the messages.

There are more than twenty different programs and services that this member could attend every week. What this means in practice is that if she misses anything at all, it will come around again. The same holds for weekend service: if she misses the Saturday evening service at 4:30, there will be six others that weekend. And if she has not attended small group in such a long time that she would feel awkward going back, there are over 3,800 other small groups to choose from. And these small groups? They are in homes scattered across southern California. Chances are there is a small group meeting in a home a couple of blocks away. What this means is that the religious community at Saddleback is no *gemeinschaftlich* (community-like) gathering, bound by repetition, ritual, and homogeneity. Like its surrounding postsuburban environment, Saddleback is a dispersed, multi-nodal, multi-scaled network through which individuals link up in varying degrees with other individuals.

The linking of individuals at Saddleback is never taken for granted precisely because there is no communal center. There are, of course, the weekend services and the central "worship center." But in a paradoxical inversion that fits perfectly with the logic of postsuburbia, the weekend services at the worship center are seen by Warren and his staff to be peripheral to the "core" of Saddleback. During interviews with Saddleback pastors and staff, I was often referred to Warren's "5 Circles of Commitment" (see fig. 1. 1) in efforts to explain how different programs were targeted to different types of churchgoers. It was striking to me that the weekend service and church campus—the spatial and performative center of Saddleback Church—are designed to appeal to the periphery of this concentric ring model, particularly the "community" and "crowd." The community is the mass of individuals within reasonable driving distance of Saddleback, while the crowd is the group of people who attend weekend services but do not get further involved. The most spatially diffuse programs—small groups in members' homes and global missions work—were designed for the center of the concentric rings, the "congregation," "committed," and "core." The closer one gets to the "center" of the Saddleback practice of Christian faith, the farther away this practice is from the spatial center of the PDE church.

Saddleback and the Performance of Secular Postsuburban Space

American Protestantism has suffered a steady delegitimization over the course of the twentieth century. This story is told in a number of ways that

cohere around the theme of pluralization. A proliferation not only of disparate lifestyles but of disparate life-spaces has led, in the words of the sociologist Jeffrey Alexander, to a "de-fusion" of legitimating rituals for all large
scale institutions.[40] In other words, the fragmentation of shared meaning has
made "authentic" performances very difficult to enact because, for a large-
scale audience, there is little chance of fusion between background cultural
codes and cultural action. From a geographic perspective, the finer the scale
and more localized an audience, the greater the chance that cultural codes
will be shared and thus a proficient performance will fuse these elements
together in a seemingly "authentic" way.

"Performances in complex societies seek to overcome fragmentation
by creating flow and achieving authenticity," writes Alexander. "They try
to recover a momentary experience of ritual, to eliminate or to negate the
effects of social and cultural de-fusion."[41] In this sense, secularity is the state
of widespread social and cultural de-fusion. It is an environment in which
the background cultural-religious codes are no longer fused with shared
narratives, symbols, and performative acts. The challenge then for religious
entrepreneurs is to find ways to re-fuse these elements.

The innovative success of PDE churches have come through a conspicu-
ous amalgamation of widely shared secular narratives, symbols, and places
with narrower, explicitly evangelical Christian narratives, symbols, and
places. Whereas Marx's moderns "anxiously conjure[d] up the spirits of the
past to their service,"[42] these PDE churches conjure up the spirits of the present to serve doctrines and liturgy of the past. This dynamic appropriation
of contemporary, secular culture by evangelicals has been widely noted.[43]
But such appropriation is largely seen as aesthetic, as a change in musical
style, architecture, or multimedia use. From a cultural geographic perspective, however, the performance of secularity by PDE churches has meant a
fundamental transformation in the spatiality of the church. An effective re-
fusing of religious performance with its socio-spatial environment requires
that the church enacts the spatial fragmentation of postsuburbia. Performing
secularity, then, is not just about adding a hard rock venue on Sunday or
designing the "worship center" (not a chapel or cathedral!) in the image of
a shopping mall. It means that the church must become as diffuse, localized,
and fragmented as its urban environment.

At Saddleback, the performance of postsuburbia is held in three acts. The
first act is produced for the outer two rings of Warren's "5 Circles of Commitment" (see fig. 1.1). The weekend service is designed for the "community"
and the "crowd," specifically to appeal to the "unchurched" community and
encourage them to become part of the Saddleback crowd. The design and

FIGURE 1.1 Saddleback's "5 Circles of Commitment." Adapted from Warren, *Purpose Driven Church*, 130.

production of these weekend services and other main campus programs work to reconfigure major postsuburban themes of expressive individualism, loneliness, gender identity, and work/life balance. These themes are *re*-presented as thoroughly spiritual ones that are fully understandable only when linked to larger evangelical narratives of salvation, sin, and the necessity and fulfillment of a personal, intimate relationship with Jesus Christ. The latter narratives are worked over in countless ways on the main campus, through themes of masculinity (in Thursday morning's men's Bible study called "The Herd"), self-improvement (as in "Leadership Training" classes), or self-therapy (through sermons titled "Life's Healing Choices," "You Really Can Change," and "A Lifetime of Growth").

The second act is staged in the residential home. Every week more than 3,800 Saddleback small groups meet in homes around southern California. These groups—in other PDE churches they are referred to as "cell groups," "life groups," "community groups," "neighborhood groups," or "home fellowships"—are considered by Saddleback to be the "foundation" and "backbone" of everything else the church does. This is where casual members, "the crowd," are turned into committed members, "the congregation" and "the committed." Typically made up of six to twelve members, these groups meet once a week (typically on a weeknight, but some groups meet during the weekend) and are structured for casual and even intimate social interaction. A small group meeting will typically begin with informal conversation as individuals or couples arrive. As everyone finds a seat, usually in an ad hoc circle in the family room, someone, usually the host, calls for an opening prayer. Afterward, the host, who usually undergoes hours of training overseen by Saddleback pastors, asks individuals to share about their triumphs and tragedies—"praises and prayers"—from the previous week. Following this, groups typically engage in a prepared curriculum by Saddleback or another PDE church such as Willow Creek. Sometimes groups will choose to do a month-long study of a book in the Bible, or other times choose a popular Christian book, such as *The Shack,* to read and discuss.[44] These groups, however, do more than "close the back door of the church," in the words of Warren. They are sites where individuals are encouraged to integrate the disparate narratives, symbols, and places of their own fragmented lives within a coherent narrative of evangelical holiness. This holiness, in earlier evangelical generations, was tied to visible self-improvement through the grace that comes from a personal relationship with Jesus Christ. The term "holiness" is rarely used in PDE performances, but its central theme of tangible, evident behavioral transformation through a relationship with Jesus is the touchstone of PDE practice. When Warren writes and speaks of "The Purpose Driven Life," this is what he means. The practice of holiness is meant to be complete and holistic, and is meant to cover every aspect of one's life. This integrative all-encompassing aspect becomes a crucial element in the performative recasting of secular postsuburbia into sacred space.

If the first two acts are staged at the scale of the home and the urban region, the final act attempts to stage itself at the global scale. The most ambitious new project at Saddleback, elements of which have spread to other PDE churches, is a global missionary effort in which thousands of lay members are trained and sent on short-term missions abroad to work with local churches. Its innovative nature lies in the fact that it is effectively a democratization of missionary work. The history of Christian missions is one in which the central actors have been denominations, para-denominational missionary organizations, quasi-professional missionaries, and the targeted communities who were to be Christianized. For Saddleback and other PDE churches following its lead, only this last group has continued relevance. The effort to democratize missionary work, regardless of its effects on the ground in the targeted regions, is a further performance of postsuburban evangelicalism that is meant to incorporate the mundane places of home, work, and shopping within a larger narrative of world-historic, spiritual significance. From the stories and symbols of the global south—of Africa, South Asia, and Latin America—to the months-long training and preparation within classes and small groups, to the weeks-long experience itself, and finally to the reincorporation of the experience back in south Orange County, this democratization of missionary work provides one more thread that weaves together the disparate narratives, symbols, and places of postsuburban Orange County.

Methods

This project is based on participant observation conducted over the course of eighteen months, from January 2008 to July 2009, in south Orange County, California. During this time I lived in Ladera Ranch, an unincorporated master-planned community only a fifteen-minute drive from Saddleback. I regularly attended Saddleback weekend services, a small home-group in the Mission Viejo area (and visited several others), and various programs, training sessions, and conferences held on the central campus. I conducted formal open-ended interviews with five pastors, six staff members, and twenty-eight congregants in addition to having off-the-record, informal conversations, some quite in-depth, with dozens of additional staff and congregants. Interview subjects were selected through convenience sampling, that is, through meeting in church services, small groups, training seminars, or church conferences. I also met several congregants in the Ladera Ranch neighborhood, at parks and at local eateries. Most of the pastors interviewed I contacted through email but also met personally either on the church campus or at nearby eateries. I collected weekend brochures, training materials, small-group study guides, various handouts, and a vast amount of website material (mostly Saddleback websites, blogs, and twitter feeds). I also took detailed notes on my daily experience of the people, places, and landscapes of south Orange County. I coded and analyzed all interviews, textual material, and notes using an inductive coding scheme that drew on both "sensitizing concepts" (themes, terms, and symbols used from theoretical and historical research) and "indigenous concepts" (themes, terms, and symbols that emerged from the data).[45]

Outline of the Book

The early chapters of this book are devoted to elaborating on the theoretical groundwork of the main argument: that Saddleback and PDE churches more generally have incorporated postsuburban strategies for making religious meaning in and through a larger environment of secularity. In chapter 2, we see that secularization theory may not explain or predict an absolute decline in religiosity. It is, instead, a set of descriptions and explanations of how Western societal differentiation and pluralization has led to a relative decline in religious authority and legitimation. This means that on a macro-social scale, churches are hindered from enacting effective cultural performances, but on the local scale a host of opportunities are still present. For Saddleback and other PDE churches, effective performances will speak to narratives of individuality, family, and local place instead of larger societal matters related to the state, the market, and civil society.

Chapter 3 elaborates on the analytical role culture and performance play in understanding the innovative spatiality of PDE churches. Through the lens of cultural performativity, we can see that the socio-spatial actions of a church like Saddleback can be analyzed as a series of differentiated and fragmented performances designed to make meaning out of a differentiated and fragmented socio-spatial environment. I go on to focus on how this environment—postsuburban local place—is assembled into meaningful performances by evangelical churches. Postsuburban evangelical congregations do not just "make community" (as it is often said)—these churches actively mobilize both cultural texts and the socio-spatial environment in ways that make postsuburban life meaningful—but only rarely in a traditionally collective sense. The PDE assemblage of the discursive and material environment is woven into a panoply of church programs that are narrowly focused and continuously evolving. A performative collaboration between church organizers, postsuburbanites, and postsuburbia-as-a-place opens up spaces for a flexible, fluid, and dynamic religious community.

The next chapters offer examinations of the performances of postsuburban place at Saddleback Church. Chapter 4 explores the weekend services where the collective narratives of Saddleback are presented seven different times over two days, at five different campuses around Orange County, in eight different demographically targeted styles (called "venues"). From the laid-back coffee shop atmosphere of the "Terrace Cafe" service to the ear-splitting rock music of "Overdrive," the Saddleback churchgoer can shop around on Sunday morning (or Saturday night when two services are held at 4:30 p.m. and 6:00 p.m.). The venues are spread around the campus and range from an ad hoc tent revival feeling to a highly produced, MTV-style set. The main service in the "worship center" aims for the broadest audience. The building itself looks like a conservatively designed civic performing arts center, both inside and out. Although each venue attempts its own unique feel, they are all designed with the singular, unified purpose of moving individuals from the "crowd" to the "congregation" and the "committed."

This movement is initiated during the weekend on the main campus (or at a satellite campus) but is completed during the week by participating in a small group in a member's home. Chapter 5, explores the fragmentation and diffusion of the PDE church through the small group. In members' homes every week, thousands of Saddleback members meet and enact their own performances and counterperformances of an evangelically inspired post-suburban life. This weekly diffusion of the church allows for many challenges to arise to the structural and narrative hegemony of the central church. Yet, this very vulnerability allows for rapid and dexterously adaptive responses by the church, through the small-group host in real-time, and also through feedback the hosts give to Saddleback staff and pastors. The dynamic interactions that take place during the week in homes around southern California lead to equally dynamic performances on the weekend.

Chapter 6 follows the intended journey of the Saddleback member to the "core" of the "5 Circles of Commitment" by focusing on the most spatially diffuse program at Saddleback, "Global P.E.A.C.E." The program is a rather innovative effort to democratize missionary work by training and sending abroad lay members to work with local churches around the world. What this chapter looks at is not the effects on the ground of Global P.E.A.C.E. but rather how the program is presented, received, and incorporated within the context of daily life in south Orange County. In this way, I interpret P.E.A.C.E as an additional thread in the weaving together of the disparate, differentiated, and fragmented aspects of postsuburban life. In other words, P.E.A.C.E becomes another way to orient oneself in a centerless cultural-material environment.

It might seem that the focus of this project on the local performance of place belies the recent national and state political involvement of Saddle-back Church and its pastor. How could I argue that the performances of Saddleback are local when it has injected itself into a presidential political campaign and a state ballot proposition controversy? Chapter 7 examines the way Warren and Saddleback Church deftly incorporate supralocal structures, interests, symbols, and narratives without using them in the service of supralocal ambitions. This chapter shows that Saddleback's politics are not political at all. In the end, such events as the "Saddleback Civil Forum on the Presidency" in which Barack Obama and John McCain appeared together for the first time in the 2008 presidential campaign, are rather elaborate performances meant to retell secular stories in a religious key and religious stories in a secular key. The desired result for Saddleback and Warren is not some Falwellian desecularization—a more Christian American government—but rather an increase in saved souls in south Orange County, California.

Conclusion

By looking at postsuburban evangelical megachurches as cultural performances I develop an explanation of both evangelical and megachurch popularity that does not forestall the question of meaning and culture but rather makes them central. As a human geographer, I see meaning and culture as integrally material and spatial, and so the centrality of culture in this book implies the primacy of things and places. But here, things are neither simply goods exchanged in markets, nor merely dead objects upon which culture is inscribed. And here, place is not only a bounded location in which religious firms compete for customers, nor just an inert backdrop in which real action happens. Things and places are seen as active participants in the meaning-making enterprise of religious action. If the postsuburban megachurch meets the "needs and desires," "the tastes and preferences" of its congregants (in the words of religious market oriented sociologists),[46] it does so by mobilizing the things and places of postsuburbia in service of powerful religious narratives that tell participants about who they are, where they came from, and where they are going. Some of these stories are grand, and some are small and narrow. Some of these stories push participants to look beyond their local environs while others draw them into its center, the residential home. But these stories are told through and many times about postsuburban place. Through the endlessly flexible narratives of classical evangelicalism—with themes of salvation through grace, an intimately personal relationship with Jesus Christ, or the manifestation of holiness through self-transformation—the disorienting, fragmented environment of postsuburbia takes on intelligibility, meaning, and design. In other words, it becomes a "purpose driven" place.

2

Sacred Archipelagos

Spaces of Secularization

Incorporating secularization theory into an explanation of the popularity of American evangelicalism might seem counterintuitive and hopelessly out of fashion. It is an obviously odd choice because secularization is most commonly thought to refer to the decline of religious practice. In this present study of one of the most successful and influential religious movements in the United States, secularization theory would seem to offer very little. But it is even stranger still because many observers in the social sciences believe that secularization as a historical process has been thoroughly discredited. In sociology and anthropology, secularization is démodé, while in geography it was never part of any disciplinary debates in the first place.

But if secularization theory, in the words of Christian Smith, is like an "embarrassingly eccentric uncle" whom everyone wishes would leave,[1] the "*post*secular" has been treated with warm hospitality.[2] Although it means many things to many people, postsecular has become an attractive touchstone to those who believe that secularization (as a social process concomitant with modernization), secularism (as a set of beliefs and practices with its own history and politics), and secularity (as the gen-eralized socio-political compartmentalization of religion) are marginal to interpreting and explaining modern religious expressions.[3] The main thrust of such assumptions is that recent spectacular religious expressions such as Islamic fundamentalism, global Pentecostalism, and the American Religious Right serve as prima facie evidence of the "collapse of the secu-larization thesis."[4] Another anti-secular impetus in recent scholarship is the idea that theories of secularization, secularist ethics, and socio-polit-ical secularity are all intimately bound to a modern, neoliberal, imperial-ist ethic of domination, and that postsecular ethics can provide a pivotal energy for political resistance, something that secular liberalism has failed to do.[5]

Both empirically and normatively, then, secularization theory is found to be inadequate. Not only is religion still with us, but its Other—seculariza-tion/secularism/secularity—is seen to be just as problematic. And so what could secularization, specifically, have to offer a study of contemporary post-suburban PDE megachurches? Their very existence seems to demonstrate secularization theory's irrelevance. But what most of these new seculariza-tion critics emphasize empirically is the degree of religious activity they observe, not its continual change and adaptation within specific socio-spatial environments. The term most often used in terse dismissals of seculariza-tion theory is "religious resurgence."[6] But "religion" is not simply "resurgent." Specific religious groups are growing in specific socio-spatial environments. Therefore, what is at stake in studying contemporary religion in America is not the relative growth or relevance of religion as such, but rather how spe-cific religious communities are changing and adapting in ways that allow for their growth and relevance.

From this perspective, the secularization paradigm still has much to offer if it can plausibly account for the socio-spatial environment of con-temporary religious communities in America.[7] And indeed, the most sophisticated renderings of secularization do this by outlining the socio-spatial constraints and affordances facing these religious communities. Therefore, my broader analysis of Saddleback Church and PDE churches like it will hinge on taking secularization as a socio-spatial theoretical framework seriously and not dismissing it as a legitimating ideology for European hegemony, a simplistic "subtraction story", or an embarrassing leftover from nineteenth-century social theory.[8] The secularization para-digm does not, as its critics charge, tell a simple declensionist story. It does not posit a steady emergence of moderns into the light of secularist ratio-nality. It instead sketches out a picture in which we can see that religious organizations face a different set of social limitations and opportunities in advanced, postindustrial milieux than their industrial and preindustrial counterparts did. The charge that the world is as full of religion as it ever was is beside the point of the secularization paradigm because the latter postulates a particular social environment for religion, not necessarily the responses to it. The fact that this is often overlooked in recent debates over secularity and the "postsecular" is in part the result of non-spatial glosses on the broad tenets of the secularization paradigm. But, as geographers have long argued, by spatializing social theory we can begin to see new cracks and fissures as well as new contours and potentials.[9]

Not only does the secularization paradigm have a widely agreed-upon, valid core based on differentiation theory, but this core has unexamined spatial elements and implications. The spaces of secularization are not secular*ist* spaces but are instead spaces in which religious action is constrained and liberated in different ways depending on its socio-spatial scale. The secularity of modern urban space and especially postsuburban space is necessarily partial, fragmented, and dependent upon the socio-spatial scales of religious action. Through the lens of secular differentiation, certain obstacles and opportunities for religious expression in the "secular city" become more apparent. Additionally, while secular differentiation closes off certain religious options, the new options opened up are particularly advantageous for "liturgically lite," symbolically flexible, and spatially supple religious expressions such as the postdenominational evangelicalism of Saddleback Valley Community Church.

Space, Place, and Secularization

Secularization theory is usually traced back to Max Weber and his modern rationalization and disenchantment theses. Here, Weber's "iron cage" thesis of modernity was that calculative efficiency and predictability snuffs out religious or enchanted modes of experience. This Weberian genealogy is often used to highlight secularization theory's supposed teleology. But a different genealogy would lead us back much farther in time to the sixteenth century when the French political philosopher Jean Bodin foregrounded the secularizing tendency of religious diversity. Not the iron cage, but the practical intermingling of religious traditions in an emerging global world would cause the faithful to relax their convictions.[10] It was not until centuries later that the effects of religious diversity along with the Weber's modernizing forces were refined and incorporated into what is now most aptly called the secularization paradigm.[11] Having been formulated in many different ways, its main thrust has been that the project of organized religion loses its social significance as societies modernize. The arguments that make up the paradigm usually include the same key aspects of modernization: rationalism and rationalization, pluralism, industrialization, and urbanization. These modern tendencies, proponents argue, work in conjunction to compartmentalize and privatize modern religious practice.[12] Each secularizing force of modernity is theorized to work on religious belief and practice in a different way. For example, pluralism, by Peter Berger's early account, leads to a "crisis of credibility" for religion in general as "the social definition of reality" becomes a matter of choice.[13] Because no single religion is completely hegemonic in modern societies, Berger argues, any particular religion's claim to absolute truth must always be accepted by the believer as a choice; it is a choice that can be revoked and one that constantly stands in tension with other similarly plausible, but contradictory, choices. To take another example, economic growth and stability, typically accompanying modernization, can be shown to lead to a decrease in fundamentalism and religious adherence in general.[14] Secularization theorists argue that fundamentalism, as a cultural defense of economically and socially marginal ways of life, loses its raison d'etre when incomes rise and the formerly evil ways of modern life become easily attainable.[15]

To most, especially in the fields of sociology and anthropology, the debate over the secularization paradigm has run its course. To the extent that it is still given consideration, it is used as a foil for exploring the apparent "resurgence" of religion in the West. But regardless of secularization's supposed relegation "to the graveyard of failed theories,"[16] it is still a curiously resilient set of descriptions and explanations that remains useful even to its critics. The desire to eliminate the secularization paradigm are oddly balanced by a begrudging acceptance of what is widely considered to be its valid and quite useful core.[17] This can be seen in Charles Taylor's widely discussed description of modern secularity. Despite his critical take on the "subtraction story" of secularization narratives, he accepts much of the work of orthodox secularization theory—that "religious belief and practice has declined, and that [the social significance of religion] is much less now than in the past," and that this can be explained by the Durkheimian (differentiation and pluralization) and Weberian (bureaucracy and rationalization) core in the concept of secularization.[18]

In the study of the geography of religion, however, these questions have barely surfaced. There has been no geographical contribution to the secularization paradigm because the latter is assumed dead.[19] When the idea of secularization is considered, it usually receives passive acknowledgment. It is either shorthand for the absence of religion[20] or the inhospitable nature of modern society for religion.[21] Very little consideration is given to what a secular space/place would be, how it would be structured, and what it would look like. In this way, geographers have accepted many of the dominant academic narratives about secularization, a central one being that secularization and secularity are *social* phenomena. Geographers have made an implicit division between the grounded, embodied, and emplaced religious activities that are thriving in local places[22] (and thus at first glance contradict "*the* secularization thesis") and the structuralist, disembodied, non-spatial levels and processes imputed by the secularization paradigm.

It is true that sociological debates over secularization have generally remained at the level of theoretical abstraction, and when they have been empirical they have been restricted to the "macro" levels of the nation-state or global regions. However, it is certainly not the case that proponents and critics in these debates have ignored geography. For example, defenders of the secularization paradigm, such as sociologist Steve Bruce, are careful to state that the paradigm is only valid for particular Western European and North American regions.[23] The sociologist David Martin, as well, works to explain the historical-geographical variation between and within developed and developing regions of the world.[24] And within the debate over American religious exceptionalism, the distinctiveness of North American regions, such as the "Bible belt," is often taken into account. Several studies even concern themselves with county-level data. But within the secularization debate and the new literature on secularity and postsecularism, very little interest is shown toward the embodied, material, and spatial responses to the confluence of social forces that make up what has come to be known as secularization.

A key reason for such indifference to space/place in sociological research on secularization is that the same social forces that are seen as agents of secularization are also seen as corrosive of place. John Agnew and J. Nicholas Entrikin have shown how modernization theory, of which secularization theory is an offshoot, implicitly and explicitly posits the erosion of the distinctiveness of place by factors such as urbanization, rationalization, and bureaucratization.[25] For social scientists who take modernization (as a multiple and variegated process) seriously, it is anachronistic to speak of place in modernity. If multiple modernities have a single telos, it is a bland cosmopolitanism hollowed out by transnational corporations, global communications, and itinerant populations. In this vision, the *genre de vie* of a particular location in the modern developed world is not significantly different from any other. This antipathy toward the utility of the concept of place can be seen in much of the sociological literature on secularization (for and against) as individuals, organizations, and communities seem to exist only in urban or rural space. These spatial zones practically serve as proxies for levels of modernization and therefore expected levels of secularization. (And, of course, the glee of secularization's critics when they discover the relatively high level of religious adherence in "urban" counties is unsurprising.)

The indifference toward place in the sociological literature on secularization is also a result of the same indifference in the literature on global Protestantism and American Christianity. We often assume that many Protestant congregations have "weak and insignificant" spatial ties and "no local bonds" because they are primarily concerned with voluntary fellowship that can theoretically exist anywhere.[26] Peripatetic camp meetings, revivals, and storefront churches receive as much inspiration from the Gospel passage, "For where two or three are gathered together in my name, there am I in the midst of them" (Matt. 18:20, KJV), as do Christian bestsellers.[27] But as the historian of religion, Darren Dochuk, persuasively demonstrates in his study of a suburban fundamentalist church outside of Detroit, the historical transformation of religious communities is an irreducibly geographical phenomenon.[28] The suburban congregation of Dochuk's study exemplifies the larger evangelical movement that has deftly incorporated the values, aesthetic, and function of the modern secularized suburb into its growth strategies. However, the historical and geographical specificities of mid-century Detroit in Dochuk's study determine how, why, and to what extent such strategies are conceived and enacted.

Such growth strategies are conscious decisions on the parts of local congregations to adapt to their secular socio-spatial environment. In what Charles Taylor calls this "age of mobilization," religious organizations must actively strategize to make transcendent belief relevant and plausible *in a particular place.*[29] Liturgically "lite" and flexible religious groups such as evangelical megachurches have made no apologies for taking such work seriously. For example, Warren writes about the door-to-door polling he did in the months before starting his eventual megachurch, and he strongly advocates demographic profiling for geographically sensitive marketing of church services. In his initial study of his church's "community," he found that his denominational ties to the Southern Baptist Convention would be problematic. "In our surveys of the unchurched," wrote Warren, "we found that denominational labels carried a lot of negative baggage for many of the unchurched in southern California. This caused us to choose the neutral name 'Saddleback Church.'"[30] This sort of sensitivity to local place can be seen in nearly every detail of the church, from its architecture, pastors' clothing, and of course sermon content and style. But this in itself is only a minor aspect of religious responsiveness to secularized socio-spatial environments. In order to see what difference a spatialized understanding of secularization makes, it is necessary to take a closer look at the much disparaged secularization paradigm.

The Core of the Secularization Paradigm

The growth that has come from such evangelical organizational strategies as Warren's is often seen as a refutation of the secularization paradigm altogether.[31] In both academic and popular literature, American evangelicalism is seen as an obvious sign of modern religious vitality. Its combination of conservative theological doctrine—centered on individual salvation through Jesus Christ, personal piety, and biblical literalism—with contemporary music and fashion, an individualistic, therapeutic style of worship and biblical interpretation, highly designed and demographically focused worship services, and an emphasis on weekly small-group meetings in members' homes, is often seen as a major innovation in American culture.[32] Several recent reports also suggest that to the extent that religious adherence in the United States is growing at all, it is growing in the style of evangelicalism.[33] Because these groups are mobilized, sometimes politically active, and growing at the same time that more traditional forms of Christianity are shrinking, leads critics of secularization to conclude that the secularization paradigm's flaws are obvious and irremediable. This particular framing is plausible only if we use the simplest and least theoretically informed sketches of the process of secularization.

Critics of the secularization paradigm often refer back to the writings of Auguste Comte, Herbert Spencer, or Sigmund Freud in an effort to show what they believe to be the necessary link between secular*ization* and secular*ism* (i.e., between modernization and the growth of anti- or non-religious ideology). And doubtless, the secularist agendas of these thinkers are plain to see in their writings on religion. But secularization as a theory was not on their agenda. Until sociologists of religion such as Bryan R. Wilson, Peter L. Berger, Thomas Luckmann, Larry Shiner, and David Martin took up secularization as a theory-building project did the concept ever receive serious attention. While important differences arose between these and other theorists of secularization, they all cohered around the central idea that, in the words of the sociologist of religion Steve Bruce, "Modernization creates problems for religion."[34] Far from the antagonistic secularism of Comte, Spencer, and Freud, the serious work on secularization theory that began in the 1960s and 1970s was concerned with how religious thought and practice *changed* in relation to the problems that modernity produced.

Perhaps the simplest way to order such change can be found in Jose Casanova's well-known disaggregation of secularization theory.[35] In Casanova's schema, secularization refers to three distinct propositions: (1) the *decline* in individual religious belief and practice; (2) the *privatization* of religious belief and practice; and (3) the institutional *differentiation* of social systems (such as the state, market, institutional education, science, and, most importantly, religion). The first proposition is perhaps the most debated point between critics and proponents, with statistical and definitional ambiguity providing much room for disagreement. The second proposition—the privatization of religion—has proven to be a much more nuanced point of disagreement largely because the definitional variations in "public" and "private" are so great that critics and proponents easily and often talk past each other. But the third proposition—secularization as differentiation—is almost universally accepted as a valid statement of modernity's effect on religious belief and practice.[36] While there are several different formulations of modern social differentiation, the most common thread holds that as social institutions respond to increasing complexity, they develop and express their own internal rationality and thereby begin to separate themselves from other institutions or spheres.[37] Most importantly, for secularization theory, social differentiation entails the separation of non-religious spheres from the authority of the religious sphere. Although it is formally a foundational tenet in modernization and social systems theory, differentiation can be seen as equally foundational to historical secularization because it technically indicated the transfer of ecclesiastical property to the state.[38]

Proponents of the secularization paradigm hold differentiation to be at its center. Bruce, one of the paradigm's most vocal proponents, describes secularization as "the declining importance of religion for the operation of non-religious roles and institutions such as those of the state and the economy."[39] For the sociologist Mark Chaves, secularization is the declining religious authority over non-religious spheres of social life.[40] Similarly, but more formally, the sociologist of religion Karl Dobbelaere explains secularization as "only the particularization of the general process of functional differentiation in the religious subsystem."[41] More plainly, David Martin argues that secularization theory should be thought of as a "sub-theory of social differentiation."[42] Far from being a recent rearguard action in response to critics, differentiation has been at the core of almost every major formulation of secularization. Peter Berger—his later disavowal notwithstanding—articulated it in his well-known *Sacred Canopy*:

By secularization we mean the process by which sectors of society and culture are removed from the domination of religious institutions and symbols. When we speak of society and institutions in modern Western history, of course, secularization manifests itself in the evacuation by the Christian churches of areas previously under their control or influence.[43]

Even farther back, Durkheim argued:

If there is one truth that history teaches us beyond doubt, it is that religion tends to embrace a smaller and smaller portion of social life. Originally, it pervades everything; everything social is religious; the two words are synonymous. Then, little by little, political, economic, scientific functions free themselves from the religious function, constitute themselves apart and take on a more and more acknowledged temporal character.[44]

Interestingly, this is not the secularization with which most critics disagree. Some of the paradigm's staunchest critics, such as Roger Finke and Rodney Stark, allow that differentiation is an entirely valid definition of secularization.[45] They contend most strongly with Casanova's first definition, secularization as the decline in religious belief and practice, but "so long as [secularization] is limited to the differentiation of religious and other primary social institutions," Finke and Stark write, they "accept it."[46] Another critic of secularization theory, the sociologist Christian Smith, writes that despite it relying on questionable historiography, strong structural determinism and unnecessarily high levels of abstraction, secularization-as-differentiation describes "something real at the level of macrosocial change . . . [that] has actually happened in history."[47] As for proponent-turned-critic Peter Berger, his repudiation of his earlier work in secularization theory does not extend to critiquing differentiation. Instead of talking about differentiation he uses "pluralization," but the meaning and effects are the same:

I would argue that modernity very likely, but not inevitably, leads to pluralism, to a pluralization of worldviews, values, etc., including religion, and I think I can show why that is. It's not a mysterious process. It has to do with certain structural changes and their effects on human institutions and human consciousness. I would simply define pluralism as the coexistence in the society of different worldviews and value systems under conditions of civic peace and under conditions where people interact with each other. Pluralism and the multiplication of choices, the necessity to choose, don't have to lead to secular choices. They can lead to religious choices—the rise of fundamentalism in various forms, for example—but they change the character of how religion is both maintained institutionally and in human consciousness.[48]

Talal Asad is one critic of secularization who does not accept the validity of social differentiation. As a key contributor to current debates over secularity and secularism, Asad criticizes Casanova and others for their easy acceptance of functional differentiation. Asad writes:

> When religion becomes an integral part of modern politics, it is not indifferent to debates about how the economy should be run, or which scientific projects should be publicly funded, or what the broader aims of a national education system should be. The legitimate entry of religion into these debates results in the creation of modern "hybrids": the principle of structural differentiation [therefore] no longer holds.[49]

However, various differentiation theories account for religious input into public policy decisions (e.g., Niklas Luhmann's concept of "leakage," Richard Münch's "interpenetration,"[50] or the liberal political ethic that is embedded in the idea of differentiation, which includes the civil right of religiously inspired political speech)[51]. One way of gauging secular differentiation's reality is whether, in a particular society, religious reasons are accepted as authoritative in non-religious spheres. In the United States the influence of the Christian conservatives notwithstanding, the answer must be no. Steve Bruce notes that religiously inspired policy proposals are nearly always promoted using non-religious justifications.[52] For example, abstinence-only sex education is typically defended on pseudo-scientific grounds, not on the inerrancy of the Bible, divine revelation, or even religious tradition.[53] That these latter reasons motivate religious adherents is irrelevant so long as they are compelled by the pluralistic and differentiated nature of their sociospatial environment to give generalized and secularized rationales for their positions.

But Asad also rejects differentiation theory on the normative grounds that accepting it would require "equating secularization with modernity" and thus accepting a "teleological theory of religious development."[54] But differentiation does not necessarily lead down a single pathway toward an ultimate demise for religion. It instead suggests that new problems and opportunities, restrictions and openings, present themselves to religion in advanced, differentiated societies.

The question, then, is not *whether* secular differentiation has occurred, but rather *what* are its ultimate effects? For the "new paradigm" in the sociology of religion, social differentiation typically leads to a free market in religion where religious organizations are forced to compete for customers. But this view too easily glosses over the ambiguous and contingent nature of social differentiation. Indeed, *freer* markets in religion are created when the spheres of religion, state power, capital, institutional education, and media each achieve some relative autonomy. But social differentiation has other effects, and many of these are expressed spatially, and ultimately favor certain religious traditions and adaptations over others. Successful modern religious organizations are not simply superior marketers who have found appealing ways to meet a universal demand for spiritual rewards.[55] They are able, for a variety of reasons, to maximally fill the limited space (both geographic and social) available for plausible and relevant religious meaning in the modern world.

Differentiation, Secularity, and the Fragmentation of the Sacred

While differentiation theory fell out of favor along with functionalism in the social sciences in the 1960s and 1970s, it continued to remain at the core of secularization theory. The reason for this is that the historical reality of secularization and differentiation in the West lies in their widely agreed-upon political-geographical origin: the transfer of ecclesiastical territory to the early modern European nation-state. Between the seventeenth and nineteenth centuries, Europe and North America saw the steady practical separation of science, economic markets, cultural production, and formal education from organized religious activity. From the "emancipation" of the state from religion down to the specialization and separation of "semi-discrete sectors of social life . . . [such as] social control, social legitimation, communication, health and education," differentiation is seen as the removal of most non-religious aspects of social life from religious authority.[56] But if the religious sphere had some overarching authority in pre-differentiated societies, then the new differentiated situation did not simply produce a new hegemon. Instead, religion became one of several differentiated institutions competing for authority. For Niklas Luhmann and the revised differentiation theory presented by Jeffrey C. Alexander and Paul B. Colomy, the modern social order cannot be reduced to capitalism, state bureaucracy, technocratic instrumentalism, or even a neoliberal variation of the three. Modern society is an irreducibly fragmented patchwork of differentiated institutions.[57]

The secularization paradigm, then, is founded on this differentiated patchwork that does not lead simply to a decline in religious belief and practice but rather to their fragmentation and privatization. Even Marx—sometimes painted as a crude secularizationist—argued that differentiation did not destroy religion but rather relocated it:

> Man emancipates himself *politically* from religion by expelling it from the sphere of public law to that of private law. Religion is no longer the spirit of the *state*, in which man behaves, albeit in a specific and limited way and in a particular sphere, as a species-being, in community with other men. It has become the spirit of *civil society*, of the sphere of egoism and of the *bellum omnium contra omnus*. . . . Thus political emancipation does not abolish, and does not even strive to abolish, man's *real* religiosity. (Italics in original)[58]

Picking up where Marx left off, Berger and Luckman both argue that such political emancipation had joined with economic emancipation to create "a 'liberated territory' with respect to religion."[59] As secularization "moved 'outwards' into other areas of society" religious belief and practice became more private and more localized.[60] Whereas Marx had at least allowed religion a certain potency and relevance in civil society, twentieth-century theorists could see only a continuous fragmentation and privatization of religious life to the point where the nuclear family served as the final bulwark. "The world-building potency of religion," writes Berger, "is thus restricted to the construction of sub-worlds, of fragmented universes of meaning, the plausibility structure of which may in some cases be no larger than the nuclear family."[61]

The fragmentation of these "universes of meaning" is seen to occur broadly on three different "social levels." First, the macro-social differentiation of institutional specialization reduces the political, economic and cultural power of religion as it becomes "just another sphere, structured around its own autonomous internal axis."[62] Whereas in medieval Europe, several social functions (e.g., education, healthcare, welfare) were the exclusive domain of the Church, by the end of the nineteenth century, these functions were largely the domain of secular specialists. Religious institutions maintain their position as specialists of sacredness, but the social relevance of such sacredness has been greatly restricted in comparison to religion's pre-differentiated status.

The second level on which the fragmentation of the sacred becomes relevant is in civil society, broadly conceived as a realm of voluntary association outside of the state and kinship. On this level, the macro-level differentiation of religion and the state opens up an arena for the development of and competition between more or less independent religious organizations (denominations). Fundamental qualities of the sacred are now contested as denominations compete for adherents and social influence. The resulting fragmentation of the sacred in civil society, however, does not necessarily mean a concomitant diminution of the sacred in civil society. While orthodox secularization theorists like Bruce argue that such pluralism more often relativizes different religious options by showing them to be a matter of choice, there is a respected body of research that suggests that pluralism also leads to innovation and growth.[63]

Finally, on the micro-social level, fragmentation of the sacred into individualized belief systems can be seen as the result of the political and social privatization of religion. Because religious adherence is not a prerequisite to participating in the most important social subsystems, it is easily compartmentalized into a private, personal realm of belief and practice.[64] The paradigmatic expression of this can be seen in Robert Bellah's famous account of "Sheilaism":

> Today religion in America is as private and diverse as New England colonial religion was public and unified. One person we interviewed actually named her religion (she calls it her "faith") after herself. This suggests the logical possibility of over 220 million American religions, one for each of us. . . . "I believe in God. I'm not a religious fanatic. I can't remember the last time I went to church. My faith has carried me a long way. It's Sheilaism. Just my own little voice."[65]

Far from spelling the end of religion, personalization, fragmentation, and compartmentalization serve as the social context within which religious organizations in civil society must adapt.

It should be clear that differentiation does not result in the fragmentation, privatization, and compartmentalization of religion simply because other social spheres are hostile to it. It is rather the radical pluralization of social life and the erosion of widely shared structures of inter-subjective meaning that cause a general fragmentation and privatization of cultural life in general.[66] Differentiation theory is often seen as foundational to modernization theory. As such, it is often linked with increasing cultural homogeneity, hegemonic social and political control, and a "colonization" of local life-worlds. But seen through the lens of secularization theory, secular differentiation produces quite the opposite. As the daily lives of modern individuals are increasingly divided among overlapping, interpenetrating, and conflicting differentiated spheres, homogeneity and hegemony are far overshadowed by fragmentation, pluralization, and eclectic pastiche.[67] Even the commonly assumed

differentiation of state/civil-society/family implies the starkly different roles
moderns must inhabit on a daily basis. Once this fundamental tripartite division of modern society is expanded to more accurately reflect the level of
differentiation imputed in the secularization paradigm, it is easy to see how
pluralization and fragmentation are the ultimate product of differentiation.[68]

Perhaps the chief criticism leveled against secularization theory is that it
assumes a causal link between the obvious and widely accepted macro-social,
secular differentiation and a quite contentious and variable micro-social secularization. As Berger, who has become a critic of secularization theory, now
states, "Secularization on the societal level is not necessarily linked to secularization on the level of individual consciousness."[69] This is clearly the case:
macro-secularization does not necessarily lead to micro-secularization. But
the reason for this is that advanced levels of social differentiation do not
destroy communal life-worlds, they radically pluralize them. In terms of the
sociology of religion, this means that the survival of religion at the micro-
social level or "the level of individual consciousness" depends above all on its
relevance to these fragmentary, pluralized life-worlds. Thus, Berger was originally correct in diagnosing the end of a "sacred canopy" that served as a uni-
fying religious-meaning system for society, and was also originally correct in
positing the continuous relevance of religious "sub-worlds" and "fragmented
universes."[70] Writing of contemporary American evangelicalism, Christian
Smith describes how, in the absence of a sacred canopy, evangelicals have constructed a much smaller, less expansive "sacred umbrella."[71] One reason such
discrete social groups with their localized umbrellas of meaning have relevance
and efficacy for their members is that the correlates of fragmentation and individualization are autonomy and the expansion of choice. But this fragmented
social environment is obviously *not* one of total autonomy and free choice. It is
one with specific contours, textures, openings, and blockages. And while sociologists of religion have long been interested in outlining the social features of
this environment, very little attention has been given to its spatial, material and
embodied dimensions. In what ways can we begin to think of the social differentiation that leads to "sacred umbrellas" as being an abstraction of spatial
differentiation that leads to "sacred archipelagos"? In other words, what does
secular differentiation look like on the ground?

Locating Religion: Social Levels and Spatial Scales

A good way to begin thinking through the transition from the sacred canopy to sacred archipelagos is through the social levels mentioned earlier. The
secularization paradigm depends heavily on the idea of social levels and the

effects of social relationships at one level on others. For example, Karl Dobbelaere argues that macro-social differentiation ("laicization") has created
meso-social organizational change ("religious change"), and has transformed
the nature of individual religiosity ("religious involvement"). The structure
of the top social level appears to have trickle-down effects that shape the constraints of action for groups and individuals farther down.[72] As the religious
sphere is stripped of its authority at the macro-social level, religious groups
in the meso-social level adapt by reframing both their macro-social discursive presentations (by becoming more "civil" in the Habermasian postsecular
sense[73]) and their micro-social ones as well (by becoming more intimate and
therapeutic).

One effort to ground the neo-functionalist concepts of the secularization paradigm can be found in Christian Smith's criticism of the latter. He
argues that the question of agency presents a special problem for a theoretical framework that relies so heavily on macro-social structures. Without a
more concrete understanding of how and why individuals acted to produce
secular differentiation (and were not just its passive objects), the secularization paradigm is "badly incomplete."[74] Smith focuses on individuals in centers of power as agents of secularization, thereby framing secularization as a
process occurring *in specific places*, rather than through large, gradual, anonymous institutional change. Smith argues that secularization is not simply
"a byproduct of modernization" but the result of the decisions and actions
of particular individuals in particular places. For instance, the secularization
of institutional education in the late nineteenth and early twentieth century
was not, in Smith's view, some putative effect of macro-level structural differentiation. Instead, specific historical actors with ideological grievances and
access to specific levers of power in particular locations carried through the
institutional secularization in America.

Smith sees his general approach as an alternative to secularization theory.
However, his focus on historical agents appears more clearly to be a refine-
ment rather than a refutation. The individuals in Smith's account are not free
agents but confront socio-spatial constraints and resources that are alluded
to in the neo-functional language of the secularization paradigm. While
Smith's approach fits much better with this paradigm than he acknowledges,
his work has brought us closer to a spatial, material, and embodied understanding of secularization. But a sizable gap needs to be bridged in order
to account for how a top-down social theoretical approach to secularization
can be fitted with a grounded approach to its spatiality. In other words, how
is one to map the social levels of the conventional secularization paradigm
on to the embodied places that constitute a broader secular environment?

One way to approach this problem is through the geographic concept of scale. In the past decade, human geographers have come to see scale as a category of spatial imagination that describes how geographically extensive an actor understands her or his actions to be.[75] Scale in human geography does not describe how spatially extensive actions really are but are instead the spatial extension within which actors understand themselves to move. Therefore, it is more apt to speak of scalar logics and scalar frameworks social actors use rather than "the scale of social action." In this way, religious action is partially structured by the scalar logic of social actors: Do individuals, discretely or in groups, see themselves acting at a local, regional, national, or global scale? Are their narratives framed at the scale of the body, the family, the neighborhood, or the globe?

The geographical scales of a secularized environment, then, are not the same as its social levels. Groups and nation-states do not "exist" at a particular scale as they do at a particular social-theoretical level. And the geographical scale of the nation-state or the globe does not have the trickle-down or knock-on effects of the macro-social level imputed by differentiation theory. Rather, actors and groups present themselves to others by drawing on particular scalar frameworks or logics: first, by understanding themselves to be working at a particular scale or scales, and second, by understanding their audience to exist at a particular scale or scales. For example, the American-based evangelical missionary organization, Campus Crusade for Christ International (CCCI), sees itself working at both the global scale and various local scales. Its agents imagine themselves carrying out the Great Commission that is seen to command Christians to "go and make disciples of all nations, baptizing them in the name of the Father and of the Son and of the Holy Spirit" (Matt. 28:19, NIV). The phrase "all nations" provides the scalar limits of CCCI's performance, while the intimate, pietistic, and voluntarist nature of evangelical conversion informs the local scalar frameworks of their activity. Motivated by this multi-scalar imaginary, CCCI has grown from a local, American college-based group in the 1950s into a transnational missionary organization with more than 3,300 full-time staff claiming to reach over 8 million individuals around the world in 2009.[76]

CCCI is evidence of the failure of the secularization paradigm only if we ignore the scalar logic of its self-constitution and, of course, its effects. CCCI, as with Saddleback's own missionary activities (see chap. 6), does not imagine itself to be acting at the scale of the nation-state. It does not, in other words, imagine itself to be acting toward expanding the significance of religion into the social spheres of the state, law, market, and other discrete, secular modes of activity. And its effects, as far as they are real and lasting, are

measured at the level of the individual. CCCI's bottom line, when account-
ing for their effectiveness, is individual "decisions." For Saddleback it is "lives
changed." A global imagination that has as its desideratum individual religious conversion is fully accounted for within a spatially sensitive theory of
secularization.

From this spatially sensitive angle we can see that secular differentiation
describes a structurally pluralized environment that opens up certain scalar
possibilities for religious action and restricts others. Thus the effect on religious organizations in the move from existing under a sacred canopy (i.e.,
from having broad religious authority) to working under countless sacred
umbrellas in countless sacred archipelagos is dependent upon the particular
scales at which they imagine themselves to work. For example, counter-sec-
ularizing efforts (ranging from congregational growth strategies to political
campaigns of de-differentiation) of particular religious organizations like the
late Jerry Falwell's Thomas Road Baptist Church heavily incorporate scalar
elements of the nation-state into their performances.[77] But in a differentiated
environment like the United States, the performances are not designed to
work at the social level of the nation-state—that is, an effective transformation of the differentiated sphere of state politics is not the goal—but instead
use the *scalar logic of the nation-state* to effect local individuals and communities as such. Falwell's de-differentiation attempts yielded little institutional
change; instead, his famous efforts as a warrior of the Religious Right seem
to have worked as a very local church growth strategy. Already in 1983 his
church reported weekly attendance of 17,000.[78]

Religious movements such as Falwell's only appear to be counter-sec-
ularizing incursions into the social domains of the state, markets, institutional education, and so forth. Seen through the lens of geographic scale,
it becomes clear that these movements are performed within a multi-scalar
framework that flexibly adapts to the discursive demands of particular social
subsystems. Counter-secularization strategies are, by necessity in Western modernized states, confined to scales where their expression does not
make *practical* claims on the authority of the state, corporations, or scientific
expertise. What is at stake for these religious movements are the body, home,
and local community.

Much excellent work has been done in the geography of religion precisely
at these locations. It is not coincidental that the private space of the home has
been a key site for the study of contemporary geographies of religion.[79] And
recent geographical engagements with the body have coincided with a recent
focus on the embodied nature of certain religious ethics.[80] But little attention
has been paid to how such religious action is bounded and also authorized

by secular institutions and practices. Religious action does not simply fly under the radar of macro-level secularizing forces. The body or local communities are not liberated spaces for religious action but are instead underdetermined by secular subsystems. While it is at the macro-social level that secularizing forces are most clearly dominant and effective, there are still well-researched manifestations of secularization at the micro-social level. As mentioned earlier, Norris and Inglehart show that broad increases in economic security, a hallmark of modernization, are correlative with decreases in both the social and individual significance of religion. Bruce demonstrates how the privatization and individualization of religion, evinced in New Age beliefs and practices and a "spiritualization" of traditional religion, is unstable and difficult to reproduce.[81] The loss of an overarching sacred canopy has provided room for countless variations on new and old forms of religious expression. This religious diversity works to intensify both the limitations and affordances macro-level differentiation presents for religion. This is all to say that secularization-as-differentiation occurs across social levels and thus affects the scalar logics of religious actors in many different ways. What this ultimately means is that the scalar imagination is most liberated and effective at the smaller scales of the individual, home, and local community, and so it is here that efforts to halt the shrinking of sacred archipelagos is at its most intense. This is why it is so important to conceive of secularization as a variable process that works in abstract social levels as well as spatially performative geographic scales. This socio-spatial perspective is key to understanding the context in which local religious organizations must work, strategize, and survive.

Placing Social Levels and Spatial Scales

Social levels and spatial scales describe the discursive and performative context in which religious (indeed, any human) action occurs. But geographers of religion also work to highlight the material context of religious action. A clearer view of religious action requires a perspective that can account for its emplacement, that is, the way social actors draw on their material location in order to make themselves and others understandable and meaningful (see chap. 3). By drawing on differentiation theory and the concept of scale, these local sites of religious action need not be seen as simply where action occurs. Instead, the local site has particular discursive and performative resources that become less available as the geographic area of action expands.

Influential PDE megachurches such as Joel Osteen's Lakewood Community Church in Houston, Texas (47,000 weekly attendees), or Bill Hybell's

Willow Creek Community Church on the periphery of the Chicago metro-politan area (23,500 weekly attendees), and, of course, Warren's Saddleback are perfect examples of how religious organizations, drawing on the logic of a variety of scales, are subject to varying and sometimes contradictory secu-larizing pressures. At the macro-social level of the nation state, many Ameri-can megachurches appear to be expanding in power and influence.[82] Such apparent expansion could be interpreted in terms of inter-systemic conflict, that is, as desecularizing incursions by religion into politics and civil soci-ety. For example, Warren's Saddleback Church hosted the first-ever, church-sponsored presidential candidate event in the summer of 2008.[83] And shortly afterwards, Warren was chosen by president-elect Barack Obama to give the invocation prayer at his inauguration. Warren could be seen here as working to sacralize U.S. national politics and alloy religious authority with political authority by not only setting the terms of electoral deliberation in the August event but also sanctifying the outcome with his inaugural prayer. However, a closer examination of the local context of Saddleback Church in Orange County suggests that all along Saddleback Church pastors' actions were directed toward and justified by local proselytic efforts (see chap. 7). Both political events were used intensively by Saddleback pastors and staff to mar-ket the local Sunday services surrounding the events. And while the Sunday services after each political event were some of the most heavily attended of the year, the sermons were clearly apolitical.[84] In other words, their goal was not to sacralize politics but to give some popular relevance to their regular weekend services. Following the August forum between the presidential can-didates, Saddleback embarked on a two-month-long series of sermons on how to have better relationships with one's family and friends. It was not an effort to build on any desecularizing momentum.

Again, evangelical churches like Saddleback are growing in the United States while other denominational varieties are shrinking or stagnant.[85] They are intimately connected to the local daily lives of their constituents through a variety of such measures as demographically sensitive church services, small groups in homes, parks, coffee shops, and workplaces, and continu-ously updated outreach programs. But they are also connected to churches around the world, sharing successful organizational strategies.[86] Saddleback, for example, holds several conferences a year at its Lake Forest, California, campus, which are devoted to marketing different aspects of organizational structure and style and claims to have trained 500,000 pastors around the world in "Purpose Driven" ministry.[87] Further, Saddleback's executive pas-tor, Rick Warren, has formulated and promoted what he calls his "Global P.E.A.C.E. Plan" (see chap. 6), the goal of which is to train lay members and other Christian churches to travel to underdeveloped regions of the world not only to work with local churches but also to cooperate with governmental, nongovernmental, and private enterprise organizations to alleviate poverty, disease, and illiteracy.

It would appear that the size and dynamism of evangelical church networks would refute any theoretical paradigm that suggests religion's marginalization in modern society. But only by separating out the scales and levels of evangelicalism, and then grounding them in specific place-based practices, can we see that secular marginalization varies at different scales and levels. Warren and Saddleback are limited in their ability to act on a macrosocial level (for the reasons elaborated earlier, regarding secular differentiation). But when they do act, it is directed toward the growth of their local congregation in south Orange County, California—their own sacred archipelago. Their national and global efforts are used explicitly to engage the local postsuburban narratives of identity formation and self-fulfillment that are so salient to their targeted local demographics. Secularization theory, then, highlights the different opportunities and limitations at different scales for religious actors in advanced differentiated societies.

Conclusion

Clearly, social differentiation is not a simple social process. Its most advanced formulations break with its theoretical origins in functionalism and instead highlight its uneven and contingent processual nature and its dialectical production of an open, yet fragmented, environment for religious organizations and individuals.[88] Three important qualifications must be made in order for the concept to be put to work in analyzing contemporary, embodied, and grounded geographies of religious practice.

First, social differentiation is not simply a structural or evolutionary social process. Against the functionalist and evolutionary perspective of Talcott Parsons and to a lesser extent Niklas Luhmann, some sociologists have formulated social differentiation as a historically contingent process grounded in the action of individuals and organizations with particular interests and resources. The collection of neo-functionalist approaches to differentiation theory brought together by Jeffrey Alexander and Paul Colomy addresses this issue through various historical analyses of "blunted," "uneven," and "unequal" differentiation, as well as resistance movements of "de-differentiation."[89] Such analyses shifted the terms of debate from teleological and evolutionary progress to the contingent nature of conflict and cooperation between and within various societal institutions. Instead of differentiation being a social evolutionary principle, it is now viewed as a historically and geographically variable product of multi-dimensional complexity.[90] This means that the future prospects for religious action are unknowable. They will depend in part on the scalar frameworks and social levels with which religious actors seek to work.

The second qualification that must be made is that social differentiation is not a dialectical antecedent to integration. Colomy writes that "Earlier renditions of differentiation theory concentrated on two primary consequences of structural change: increased efficiency and reintegration."[91] But revised differentiation theory takes as its premise that modern functionally differentiated societies are not, and need not be, unified or re-integrated under a more expansive moral community or the hegemony of a particular subsystem, such as the state or market. Instead, society is seen as an "interinstitutional system" where the "whole is less than the sum of its parts."[92] "In other words," writes Luhmann:

> the functionally differentiated societies cannot be ruled by leading parts or elites as stratified societies (to some extent) could be. They also cannot be rationalized by means/ends chains as a technocratic conception would suggest. Their structural complexity can be adequately formulated only by models that take into account several [differentiated spheres] at once.[93]

For modern religious entrepreneurs this means that there is little hope for a fundamentalist recovery of religious hegemony. The scale of the nation-state, for example, is a highly restricted performative arena for religious actors because religious actors must justify themselves in terms of other non-religious social subsystems. Doubtless, there are "leakages" and "interpenetration" in which religious justifications find acceptance in other spheres of action, but generally subsystems are kept from "presenting unsolvable problems" for the others.[94] "Its just business," "the science says . . ." or "the necessity of political compromise" are common phrases that maintain "buffers" between differentiated spheres of action *when the action is designed and performed at the scales of political territories*. Theoretically, as long as religious actors observe such boundaries at these scales, they will continue to have a relatively autonomous and undetermined relationship with these other spheres.

Finally and most importantly, social differentiation has material and embodied effects in everyday lived places. These effects will be sketched in more detail in chapter 3, but they can be most easily identified under the rubrics of specialization and individualization. One common historical origin of modern social differentiation is the separation of work life and family life. Sometimes abstractly conceived as a moment in the modernization of the public/private binary or in the creation of modern civil society, this separation was irreducibly material and spatial. It was the physical movement of the early bourgeois family from a live/work site of residence to a "home" that was spatially and functionally separated from work. This movement was a response to growing density and complexity in work relations, and it eventually led to the apotheosis of market/family differentiation in the modern suburb.[95] That social differentiation is coterminously material and embodied spatial differentiation can be seen in countless examples. A critical moment in state/religion differentiation is found in the transfer of territory in the negotiations of the 1648 Peace of Westphalia, which, in effect, created the modern European state, and was a landmark in the separation of political and religious authority in Europe.[96] To use another example, secularization was once used describe the transfer of priests to local parishes. This movement from centers of religious education or religious bureaucracy out into places where non-religious institutions held sway was and still is fundamentally spatial.

These caveats to the general concept of differentiation as it is used in the secularization paradigm point to the broader issues of agency and place. It is not just that agency and place matter in a general way and are necessary concepts in any case: agency and place matter particularly in the context of religious belief and practice in contemporary advanced differentiated societies because social differentiation has uneven spatial effects. At the places of the body, the home, and the neighborhood, religious entrepreneurs are free agents. The localized places of everyday life are left open for sacralization in countless ways, as evidenced by the ever-increasing offerings at evangelical megachurches for evermore finely tuned demographic niches.[97]

Although religious entrepreneurs are continuously filling these open social spaces, it is not true that such spaces are boundless. Research on contemporary Western religious practice suggests that sites of sacralization proliferate easily and rapidly on the local scale—from suburban American house-church groups to rustbelt American storefront churches and Australian mall-like megachurches.[98] However, it is by no means clear that such practices are an indication of larger scale sacralization. These changing spatial practices of sacralization leave much to be studied, but their proliferation does not bespeak the end of secularization. Instead, their very success suggests a multi-dimensional and multi-scalar complexity that many secularization theorists have been arguing for all along.

Of course, not all PDE churches like Saddleback restrict their activity to local scales. Warren and Saddleback have become well known for their ambitiously global mission activity: the Global P.E.A.C.E. Plan, as well as for their national political involvement in the 2008 U.S. presidential elections. When on August 16, 2008, Warren convened the "Saddleback Civil Forum" in which presidential candidates John McCain and Barack Obama participated in the first joint presidential campaign event to be held at a house of worship, many observers worried about the anti-disestablishmentarian subtext of the event. And when Warren talks about his P.E.A.C.E. Plan in which the church and its lay members hope to enter into partnership with governments around the world to provide development aid, it appears that de-secularization is precisely what is taking place. But these types of efforts are targeted to the very local hopes, desires, fears, and dreams of Saddleback's constituency in southern Orange County, California (see chaps. 6 and 7). The scales of the national and global are not territories for the expansion of evangelical religious authority. Instead, they are culturally constructed as loci of meaning for Saddleback congregants. "The nation," "Africa," "The West," and "The Global South" all become constructed participants in a performance of contemporary evangelicalism in localized postsuburban places.

In the sprawling expanse of postsuburban Orange County, many of the categories that make up localness are inverted, effaced, or otherwise transformed. In order for Saddleback and other postsuburban churches to serve the needs and desires of a local community, a sensitive reinterpretation of the terms "local" and "community" must take place.

3

Sacred Scenes

Postsuburbia and Evangelical Performance

If secularization implies a de-fused and fragmented socio-spatial environment for religious action, then what sort of analytical advantage is gained
by the concept of performance? For proponents of the religious market
approach, performance tells us little more than do the concepts of "marketing," "responsiveness," or "adaptation." In this latter view, the relationship
between suppliers and consumers of "religious goods" is straightforward.
From Roger Finke and Laurence R. Iannacone's assertion that "a particular
religious firm will flourish only if it provides a product at least as attractive as
its competitors"[1] to Shayne Lee and Phillip Sinitiere's use of the metaphors of
"packaging and delivery,"[2] religion is seen as an effective exchange as much as
an affective relationship. Of course, this is a neatly parsimonious interpretation of religious action; but its parsimony leaves its proponents silent just at
the moment when the heart of the analysis should begin.

The religious market principle that religious action in advanced societies
consists of consumers ("current and potential followers"), suppliers ("religious organizations"), and product ("religious doctrines and practices") only

brings us to the beginning of the question.[3] It may be able to tell us about the crude effects of state sponsorship of religion (that it often depresses religious innovation and a general interest in organized religion) or the results of focused, organized proselytism (that it tends to work), but the net gain of such an approach is negligible. What can proponents of this approach tell us about the lived experience of religious followers, and more specifically, the millions of Americans who are attempting to build a "purpose driven life" in Saddleback-like churches? Surely, the conclusion that if religious organizations "work harder, they are more successful" does not get us far.[4]

What we need instead are conceptual tools that allow us to analyze the relationships that are built in churches like Saddleback. These relationships obviously consist of overtly religious doctrines and rituals, but they are also integrally connected to webs of meaning in the larger socio-spatial environment. We need tools that will allow us to take into account the depth and range of cultural meaning that undergird the decision to attend a church service, become a church member, lead a small group, or travel abroad on a short-term mission. In this chapter I use Jeffrey Alexander's theory of cultural pragmatics to examine the socio-spatial environment in which these decisions are made, namely in postsuburban America.

The model of cultural pragmatics shows how its dramaturgical concepts allow us to take stock of the ideal and material, social, and spatial dimensions of lived religious action. Then we look at the "transition and tension" that Warren explicitly sees as the felicitous backdrop to Saddleback's performance, which I believe is a product of social differentiation (see chap. 2) as well as spatial differentiation, defined as the increasing functional specialization of place-making. Social differentiation is not only a macrosocial process that abstractly restricts the authority and resources of the religious societal subsystem. It is also a process of material and embodied specialization, fragmentation, and—in cultural pragmatic terms—de-fusion, in response to socio-spatial complexity, density, and diversity. This means that social differentiation not only has material, embodied, and spatial effects but that it is dialectically produced by these same effects. To speak of social differentiation is to also speak of spatial differentiation. In the spirit of neo-functionalism, however, this relationship should be seen as a negative dialectic without any necessary resolution. Just as neo-functional social differentiation results in fragmentation, privatization, and individualization (not a Parsonian equilibrium), neo-functional spatial differentiation can be seen to produce decentralization, buffering, and isolation (not an ecological equilibrium). In contemporary urban form, then, the abstract societal subsystems of differentiation theory can be seen also as the internal differentiation of the metropolis into discrete, functionally specialized spaces of domesticity, wage labor, functional and recreational consumption, and physical mobility.

This idea of dialectical *socio-spatial* differentiation has a long pedigree in urban studies. Although it has fallen out of fashion as a central organizing concept along with non-spatial social differentiation, it is still accepted as a commonsense concept. My reason for resuscitating it is that it provides an important connection, which allows us to speak of cultural pragmatic "de-fusion" (the fragmenting of cultural meaning) as a social *and* spatial process. Socio-spatial de-fusion provides us with a conceptual apparatus to think through the cultural geography of the places in which PDE religiosity is so vibrant. These places are often considered to be "the suburbs." And while the suburbs were indeed home to an older evangelicalism, today's postdenomi-national evangelicalism resides in a less coherent and more fragmented version called postsuburbia. The elite differentiation of work life from family life, as represented in the classic suburbs west of eighteenth-century London or outside of nineteenth-century New York or Chicago, can be seen as the beginning of a demographic, spatial, and functional expansion of urban space that has now resulted in a decentralized patchwork in which domesticity, work life, consumption and mobility have no *necessary* spatial (i.e., center-periphery) relationship. The increasing differentiation of these socio-spatial spheres is interpreted in PDE churches through Warren's language of "transition and tension." Pastors and members at Saddleback often refer to "balancing" the different parts of their life. And while the work/family balance comes up most often, every sphere of social life is implied in this dichotomy.

Postsuburban place has a "betweenness," like all places. From this view, place has a symbolic *and* instrumental quality, is experienced as both meaning *and* material, and has an internal *and* external environment.[5] While acknowledging the *material* qualities of postsuburbia (its functional networks, morphology, and demography) is essential to understanding Saddleback and other PDE megachurches, understanding the *symbolic-cultural* dimension of postsuburban place is just as important, if not more so. Although postsuburbia is marked by recent fundamental material changes, it is still culturally dependent on the myths and narratives that were foundational to an older, classical suburbia. The problem for the PDE megachurch is in deploying the old cultural narratives of suburbia within the new realities of postsuburbia. The neatly ordered suburban binaries of private/public, domesticity/work, consumption/production, and autonomy/heteronomy are scrambled in the fragmented patchwork spaces of postsuburbia. Whereas the suburban church of the early to mid-twentieth century served as a

legitimizing institution for a common suburban experience,[6] the contemporary postsuburban megachurch can only hope to contextualize the countless
fragments of its diverse constituents' lives. The successful PDE megachurch
does not serve as an "integrating" overarching system for a differentiated,
de-fused postsuburbia because such a solution appears not to exist. Instead,
PDE churches work to connect these fragments in a way that make the transitions and tensions of postsuburbia not just bearable but meaningful.

Performing between Society and Space

Membership at Saddleback is a very flexible and variegated undertaking. It
has many of the elements of classical evangelicalism: the espousal of traditional evangelical doctrines of sin, grace, and salvation; the cultivation of a
personal relationship to Jesus Christ through prayer and worship; communal
bonding through singing and sermonizing; and evangelizing non-members
in both organized and non-organized ways. But these and many other elements stand in dynamic tension with the broader socio-spatial environment in which the method (where and how), content, and existential status
of prayer and worship are by no means given; in which the audience reception of any given sermon is dependent on the level of the former's diversity
and fragmentation; in which evangelism (proselytism) is largely disdained;
in which the church campus is not a spatial center for its members but one
node in a much larger postsuburban web of daily urban action. This, therefore, is a broad socio-spatial environment that challenges the construction
and maintenance of widely shared meaning.

The central question of this book is this: How can we account for the
embodied, historicized, and especially emplaced success of Saddleback
Church and churches like it? Any substantial answer must take into account
the way these churches build meaning. A fundamental way meaning has been
built in religious communities is through ritual. For Émile Durkheim, ritual
was a social glue whereby "individuals [are] reunited . . . [and] common feelings [are] re-experienced and expressed by common acts." Rituals are "above
all, the means by which the social group periodically reaffirms itself."[7] The key
to ritual, for Durkheim, lies in the set of followed rules that allow individuals
to objectively represent the social order to themselves. This insight allowed
Erving Goffman to profitably elaborate the modern, secular concept of "interaction ritual" in which "societies . . . must mobilize their members as self-
regulating participants in social encounters."[8] But Goffman's work on ritual,
which is focused on modern societies, suggests just how much has changed
in ritual from preindustrial, less-differentiated eras. His work is just as much

about individual manipulation, gamesmanship, bad faith and social fragmentation as it is about solidarity, integration, and social cohesion.

The problem with continuing to use ritual as a central analytical category in the study of contemporary American religion is that it is both too broad and too narrow to capture the production, negotiation, and maintenance of meaning in complex societies.[9] Jeffrey Alexander argues that

> Societies still seem to be permeated by symbolic, ritual-like activities. . . . But we also clearly sense that these [activities] are not rituals in the traditional sense (cf. Lukes 1977). Even when they affirm validity and authenticity and produce integration, their effervescence is short lived. If they have achieved simplicity, it is unlikely they will be repeated. If they are repeated, it is unlikely that the symbolic communication can ever be so simplified in the same way again.[10]

Alexander is concerned with how to account for the "ritual-like" symbolic action in complex societies—action that is always in danger of producing fragmentation as easily as integration. Drawing on a rich tradition of dramaturgical theory (not least Goffman's contribution), Alexander outlines a social theory of performance in which social interaction, to be effective, must tightly bind together the elements of performance into a "fused" whole. This performative "fusion . . . display[s] for others the meaning of their social situation."[11]

What exactly becomes fused together in an effective social performance? Alexander outlines seven distinct elements: (1) background symbols; (2) foreground scripts; (3) actors, both individual and collective; (4) observers/audience; (5) means of symbolic reproduction; (6) *mise-en-scène*; and (7) social power.[12] Background symbols are essentially deep Durkheimian cultural binary codes. If sacred/profane is the most fundamental binary code, then what Durkheim called "secondary species," such as masculine/feminine, clean/unclean, public/private, are more apparently foundational to Alexander's foreground scripts. The latter are more articulated "scripts" and "narratives" that "reflect the relative freedom from background representations." Within the broad and intuitively recognizable deep cultural binaries, actors have a wide range of possibilities to choose from. For example, the American politician can choose from an array of possible political characters and binaries. And from these she can craft a fitting narrative and still has even more freedom of choice in constructing a precise script. Obviously, she does not have a limitless range of choices, but they are not nearly as circumscribed as in a less differentiated, more fused society.

These deep cultural binaries, foreground scripts, and narratives are the cultural structures that allow actors to effectively represent themselves and their projects to others. Background symbols, scripts, and narratives are resources and do nothing in themselves; they need actors in order to be activated. This relationship between actors and culture structures must appear not as a relationship but rather as an undifferentiated whole in which actors *are* the symbols they represent. On the part of the actor this requires a deep, visceral understanding of the symbols, scripts, and narratives being deployed as well as the performative skill to project these as simply natural.

But even if a performance is masterfully executed, its effectiveness is still unsecured because of audience reception. An audience may be disinterested, distracted, or otherwise contextually out of tune with the performance. Perhaps most important in the contemporary American political context, critics may disrupt the audience's identification with the performer. For a host of reasons, the fusion between the audience and actor is just as contingent as it is between actor and background symbols, scripts, and narratives. An effective performance, then, is a "double fusion" in which the actor is fused (and has the skill to display this fusion) with her background symbols, scripts, and narratives, and the audience is fused with the actor through "psychological identification."[13]

As important as performative skill and felicitous audience reception are, it is the socio-spatial context that determines whether an effective performance is even possible. The elements of this context are captured by Alexander through the concepts of "means of symbolic reproduction," "mise en scène," and "social power." The means of symbolic production are the material and mediatic equipment that allow for a performance to be executed. These can range from clothing and props to the place of performance, from media transmission to techniques of staging.[14] Mise en scène quite literally puts these things together with a script and an actor into a particular scene. It is to "sequence temporally and choreograph spatially" all of the elements of social performance. But the ability to "put into scene" a performance is fundamentally tied to social power. It is bound up with not only the power to produce a performance (obtaining access to all of the material resources an effective performance requires) but also the power to distribute and transmit the performance.[15]

A spatial approach to Alexander's cultural pragmatics must emphasize the materiality of an effective performance. This is not just in reference to the staging, the props, the mise en scène, or even the embodiment of actors. It is to recognize that even the immateriality of cultural binaries, foreground scripts, and narratives is connected intimately to the material world. In anthropology and archaeology a "new materialist" approach has emerged over the last twenty years, which has demonstrated both theoretically and empirically how cultural representations are fundamentally relationships between the ideal and the material.[16] As the anthropologist Daniel Miller has argued, "There is no (cultural) subject prior to the process of objectification through which it is created."[17] This is true for such surficial cultural performances as being the U.S. president[18] as it is for deep cultural binaries such as sacred/profane.[19]

The performances of PDE churches are no less material. They refer consistently to the immaterial, allude always to the dangers of worldly materialism and idolatry, and focus sharply on divine, unearthly rewards. But the effectiveness of these performative elements not only depends on their very material staging within postsuburban space but also the spatiality of their deeper cultural undergirding. This means that any cultural performative response by PDE churches to their local postsuburban communities must be thoroughly spatial *and* material.

Praying on the Edge: PDE Megachurches on the Metropolitan Fringe

In order to understand the spatiality and materiality of the contemporary PDE church, we must begin by examining a common descriptive term for these churches: "seeker." Whether it is part of an historical narrative of transition from an older "dwelling" religiosity to a newer "seeking" spirituality or the emergence of a "quest culture," or the description of culturally contemporary congregations as "seeker churches," there is a strong tendency in recent studies of American Protestantism to view fast-growing religious organizations as successfully adapting to a market of consumers who are actively searching to meet their religious/spiritual needs.[20] These consumers are seen as largely untethered from religious traditions and rooted religious communities and are therefore either seeking to re-create these idyllic enclaves or are looking for updated and specialized communities. One is much less likely to find an appreciation for an alternative interpretation of the seeker church, where it is not the religious "consumer" but the religious "entrepreneur" that is doing the seeking. Despite the heavy use of the "seeker" motif to describe religious consumers, church growth experts like Rick Warren view their market as remarkably uncommitted and ambivalent. Without extensive outreach programs, highly organized children services, well-researched and culturally specific worship services, and immediately relevant sermons, their congregations, they believe, would not grow. It is not a matter of churches presenting their organization to the "seeking" masses, but rather of actively seeking the masses out.[21]

Put in cultural pragmatic terms, evangelical church growth has largely resulted from churches seeking out specific audiences and performatively responding to their material and symbolic worlds. Much of the literature on American evangelicalism in the last thirty years has told this story through the tropes of cultural accommodation and resistance. The relatively rapid pace of Protestant restructuring in America during the 1960s, 1970s, and 1980s—an era when mainline denominations saw steady decline, fundamentalists emerged from their self-imposed exile, and evangelicals claimed a broad middle ground between these two—was explained by many religious sociologists as the product of an intentional (but not always careful) blend of resistance and accommodation to the culture of a diverse, secular, modern world.[22] Because striking the right balance in any particular context required sensitivity to a diverse and fragmented audience, national denominational structures were seen as increasingly irrelevant.[23] Once the bedrock of American religiosity, denominations appeared slow-footed in relation to the new evangelical nondenominational seeker church.

These stories often overlooked the material socio-spatial environment in which the changes were taking place. The rise of nondenominational evangelicalism and church growth methodology in the last half of the twentieth century was closely tied to the steady expansion of suburban and postsuburban space. As early as the 1920s, observers found that suburbs provided a unique environment for church growth because rapid suburban in-migration was comprised of churchgoers with disparate denominational backgrounds. Hence, church growth was coupled with internal church fragmentation. Suburban churches' "constituencies are broken up into so many small social groups," writes H. Paul Douglass, a clergyman and sociologist of religion, "that the church infrequently serves them all at once."[24] Decades later, William H. Whyte, in his classic study of suburbia, found that suburban communities dealt with denominational diversity through a pragmatic focus on "a useful church." "To emphasize theological points," Whyte wrote, paraphrasing a suburban land developer, "was to emphasize what is not of first importance and at the price of provoking dissension."[25] This emphasis on usefulness—what a church could do for its constituents—was manifested in the church-growth movement of the next decade. Surveys, organized competitions, statistical models, motivational speeches, and formal curricula all became part of suburban church-growth methodology that saw the confluence of rapid population growth, displaced young families, and the loosening of denominational ties as providing an ideal stage for their performative innovations.[26]

While the suburban church-growth boosters were busy taking market surveys and planting churches, a cottage industry of suburban church criticism arose. H. Paul Douglass's subtle critique in *The Suburban Trend* was replaced by clear polemics that argued that the suburban church, while bursting at the seams with new members, has abrogated its moral and spiritual responsibility to communities left behind in the city's urban core.[27] Much of this frustration might ultimately have had to do with *which* churches were thriving in the suburbs, rather than the "suburban church" in general. By the 1970s it was clear that many of these growing suburban churches were not of the staid mainline denominational variety.[28] They were theologically conservative (sometimes expressly fundamentalist) congregations that were either nondenominational or loosely denominational (of a Southern Baptist or a Pentecostal variety). Observers noticed that because independent churches were more flexible and could move quickly and decisively, they could speak to the rapidly changing worlds of these newly formed local communities. In this environment, denominationalism had no clear advantage.

Rick Warren's story and his theory of church planting are practically perfect illustrations of this postdenominational shift. For Warren, newly formed, rapidly growing communities represent an untended but primed and receptive audience. In these high-growth areas, individuals and families are often in transition, without support groups and under an unusual amount of stress. "Who are the most receptive people?" Warren asks. "I believe there are two broad categories: people under transition and people under tension."[29] Warren didn't need to do a heavy amount of research to find out where this sort of population resides. At the end of his seminary education, according to Warren:

> I discovered that the Saddleback Valley, in Orange County, southern California, was the fastest-growing area in the fastest growing county in the U.S. during the decade of the 1970s. This fact grabbed me by the throat and made my heart start racing. I knew that wherever new communities were being started at such a fast pace there would also be a need for new churches.

Warren described this momentary confluence of demographical and spiritual inspiration:

As I sat there in the dusty, dimly lit basement of that university library, I heard God speak clearly to me: "That's where I want you to plant a church!" My whole body began to tingle with excitement, and tears welled up in my eyes. I had heard from God. It didn't matter that I had no money, no members, and had never even seen the place. Form that moment on, our destination was a settled issue.[30]

It is precisely in these new communities "that people are more receptive to the Gospel when they face changes like a new marriage, a new baby, a new home, a new job, or a new school. This is why churches generally grow faster in new communities where residents are continually moving in than in stable, older communities where people have lived for forty years."[31]

Warren describes the cultural geographic dimension of the well-known twentieth-century shift in American Christianity. The Roman Catholic Church and virtually every mainline Protestant denomination in the United States steadily lost members, while PDE churches like Saddleback continuously grew.[32] There are differing opinions about whether this growth is simply siphoned from other shrinking congregations or whether all megachurches are the product of real economic conditions (i.e., rising costs but flattened efficiency leads to a dominance of large firms).[33] Outside of such debates one thing is clear—there is a peculiar geography to PDE megachurches. Such peculiarity has little to do with their regional distribution; in the last thirty years regional evangelical distribution has remained remarkably stable (see fig. 3.1). We can assume a similar stability for the diffusion of megachurches over time because the most recent data show megachurch regional distribution tracking closely with general evangelical distribution (see fig. 3.2). The interesting geographical characteristics of the PDE megachurch can best be detected at the urban scale and below. Of the largest fifty PDE megachurches, all but six are set on the residential fringe of large metropolitan areas (see the appendix). And in the past decade, the percentage of megachurches on the metropolitan fringe has only increased (see fig. 3.3). In the popular imagination this has created the notion of the "suburban," "exurban," or "regional" megachurch sprouting up alongside barely finished subdivisions and freeway exit ramps.[34] Even if we map the one hundred largest megachurches of any denominational stripe, not just the postdenominational ones, we still find a solid majority (69) on the metropolitan residential fringe, with the remainder scattered between dense urban cores (18), industrial clusters (5), and older working-class suburbs (7) (see the appendix).

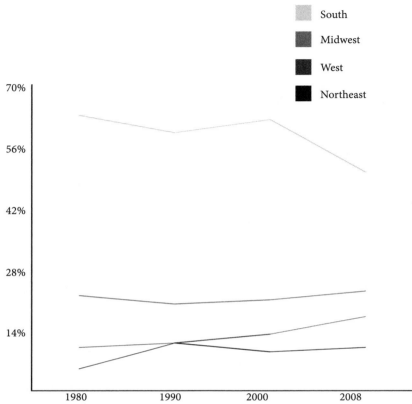

Figure 3.1 Percentage of evangelical religious adherence by region, 1980–2008. Source: U.S. Religious Landscape Survey, 2007. *Pew Forum on Religion and Public Life*. Available at http://religions.pewforum.org/portraits.

There is a high correlation between the styles of megachurches and their urban locations. For instance, churches that closely match the PDE style of congregational organization—which includes a majority white membership (see chap. 1)—are overwhelmingly likely to be on the residential fringe of a large metropolis near a freeway. But if the megachurch has a majority African American membership, or is a culturally conservative white congregation, it is much more likely to be in an urban cluster or in an older suburb (see figs. 3.3 and 3.4). Thus, the demographics of a congregation will not differ significantly from the demographics of the surrounding community. It is obvious that these megachurches are founded on the fast-growing urban fringe because that is where the people—with money and kids, especially—are increasingly located. But it is clearly not as simple as "build it and they will come." Megachurches are not just day-care centers with adult-contemporary

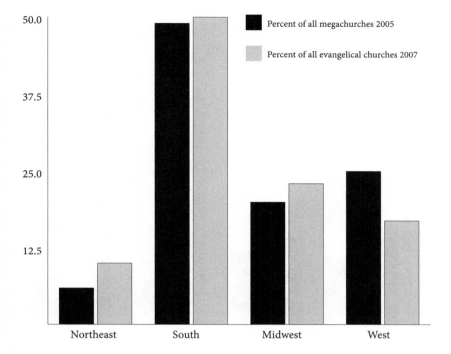

Figure 3.2 Churches by region, 2005 and 2007. Compiled from, Scott Thumma, Dave Travis, and Warren Bird, "Megachurches today 2005: summary of research findings," Hartford Institute for Religion Research (2005), available at http://hirr.hartsem.edu/mega-church/megastoday2005_summaryreport.html; "U.S. Religious Landscape Survey," Pew Forum on Religion and Public Life (2008), available at http://religions.pewforum.org/.

music on Sundays: they are meticulously ordered, demographically diverse, strategically positioned, and reflexively adaptive organizations that constantly revise their performances.

Older congregations in established neighborhoods, what Rick Warren calls "family reunion churches," can draw on generational inertia to ensure the meaningfulness of their performances. But PDE churches on the metropolitan fringe must continually reassess each performative element—background symbols, foreground script, staging, setting, costumes, *mis-en-scène*—for not only do they lack the taken-for-grantedness of tradition, but tradition works against PDE churches' desideratum: contemporary relevance. The highly mobile character of its population and environment force megachurches to continuously innovate and discard programs, styles, practices, and organizational structures in order to seamlessly blend into the daily rhythm of their ever-changing constituents' lives.

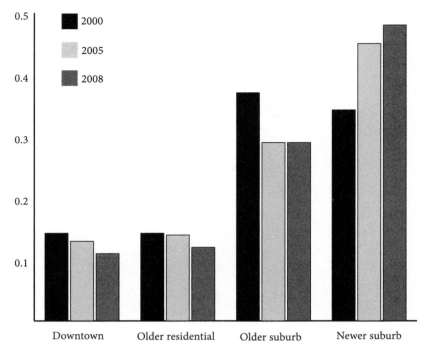

Figure 3.3 Megachurches in self-described urban location. Source: Thumma, Scott. Megachurch Research. Hartford Institute for Religion Research. Available at http://hirr. hartsem.edu/megachurch/research.html (last accessed February 17 2009).

In the absence of long-standing tradition and intergenerational ties, PDE congregations must find ways of making theologically conservative Protestantism meaningful to contemporary life in postsuburban places. They cannot rely on the unquestioned, automatic membership of younger generations into the older generations' family church, nor on larger societal pressure of belonging to *some* church. Instead, they must rely on their ability to craft meaningful performances that achieve fusion with an audience assembled from a radically de-fused socio-spatial environment.

Before the "Post": Evangelicalism in Suburbia

The relationship between evangelicalism (broadly conceived) and the residential metropolitan fringe predates Saddleback by almost two hundred years. To a significant extent, modern suburbs and evangelicalism have grown hand in hand. One of the first true modern suburbs in the world was created in Clapham, a sleepy hamlet five miles outside of eighteenth-century

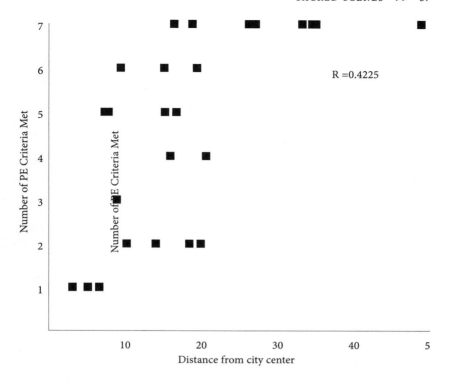

Figure 3.4 Scatter plot of twenty-five largest U.S. megachurches, measured by level of adherence to postdenominational evangelicalism and the driving distance from their metropolitan core. The latter is a crude and highly imperfect measure of suburbanity and postsuburbanity (see especially Fishman, *Bourgeois Utopias*, 6–8). Here it is used as one illustrative example among many.

London.[35] As wealthy merchants from London began locating their country villas close enough to the city to make them permanent residences, Clapham quickly became a *sub*-urban residential community. It was centered physically around the verdant Clapham Common and morally around the virtuous nuclear family. By the 1790s it was home to some of the most important evangelicals in England, including William Wilberforce (MP, influential abolitionist), Henry Thornton (MP, son of the influential evangelical John Thornton), John Venn (son of another important evangelical, Henry Venn), and Zachary Macaulay (editor of the evangelical periodical the *Christian Observer*). These founding evangelical suburbanites (known popularly at the time as the "Clapham saints" or "Clapham sect") were best known for their passionate opposition to slavery. Equally important to them was a campaign to spread a domestic ideology centered on a hierarchically divided nuclear

family and personal devotion to Bible study and prayer. These were not
the hot-blooded evangelicals of camp revivals in America but represented
a "patrician evangelicalism," which focused as much on bourgeois values of
order, hard work, and restraint as on spiritual reform.[36] Nevertheless, their
determined advocacy for personal, inward spirituality differed in no significant way from early evangelicals like Jonathan Edwards, George Whitefield,
or John Wesley.

This personal spirituality for Clapham evangelicals was expressed
through daily spiritual practice, which was centered spatially on the home
and embodied in the nuclear family.[37] For such evangelicals like William
Wilberforce, true Christianity is a state "into which we must be translated; a nature which we do not inherit, but into which we are to be created anew."[38] This translation into a new creation would take place within
the warmth and strict guidance of a morally upright nuclear family. "It
is the diffusion of personal and family piety, of holiness in our domestic circles . . . that prepares for every future blessing."[39] The move from
London to Clapham, then, could be seen as an effort to purify a space for
personal and family piety—a space unpolluted by work, the bureaucratic
state, extraneous excitements, and uncontrollable contact with diverse
others. Of course, suburban Clapham was not only a project of separation
but also of new connections—between emerging expressive individualism and idyllic natural landscapes, between male heads of households and
their families, and between nuclear families and their new intentionally
constructed communities.

The functional differentiation of family life from work life for these early
suburbanites was not just a peculiar response to the particularities of life
in eighteenth-century London. Such combinations of differentiation and
integration marked the culture and politics of modern suburbs throughout the next two centuries. The urban historians Robert Fishman and Kenneth T. Jackson chronicled this trend from nineteenth-century Manchester
and Philadelphia to early twentieth-century suburbs of New York City and
Chicago.[40] These sites of classic suburban life in Riverside, Illinois, or Westchester County, New York, were, like Clapham, idyllic refuges for wealthy
and upper-middle-class rail commuters. It was not until the invention of
affordable automobiles and mass-produced Levitt-style subdivisions that the
exclusivity of suburbia became available to many. As the suburbs became an
increasingly common place to interpret the American dream in the middle
of twentieth century, it began to be seen as the cause of countless and sometimes contradictory maladies such as conformity, ennui, isolation, psychosis,
aesthetic indifference, and general anomy.[41]

Among these suburban ills was the "captivity" of Christian churches by an insular, instrumental, and somewhat shallow suburban way of life. Gibson Winter, an Episcopal priest and theologian, and the sociologist Peter L. Berger both argued in the early 1960s that as urban churchgoers moved out to the suburbs, the scope of Christian charity and the seriousness of religious practice would dwindle.[42] They saw the concerns of the suburban church turn more toward sanctifying the social status quo and patching over the tensions and contradictions of life in post–World War II America. The organization man of the suburbs had simply constructed around him the "organization church."[43] The difficulty in suburbia for congregations (denominational and nondenominational alike) and their adherents was that the assumed requisites of local community appeared to be absent. Spatial proximity, low geographic mobility, historical ties to a place and a community, strong extended kinship networks, and integrated traditions hardly seemed characteristic of these new suburban places.

Winter's and Berger's polemics notwithstanding, the suburban church's rise in congregational numbers, membership, and influence continued apace. Other church practitioners saw as much opportunity as peril in churches moving to the suburbs. Frederick A. Shippey, a sociologist and United Methodist minister, saw the suburban church playing a critical role in its social environs by growing communal solidarity and maintaining the structure of the nuclear family. In helping new suburbanites cope with the stresses and vagaries of life in these "instant communities," churches could demonstrate the reality of "God's word," that "this is God's world and all men are brothers."[44] Harvey Cox's well-known 1965 treatise *The Secular City* is similarly optimistic but politically opposed. While not strictly speaking to the suburban church, Cox talks about the pace, diversity, and segregation of the modern city, and sees the resulting tensions not as something the church can and should ameliorate but rather as something that can push the faithful into a deeper, more mature religiosity.

All sides of the debate over the suburban church failed to anticipate the emerging new religious and urban landscapes that would produce the postdenominational megachurch. By the time the debates faded in the late 1960s, a new urban space was supplanting both suburb and central city, and a new church was overtaking both the denominational "organization churches" and the smaller, older "family churches." Today, and for the last fifty years, the fastest growing, largest, and most innovative churches have not been in the "suburbs" but in those vast, sprawling, polynuclear places that have sometimes been called "outer suburbs," "edge cities," "exurbia," or "boomburbs."[45] The largest megachurches in the United States are not in traditional suburbs that are economically, politically, and culturally tied to a dominant city center. From an areal perspective they are on the periphery of large metropolises, thus easily evoking the center-periphery relationship that defines "suburbia." But places like Lake Forest, California, South Barrington, Illinois, Alpharetta, Georgia, Fort Lauderdale, Florida, and Edmond, Oklahoma, are not necessarily connected to any dominant urban core. They are part of what the urban sociologist Mark Gottdiener calls a "multinucleated metropolitan region"—deconcentrated, functionally differentiated, and fragmented.[46]

Whereas suburbia refers to a residential periphery connected economically, culturally, and perhaps politically to an urban core, this new postsuburban space is only contingently connected to multiple, smaller urban cores.[47] In California, for example, south Orange County residents might commute to one of the moderately dense commercial centers in Irvine, but they are just as likely to commute to an office park in Anaheim, Newport, or Rancho Santa Margarita. Some still make the fifty to sixty-mile commute into downtown Los Angeles. There is no single dense center of shopping or the arts as these, too, are spread throughout the region. Orange County also has few large-scale, purely residential communities. More commonly, residential development exists alongside office complexes and shopping centers. Unlike their suburban forbears, contemporary residents of Orange County need not ever visit a dense and diverse metropolitan center for anything at all. Whereas Clapham and all pre–World War II suburbs existed in relation to a dense city center, postsuburban regions like Orange County have no single center. "The true center of this new city," writes Fishman, "is not in some downtown business district but in each residential unit. From that central starting point, the members of the household create their own city from the multitude of destinations that are within suitable driving distance" (see fig. 3.5).[48]

What is this new city called? Fishman uses the term "technoburb"; Joel Garreau calls it an "edge city"; Paul Knox uses "metroburbia"; others use "sprawl," "exurbia," or "exopolis."[49] While these terms direct our attention to crucial new changes in the suburban form, it is not clear that these changes are more than extensions and variations on the classic suburban form expressed in eighteenth-century Clapham. The culture of suburbia—the centrality of the nuclear family, domesticity, Edenic nature, and the ambivalent relationship with the "secular city"—is clearly present in sprawling examples like Orange County, or South Barrington, Illinois. From a demographic standpoint, there does not seem to be much of a difference either. Occupation, income, ethnicity, and age do not differ significantly, although the extreme urban periphery is home to a higher number of families with young

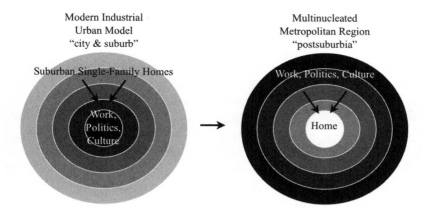

Figure 3.5 Postsuburban transformation of the classic urban concentric ring model. Adapted from Robert Fishman's description of "technoburbia."

children.[50] But most importantly, suburbia and postsuburbia are connected through socio-spatial differentiation. Insofar as suburbia is the expression of the functional and social differentiation of urban space along the lines of work life and family life, postsuburbia should be seen as its continuation. Suburbia and postsuburbia should be considered not as presently competing urban morphologies but as different perspectives on Gottdiener's "multinucleated metropolitan region." Postsuburbia in this framework is a way of talking about the socio-spatial changes—technological, economic, and political—that have effaced the older core-periphery relationship between suburbs and city center. But the term "suburbia" still adequately describes the cultural meanings, values, and aesthetic design principles that organize how Americans continue to think about home, work, family, the environment, and faith.

The End of the Center: Postmetropolis, Postsuburbia, and Urban Differentiation

The centerlessness of postsuburbia could be seen as merely the spatial expression of (secular) social differentiation where no single societal subsystem can claim primacy. Something of this view appears in corners of urban sociology,[51] but the more common view—that social differentiation is dialectically related to urbanization as a whole—has either fallen out of favor along with urban ecology or has been subsumed within a larger political economy approach to urbanism.[52] The relatively simple notion of the connection between social and spatial differentiation remains relevant, though, despite the successive revolutions in urban studies from human ecology to spatial science, systems theory, Marxian and non-Marxian political economy, and postmodern urbanism. Beginning with Durkheim, social differentiation (in terms of the division of labor) was seen as being made possible by urbanization. He saw it as the result of "dynamic" and "material density" and "social volume," that is, as a description of an agglomeration of individuals that self-regulates through dividing, separating, and specializing occupations and social roles. The conditions of urbanization (density and volume) and social differentiation, then, act back on each other in a dialectical way so that social specialization and spatial specialization become inseparable.[53]

The Chicago School urbanist Ernest Burgess developed the other side of this dialectic as advanced social differentiation was seen to lead to a particular pattern of urban differentiation.[54] His concentric-ring model, which laid out an areal pattern of urban-functional differentiation, is now considered to be irremediably flawed by postmodern urbanists who reject its "simplicity" as well as mainstream urbanists who consider it a flogged dead horse.[55] However, the most egregious problems with Burgess's concentric ring model—the imperatives of centralization, organicism, and universality—were not integral to his key insight that urban differentiation is in a "reciprocal" relationship with an increasing division of labor, cultural pluralism, and social complexity. Robert Park expressed this in a less theorized form through his famous characterization of the modern city as "a mosaic of little worlds."[56] To be sure, this mosaic of differentiated parts was divided along racial and class, as well as functional, lines. But it was this differentiation of social worlds that marked the unique nature of urban life. Louis Wirth most completely formulated the Chicago School concept of socio-spatial differentiation by linking size, density, and diversity of cities with "urbanism as a way of life."[57] In Wirth's view, urban life is made possible through "a more ramified and differentiated framework of social stratification" because the speed, volume, and heterogeneity of urban social interactions require specialization and compartmentalization. Social differentiation and urban spatial differentiation, then, are tied to the practically differentiated life of the urbanite:

> No single group has the undivided allegiance of the individual. The groups with which he is affiliated do not lend themselves readily to a simple hierarchical arrangement. By virtue of his different interests arising out of different aspects of social life, the individual acquires membership in widely divergent groups, each of which functions only with reference to a single segment of his personality. Nor do these groups easily

permit of a concentric arrangement so that the narrower ones fall within the circumference of the more inclusive ones, as is more likely to be the case in the rural community or in primitive societies. Rather the groups with which the person typically is affiliated are tangential to each other or intersect in highly variable fashion.[58]

Herbert Gans later points out that Wirth is describing something both narrower and broader than the "urban way of life."[59] He argues that as a description and explanation of a particular "settlement pattern," Wirth is only describing an unfortunate segment of the "inner city." But insofar as Wirth is writing about a way of life that is largely dependent on "secondary relationships," he is dealing with broad historical changes in social organization. Although Gans contests its explanatory validity as an ecological concept, he does not argue with functional and social differentiation as a description of urban and suburban life.

The Marxian turn in urban geography further elaborated on urban differentiation by describing and analyzing the post–World War II urban landscape produced by broad regional specialization as well as more local specialization determined by race, class, and gender.[60] Gottdiener has explained the increasing spatial differentiation of American cities in the twentieth century as the result of a private-public partnership in promoting capital accumulation. Against the ecological explanation of spatial differentiation as the product of population migration and technological innovation, Gottdiener's neo-Marxian approach paints a picture of urban fragmentation, expansion, and deconcentration as a partially planned solution to underconsumption and overaccumulation. Political devolution on the peripheries of cities, tax abatements, federal programs, and the availability of cheap land were just some of the elements that have led to the emergence of Gottdiener's "polynucleated metropolitan region." While such an analysis is ultimately economically deterministic, it was an important corrective to the organicist model that saw competition and homeostasis as the key factors in urban spatial differentiation.[61]

Gottdiener's analysis was inspired by the work of Henri Lefebvre, particularly the latter's focus on the production of space as a vital element in advanced capitalism. But Lefebvre has also contributed more broadly to the notions of postmetropolis and postsuburbia through his conception of urban "implosion-explosion" where the modern metropolis gathers all cultural, economic, and political life to it, while simultaneously diffusing into fragmented, disjointed, and defensive urban enclaves. "Our modern city is a divided city," Lefebvre writes (with European cases particularly in mind).

"On the one hand it is broken up into peripheries, into suburbs, some inner, some further out, in rings where workers and the excluded are relegated. And on the other hand, its centrality is becoming more pronounced. It has become the centre of decision-making, of information, of authority and knowledge."[62] Terms such as "urban," "suburban," and "rural" fail to capture "the historical process of implosion-explosion (a metaphor borrowed from nuclear physics) that occurred: the tremendous concentration (of people, activities, wealth, goods, objects, instruments, means, and thought) of urban reality and the immense explosion, the projection of numerous, disjunct fragments (peripheries, suburbs, vacation homes, satellite towns) into space."[63] For Lefebvre, then, urban spatial differentiation is not a recent, unique moment in the history of urban morphology. It is instead a defining feature in the development of the modern capitalist city. The very forces of socio-spatial agglomeration that created the early capitalist free towns were always simultaneously expansionist, diffuse, and centrifugal. These tendencies of capitalism were conceived of by Lefebvre as an "explosion" of space that produced an array of specialized spaces: "living space, personal space, scholastic space, prison space, army space, or hospital space."[64]

In this way, traditional suburbs—as functionally distinct spaces—can be seen as the residential fragments of the emerging polynucleated metropolitan region. Far from being uniquely suburban, the social, spatial, and functional differentiation represented in classical suburbia is interwoven into the fabric of the modern urban form. Richard A. Walker writes that "spatial differentiation, deconcentration, and the phenomenon of successive, distinct waves of urbanization have been at work since the capitalist revolution transformed American cities in the nineteenth century and have become, in absolute terms, more pronounced over time."[65] It is no longer possible to conceptualize a simple differentiation between core and periphery because the multiplier effects of differentiation, deconcentration, and expansion have created countless cores in any metropolitan region, alongside seemingly peripheral zones that have no necessary relationship with any particular core. The concepts of core and periphery have not vanished; it is rather that they can no longer be conceived of in simple territorial terms. Manuel Castells's work on the informational city is an example of how such concepts can still be used. He writes of the "dual city" where "the necessary mixing of functions in the same metropolitan area leads to the attempt to preserve social segregation and functional differentiation through planning of the spatial layout of activities."[66] Classical suburbia was the product of such preservation efforts, but today the urban dualism, according to Castells, is not between suburb and city or rural and urban but between the enclaves of cosmopolitan elite and "the tribalism of local communities." Such groups have no necessary spatial relationship with a single territorial urban core or periphery. Cores and peripheries become multiple and relative.

Following on Castells's urban dualism, Steven Graham and Simon Marvin have articulated a "splintering urbanism" in which the specialization of functions and spaces has produced and is produced by a fragmented moral vision of the urban community.[67] No longer is the city seen as a mosaic of different but connected parts, all with rights and responsibilities related to the common good of the city. Instead, the infrastructure of the city, from roads and water to energy and telecommunications, has been steadily privatized and fragmented so that access to the urban infrastructure network is a matter of private consumption rather than public citizenship. The story that Graham and Marvin tell has affinities with neo-functionalist differentiation theory: functional differentiation results not in an integrated resolution but in a patchwork, contingent, and fragile settlement.

The daily lived experience of the patchwork of postsuburbia is best summed up in the term "fragmentation."[68] The explosion of differentiated spaces is mirrored by a proliferation in the possible roles that any given individual must take on. As individuals' roles multiply, separate, and become spatially and socially specialized, a single place (home or neighborhood) can no longer be expected to integrate them all. The local place of home, then, often takes on the role of a protected enclave where a "real" integrated self can seek relief from the extraneous multiscalar networks of work life, the state, and society: all putative factors of secularization.[69] From a very different angle than the neo-Marxian analyses presented earlier, the differentiation and multiplication of social roles can be seen as part of a longer and larger process of Lefebvrian implosion-explosion. Through the centripetal agglomeration of people and capital on the one hand, and their centrifugal deployment into functionally and socially differentiated spaces and roles on the other, the postsuburban enclave is less tied to geographically local networks and more tied to complimentary but diffuse enclaves within wider networks of information and transportation. This sort of splintering was foreshadowed in Robert Park's description of the industrial metropolis as "a mosaic of little worlds *which touch but do not interpenetrate*."[70] Such fragmenting of daily life was "fascinating but dangerous" to Park because the local community in this splintered metropolis could not sustain a moral community.

At the time Park was writing, the suburbs were still a functional reality where the possibility of local community was held open by social homogeneity. Within half a century, however, the exclusivity of the suburban periphery had been transported to scattered enclaves as population and industrial migration rendered the traditional geography of core and periphery almost meaningless. According to urbanists like Robert Fishman, the core/periphery binary still had value but only if turned on its concentric-ring-modeled head. The new postsuburban reality, argued Fishman, had replaced the communally shared urban core with countless privatized and differentiated centers that were consumer-citizens' residential homes. The new postsuburban periphery is anything within "reasonable" driving distance/time.[71] This insight cuts to the heart of the functional-spatial transformation from suburbia to postsuburbia (see fig. 3.5). As the suburban landscape has fragmented, the residential home has become the de facto center. And not only is it a functional center but it is a symbolic-affective one as well.[72]

It is partially because of the contemporary symbolic power of the home, that an understanding of postsuburbia must be accompanied by an understanding of the cultural legacy of suburbia. This means that the discussion of the functional transformation of suburbia into postsuburbia should not indicate that the term "suburbia" has lost its purchase as a description of residential places on the metropolitan periphery. Postsuburban place, like all place, has a dual structure—a "betweenness" in the words of J. Nicholas Entrikin—in which its material, functional, and spatial qualities afford and bound but do not determine its subjective, affective, and cultural qualities. In other words, the values, aesthetics, discourses, and meaning of modern suburbia have not been transformed in precisely the same way as its space and function.

The Betweenness of Postsuburban Place

Structured through deep cultural binary codes such as public/private, work/family, society/community, and freedom/restraint, suburban culture has remained central to postsuburban life. The spatial and functional transformation from suburbia to postsuburbia scrambled many of these binaries so that their spatial referents such as workplace, home, shopping district, and especially church are no longer cleanly aligned with them. For example, if work is even more peripherally located in the metropolitan region than the home, then the homologic alignment of work, public center, society, and world ceases to be so clean. Early modern suburbs were such powerful models for later design because their location, aesthetics, politics, and infrastructure were more clearly aligned with both emerging and older cultural binary codes. This alignment allowed for a seamless translation of these places into the vocabulary of nineteenth-century urban life.[73] By the time the suburbs became a mass commodity in the twentieth century, its cultural codes were well established. These codes are remarkable for their staying power; they continue to fundamentally structure twenty-first century cultural understandings of house, home, neighborhood, and city.

If the culture of suburbia still has the power to order the meaning of contemporary metropolitan patterns, then postsuburbia and advanced urban spatial differentiation cannot bring us as far as we need to go in understanding the socio-spatial environment of the PDE megachurch. They do not tell us about the background symbols and scripts of postsuburban life, nor about how PDE congregations mobilize such cultural elements in a religiously meaningful way. Suburban culture, then, has a power of its own and acknowledging the death of suburbia as a functional, spatial zone should not lead to accepting the death of suburbia as a cultural mode of understanding the self and community in twenty-first-century America. The power of suburban ideas, aesthetics, and values is derived from more fundamental cultural binary codes that serve as a foundation for more elaborate cultural coding (see table 3.1). The following chapters will elaborate on this notion of

private/public (Jackson 1985; Hansen 1991; Baumgartner 1991; Archer 1997; Kumar 1997)

female/male (McDannell 1986; Beuka 2004, chaps. 3 and 4; Archer 2005)

family/work (McDannell 1986; Fishman 1987; Sies 1991; Beuka 2004, chap. 3)

nature/city (Fishman 1987; Cronon 1996; Archer 2005; Bruegmann 2005)

faith/reason (Gallagher 2003; Brooks 2004, chap. 4; Luhr 2009)

emotion/rationality (Beuka 2004, chaps. 1 and 2; Archer 2005)

home/world (Sies 1991; Morley 2000, chap. 6; Rybczynski 2007)

child/adult (Rybczynski 1985; Fishman 1987; Low 2003; Brooks 2004, chap. 5; Luhr 2009)

community/society (Whyte 1956; Jackson 1985; Fishman 1987)

order/chaos (Blakely and Snyder 1999; Low 2003; Bruegmann 2005)

homogeneity/diversity (Duncan and Duncan 1997; Teaford 2006; Knox 2008)

freedom/restraint (Fishman 1987; Cross 1997; Archer 2005; Bruegmann 2005)

autonomy/heteronomy (Baumgartner 1991; McGirr 2001; Archer 2005; Lassiter 2005)

mobility/stasis (Brooks 2004; Urry 2004; Knox 2008)

new/old (Fishman 1987; Beuka 2004; Bruegmann 2005; Knox 2008)

ownership/servitude (Jackson 1985; Archer 2005; Bruegmann 2005; Lassiter 2005)

consumption/production (Brooks 2004; Knox 2008; Luhr 2009)

Table 3.1 Suburban cultural binaries

cultural binary codes and cultural power (drawing on Alexander's cultural pragmatics) and in the process demonstrate the ways that PE megachurches draw on suburban cultural codes in an effort to weave contemporary evangelical institutions into the everyday fabric of postsuburban life.

From the perspective of the culture of suburbia rather than its spatiality (morphology, function, economic, and political networks), postsuburbia still harbors within it many of the meanings of its antecedent. As the architecture historian John Archer has pointed out, the meaning of suburbia was built on several cultural binary codes, which allowed for new agonistic distinctions to be made between the city and the suburb.[74] Early suburban developments like Clapham and New Jersey's Llewellyn Park did not simply arise out of the exigencies of emerging capitalist modes of production and reproduction, but they were also built on incipient understandings of the modern self and its proper environs. These understandings were traceable to self-conscious, modern, secularist notions of the rational and self-directed individual. But they were at the same time rooted in newly formed Protestant and particularly evangelical ideas of self-will, emotion, privacy, and civilization.[75]

Protestant evangelical binaries such as self-willed/tradition-bound, emotional connection/rational-detachment, private-cultivation/public-distraction, and civilized-discipline/contagious-degeneracy were woven into the spatiality of early suburbia, and are in fact defining features of the function and morphology of modern suburbia. The physical separation of the old city from the new suburb, the large lot space for the single-family home's nuclear family, the romantic landscaping of "natural" rolling hills and curvilinear streets, the explicit appeal to privacy at the level of the home and the secluded community, and the infrastructural dedication to cultivation, health, and order are all material-spatial counterparts to the fundamental cultural binaries by which the Anglo-American bourgeoisie began to understand themselves. The meaning of the single-family home in the polynucleated metropolitan region is still deeply embedded in these foundational binaries of autonomy/heteronomy, emotion/rationality, and family/work among others. Yet, the detachment of the suburban home with a shared, collective urban core renders many other binaries problematic.

It is possible to see that several suburban binaries are dependent on a clear center/periphery relationship (see table 3.1). For example, the private/public binary was dependent on a coherent, recognizable public sphere that had its spatial referent in the urban core. Even if we take the public sphere to be primarily mediatic, its productive activity was centered in specifically urban cores. For the Claphamites, the separation of the private space of the peripheral suburban abode from the public space of London was aligned with a host of other socio-spatial binaries. Female/male, family/work, emotion/rationality, nature/city, home/world and other binaries were used to make sense of the new world that was emerging in Clapham, London, and abroad. Wilberforce and other Clapham saints saw their suburban idyll as a fortress from which to reform the world (through legislation as much as evangelism).[76] The works of Wilberforce, Hannah More, and the Claphamite *Christian Observer* are shot through with narratives of manly self-exertion and womanly submission; self-willed reformation against degenerate heteronomy; and domestic bliss versus urban licentiousness.[77]

The "metropolitan revolution" that took place over the next two centuries would scramble such binaries so that the private no longer corresponded to a clear public, work was separated farther from family life, consumption overshadowed production in narratives of self-formation, increasing numbers of women in the workplace challenged the symbolic masculinity of work space and public space, and the bourgeois exclusivity of the suburbs was lessened as they become more geographically and economically accessible.[78] Metropolitan fragmentation has undermined many of suburbia's foundational binary codes although postsuburban space is still strongly shaped by them. Researchers of postsuburbia describe the "degenerate utopias," and "lifestyle enclaves" that commercial and residential land developers attempt to construct around themes of nostalgia, family, domesticity, and local community.[79] Although they market—for example, through features that emphasize the automobile—to a clientele that understands the fragmented and decentered spatiality of postsuburbia, architects, developers, and real estate agents still pay homage to long-standing suburban cultural codes.[80]

At the heart of postsuburban evangelical performances is the attempt to bring these older suburban mythologies into alignment with contemporary postsuburban realities. Saddleback's church structure, outreach campaigns, evangelistic strategies, and theological style are all geared toward resolving the contradictions that arise between suburban myth and postsuburban reality. Popular evangelical literature chronicles the tension between these two with book titles such as *Death by Suburb: How to Keep the Suburbs From Killing Your Soul*; *The Suburban Christian: Finding Spiritual Vitality in the Land of Plenty*; *The Jesus of Suburbia: Have We Tamed the Son of God?*; and *Plastic Jesus: Exposing the Hollowness of Comfortable Christianity*.[81] Each of these is a conservative evangelical counterpart to Gibson Winter's liberal mainline critique of the suburbs. Instead of Winters's concern with nonsuburbanites left behind in the old city, these new evangelical critiques of the postsuburbs focus on the spiritual travails of the lonely, individualized, aimless suburbanite. Naturally, these authors end on more hopeful notes for suburban Christianity. They argue that the insular privacy, disconnected anxiety, and fragmented individualism are problems that can be remedied by a local, Bible-believing church. The trick for these local churches is to transform these postsuburban problems into a meaningful spiritual condition.

4

Purpose Driven Pluralities

Variety, Consumption, and Choice in Postdenominational Evangelicalism

Much has been made of Warren's opening sentence in his mega-best-seller *Purpose Driven Life*. "It's not about you," he writes. "The purpose of your life is far greater than your own personal fulfillment, your peace of mind, or even your happiness."[1] It is one of the first things mentioned by journalists and academics alike when writing about the book and Warren's rise to fame.[2] In addition, it has spawned a cottage industry of evangelical self-help books that purport to downplay the self.[3] But in fact the design of the postdenominational evangelical megachurch is carefully crafted to meet the highly differentiated, individualized needs of the postsuburban self. If you live in postsuburban Atlanta, Chicago, Washington, D.C. or Southern California and are not outright hostile to religion, then for these PDE megachurches it is unswervingly and painstakingly *about you*.

More precisely it is about a set of performances that center on *you*. Whether it is Warren's book, the main concern of which is the classically evangelical theme of an intimately personal God who created and cares uniquely about *you*, or postdenominational evangelicalism's development of small groups to meet the unique circumstances of *your* life (see chap. 5), or even evangelical political action (see chap. 7), Saddleback and other PDE churches work intentionally to create an environment, which is in seamless unity with the postsuburban dreamscape.

The older suburban dreamscape, as described by both boosters and critics, has been summed up by John Archer as consisting of themes of escape, social advancement, and self-fulfillment.[4] According to chroniclers of postsuburbia, this dreamscape has nostalgically held fast to the older suburban version, except in the new version the negative sides of suburban cultural binaries—poverty, ethnic minorities, crime, heterogeneity—have lost their geographical bearing in the city center.[5] The "other" does not map onto an urban center-periphery as easily. More clearly, as Archer shows, the postsuburban dreamscape centers on the singular site of the residential home of the individual and his or her family.

Attempting a meaningful engagement with the material culture of postsuburbia, designers of PDE megachurches have built their institutions on concerns for the individuated self and its (real or ideal) nuclear family. Boosters frame the suburb's nurturing of the isolated self and family against purportedly degrading alternatives while critics skewer this individualized introversion as the worst symptom of a deeper moral rot.[6] Regardless of their normative standing, themes of individuation are part of the cultural-material environment for PDE megachurches like Saddleback. And these churches' popularity and very existence relies on their performatively responding to this environment. A problem that lies at the heart of this pursuit, however, is the seeming impossibility of designing and maintaining a large institution that must cater to the differentiated and finely detailed tastes and desires of these postsuburban individuated selves.

This chapter focuses on the ways Saddleback Church as a local, embodied institution solves this problem. Indeed, Saddleback Church's spatial structure mirrors that of postsuburbia, and this mirroring allows for widely diverse performances of salient suburban narratives.

The Community

One of the most frequently articulated spatial imaginaries at Saddleback is the "5 Circles of Commitment" (see fig. 1.1). Warren created this model in 1974 as a youth pastor at the First Baptist Church of Norwalk (only thirty-five miles north of Saddleback's present campus). He was looking for a way to describe how a single church might meet the needs of churchgoers with a wide gradation of commitment to Christianity. The community, in

Table 4.1 Saddleback Church outreach efforts to "the community"

Name	Location	Description
Civil Forum	Central Campus— Worship Center	Events with quasi-secular topics and special guests, which are meant to attract a broad, "unchurched" audience from "the community."
Job Fairs	Central Campus— Venue tents around the campus	Began in the fall of 2008 as the economic crisis became full blown; includes career coaching, employment databases, and networking fora.
Child and Youth Programs	Central Campus— Children's building and the "Refinery"	A foundation of Saddleback's outreach to the community from its inception; includes both weekend and weekday programs, and summer camps.
Celebrate Recovery	Central Campus— Venue tent	Although it is billed as an explicitly Christian alternative to the AA 12-step program, CR members actively recruit unchurched members from "the community."
Support Groups (different from small groups)	Central Campus— Various rooms around the campus	There are two main categories of support groups: relational and medical. The former consists of different groups dealing with problems as diverse as workplace transition, divorce, and post-abortion.
Weekend Service	Central Campus— Worship center and venue tents around the campus	The main service each week, delivered at seven different times in seven different venues around the central campus; designed to appeal to newcomers.
Personal Evangelism	A key step in personal evangelism is inviting the target to the central campus.	Personal evangelism strategies are discussed in detail in C.L.A.S.S. 401, the fourth and final membership class at Saddleback.

How may we serve you?

saddleback church

PLEASE PRINT

Date: ☐ Miss ☐ Ms. ☐ Mr. ☐ Mrs. Name: _____ ☐ 1st Time Guest

My E-mail: _____ ☐ New E-mail?

I'D LIKE PROGRAM INFORMATION ON:

☐ Bible Studies ☐ Men ☐ Children ☐ College Age ☐ Recreation/Sports
☐ Music & Drama ☐ Women ☐ Junior High ☐ Single Adults ☐ Support Groups
☐ Men ☐ Couples ☐ Senior High ☐ Seniors 60+ ☐ Online Giving

Free e-mail newsletters: ☐ Rick's News & Views ☐ Daily Devotional ☐ Slice ☐ Ministry Leader Toolbox

COMMENTS/PRAYER REQUESTS: ☐ Confidential

_____
_____
_____
_____
_____

Home: (   ) Work: (   )

I AM: ☐ Single ☐ Married Date of Birth: _____ ☐ I'm a Pastor ☐ Our Church did 40 Days of Purpose

NEXT STEPS IN MY SPIRITUAL JOURNEY:

☐ I am committing my life to Jesus today.
☐ I'd like to be baptized the way Jesus was.
☐ I'd like to join a small group:
    ☐ Couples ☐ Singles ☐ Men ☐ Women
☐ I'd like to help start a small group.
☐ I will begin tithing.
☐ I am recommitting my life to Jesus.
☐ I'd like information on how to commit my life to Jesus.
☐ I'd like information on joining the church.

PURPOSE DRIVEN LIFE CLASSES (offered once a month):

☐ Enroll me in Class 101: Discovering Membership
☐ Enroll me in Class 201: Discovering Spiritual Maturity
☐ Enroll me in Class 301: Discovering My Ministry
☐ Enroll me in Class 401: Discovering My Life Mission
☐ Notify me when Class 501 is offered

SEND ME INFORMATION ON THESE SPIRITUAL HABITS:

☐ Starting a daily quiet time ☐ Reconciling a relationship
☐ Tithing and God's promises ☐ Managing my finances
☐ Finding my place to serve God ☐ Small group fellowship
☐ Sharing my faith with others ☐ Helping the poor
☐ P.E.A.C.E. Plan mission projects ☐ Caring for the sick

I NEED PERSONAL COUNSELING FOR:

☐ Pre-Marital ☐ Marriage ☐ Grief
☐ Financial ☐ Personal ☐ Addiction/Habits

I'D LIKE TO VOLUNTEER TO SERVE WITH:

☐ Church Office ☐ Video/Audio ☐ Children ☐ Single Adults
☐ Writing/Editing ☐ Graphics ☐ Junior High ☐ Ushering
☐ Web Design ☐ Landscaping ☐ Senior High ☐ Traffic
☐ Fine Arts ☐ Custodial ☐ College ☐ Greeting

Figure 4.1 Saddleback Church visitor information card.

this model, is "the pool of lost people that live within driving distance of your church that have made no commitment at all to either Jesus Christ or your church."[7] In this definition, the *community* of Saddleback spans as far south as San Diego, as far north as the San Fernando Valley, and as far east as Riverside. On a Sunday morning, Saddleback can be reached in an hour's drive from much of southern California, and Saddleback staff focus on south Orange County as their community. When pastors speak casually of "the community" they almost always refer to the cities that make up the Saddleback Valley: Mission Viejo, Lake Forest, Rancho Santa Margarita, Tustin,

Figure 4.2 Saddleback Church, Worship Center.

Figure 4.3 Saddleback Church, Children's Ministries Complex.

Figure 4.4 Saddleback Church, Head Office Complex.

Figure 4.5 Saddleback Church, The Refinery.

Irvine, Laguna Niguel, and Aliso Viejo. Although many committed members, full-time staff, and pastors live farther out in Costa Mesa or Garden Grove to the north, Corona or Riverside to the east, and Oceanside to the south, most live nearby in the Saddleback Valley.

But the community in Warren's five circles is not primarily a geographic concept; it is a spiritual category. It is meant to indicate the spiritual condition of individuals and the church's perceived responsibility toward them. If an individual visits Saddleback even once and fills out a visitor's information card (see fig. 4.1), they are entered into a database of "hot evangelistic prospects." They will receive email updates and targeted advertising for "community events" (see table 4.1) that are designed to turn visitors into churchgoers. The spiritual condition of "the community," then, is diagnosed a priori; the question for Saddleback staff and pastors is what will lead these unchurched individuals to their salvation?

Answering this question is the self-perceived purpose of churches like Saddleback. These various churches are often grouped under the rubric of "seeker churches" because they are seen to be intensely focused on engaging individuals who are not committed churchgoers or even Christians but who are nonetheless "seeking" a religious community. But it is the PDE churches who are doing the seeking, and their evangelism is targeted far beyond the narrow band of religiously curious seekers (see chap. 3). The community, for Warren, is not just the potentially eligible unchurched "seekers" but neither is it an undistinguishable mass. It is made up of a dizzying diversity of individuals who have different desires, fears, hopes, and dreams—what one Saddleback pastor called "triggers"—that can be activated with just the right evangelistic strategies. The content of each strategy differs, whether it is the fall campaigns that have broad, quasi-secularist themes such as "purpose," "love," "community," or "health," or the individualistic evangelism that is taught in Saddleback's Class 401, the church's final class in their four-class membership series. But the geography is the same: by all acceptable means, the community must be drawn centripetally toward the church campus.

Once on the campus, the newcomer—even if attending an avowedly secular event like a Civil Forum (see chap. 7), a Christmas musical, or a job fair—will subtly be presented with the visitor's information card. Depending on the event, the card will ask about personal interests, how one heard about the event, and an email address so he or she can be contacted "for similar events in the future." The hope, according to Erik Rees, pastor of communication, is that the material environment of the church campus appears familiar and comfortable enough that a visitor to a community event will consider returning for a weekend service. The performances of Saddleback Church in these community events must be immediately intelligible and seemingly harmonious with the extended postsuburban environment.

One of the key aspects of these performances is the architecture and landscaping of the central campus. According to Rees, "Every building is a tool for us to set the table for somebody to feel comfortable enough to come." Many observers of evangelical megachurches have noted how the similarity between megachurch campuses and other suburban and postsuburban landscape fixtures such as the mall or office park achieve this very thing.[8] Saddleback is exemplary in this respect. While the campus as a whole is too large and sprawling to be taken in from a single vantage point, its various parts—from the main sanctuary (fig. 4.2), to the building for its many youth ministries (fig. 4.3), to its head office complex (fig. 4.4)—mirror the architectural design of its surrounding environment. When Warren talks explicitly about campus design, he most often speaks of "accessibility." Typically, it is used literally, as in a 2004 "state of the church" sermon in which he touted plans for a new parking garage, additional campus entrances from the major adjacent roads, and an on-ramp to an adjacent freeway. But it is also meant figuratively, to indicate the various ways Saddleback's performance is read and interpreted by newcomers.

One example of this is Saddleback's newest building, the Refinery (fig. 4.5). As the new home for the junior high ("Wild-side"), high school ("HSM"), college ("Crave"), and post-college ("Fuse") ministries, the Refinery is the performative setting for an entirely different audience from Saddleback's main worship services. Accessibility for the latter requires narrative references to the sites of everyday adult life in postsuburban Orange County: the shopping mall, office park, parking garage, master-planned subdivision, the local park. But for the children of these adults, accessible narratives will reference desires for the subversion and transgression of these sites. The Refinery, therefore, is a faux-urban pastiche of stressed brick and metal, designed to appear, in the words of Warren, "different" and "cutting-edge," and "state-of-the-art." An outdoor plaza in the rear has been transformed into a skateboard park. The bilevel interior consists of an urbanlike cafe, an intentionally makeshift eating area, several enclosed "hangout" areas, basketball courts, and an intimate theater for worship services. Its grand opening featured DJs, "hip-hop dance crews," and "beat boxers." Little in the building is made to look or feel suburban (let alone ecclesial). But these aesthetic subversions of classic suburban form are only performative reinterpretations of a very mainstream conservative evangelicalism. Accessibility can come in nearly any form at Saddleback—what is being accessed remains the same.

The Crowd

Once a casual visitor becomes a semi-regular attender (but still not a member, let alone a committed participant), he or she is considered part of "the crowd." Turning an individual in "the community" into an individual in "the crowd" requires Saddleback pastors and staff to understand what background symbols and narratives will be accessible to "the community." Warren has long shown a deep appreciation for reinterpreting evangelical themes through contemporary secular styles. As a youth pastor he was known for being "quite popular with the young folks" not least because of his knack for hip rephrasing of conventional Baptist doctrine and music. As one older pastor in the mid-1970s described him, "He uses some picturesque words like 'God busted him' (God brought him low or humbled him, and he got right) . . . [or] 'I hope the devil hates you!'" Warren's most popular song back then was "I Get so Happy in Jesus, I Have to Backslide to Go to Sleep."[9] While seen by Warren's senior pastor as a harmless appropriation of more innocent aspects of popular culture in the mid-1970s, it later became a fundamental principle of his philosophy on church growth.

"Pastors must know more about their community than anyone else," Warren wrote in *Purpose Driven Church:*

> In today's secular environment it is just as important for us to understand the culture we minister in. We don't have to agree with our [community's] culture, but we *must* understand it.
>
> Within our community there are most likely many subcultures, or subgroups. To reach each of these groups you need to discover how they think. What are their interests? What do they value? Where do they hurt? What are they afraid of? What are the most prominent features of the way they live? What are their most popular radio stations? The more you know about these people the easier it will be to reach them.[10]

Knowing about one's community, then, is necessarily to know about one's *communities.*

Warren's note regarding subcultures is off-handed in his book because he is catering to pastors of churches of all sizes, and most pastors have churches with the resources to barely target one demographic niche. But at Saddleback, the plurality of communities in south Orange County is taken very seriously. "To reach our Jerusalem, which is south Orange County,"[11] Warren told his congregation in 2004, "we're going to have to keep building venues, keep building more and more spaces."

I'll let you in on a little secret. Someday we're going to have thirty venues. Someday we'll have fifty venues on this 120-acre campus. Then you can say, "Today I think I'd like to go to the polka worship." Or, "I feel like heavy metal today. What mood are you in for?" It'll be like going over to Edwards 21 Theaters, "Now showing at 9:00, 9:15, 9:30, 9:45, 10:00." You can choose the time, the style and even the size of service you'd like to be involved in.[12]

Once a subculture in "the community" is identified (and identification is almost synonymous with understanding for Saddleback pastors because so much evangelistic and sermonic performance is created through intuition), a performative setting called a "venue" is created, replete with its own music, stage production, pastor, and title.

As of spring 2010, Saddleback had ten venues (held a total of eight times) on the main campus. This is down from the previous high of eleven venues (for budgetary reasons the Hawaiian-themed venue was canceled). The style of the venues range from the high-decibel, alternative-rock service of "Overdrive," to the old-time religion hymns at "Traditions," to the African American gospel music at "Praise!" (see table 4.2). Additionally, Saddleback has "multisite" venues in Anaheim, Corona, Irvine, Huntington Beach, Laguna Woods, Orange, Rancho Capistrano, and San Clemente. The venues altogether are differentiated by age, ethnicity, and, most recently with multisite venues, geography.

The design, maintenance, and performance of these venues comprise the first steps toward what Saddleback pastors refer to as "making a big church feel small." In Warren's "5 circles of commitment," the logic of audience differentiation works at the border of each concentric ring to move individuals into increasingly specialized and individualized relationships with both Saddleback Church in particular and evangelicalism in general. As individuals move toward the center of the concentric rings, toward a deeper "commitment to Christ," they move spatially away from the church campus and toward specialized, personal ministries. But at the first two levels of commitment they are firmly within the spatial orbit of the main campus or satellite campuses. The goal of Saddleback pastors is to draw "the community" and "the crowd" to the campus and keep them engaged there long enough to begin the individualized postdenominational evangelical journey back out into the world.

Once the differentiated individuals in "the crowd" have found their venue, the particular performances in each venue are meant to do the most difficult and most crucial work of turning a "crowd" into a "congregation." The venues are meant to signify the church's openness to expressive individualism and

Table 4.2 Saddleback Church "venues"

Venue Name	Location	Musical Style	Description
Main Service	Worship Center	Adult-contemporary	This is the central worship service, held six times over Saturday and Sunday. Warren preaches live at each service; the video feed is transmitted to each of the venues depending on their service time except for Fuel, which has its own pastor. The Worship Center holds nearly 3,000 people.
Overdrive	Main Campus—Permanent Tent	Alternative (guitar-driven) rock	Held in one of three large permanent tents on the Lake Forest campus. It is dimly lit and the music is very loud. The crowd is a mix of young adults, families with teenagers and childless middle-aged adults apparently enjoying an osmosis of youth.
!El Encuentro!	Main Campus—Permanent Tent	Spanish-language adult-contemporary mixed with traditional hymns	Located in one of the permanent tents on campus, "!El Encuentro!" is Saddleback's only non-English service. The music ranges from soft adult-contemporary to Spanish-translated English-language hymns. The message is a faithful translation of Warren's sermon, given by a bilingual pastor at Saddleback.
Praise!	Main Campus—Permanent Tent	Contemporary African American Gospel (with a gospel choir)	Held in the largest permanent tent on campus. The demographic makeup of those in attendance is quite diverse. It ranges widely in age and ethnicity, though the majority in attendance are African American. Between songs a pastor might add some welcoming words, but Praise! does not have its own sermons. Warren's sermon is simulcast to a large video screen after about a half hour of singing.
Fuel	The Refinery Theater	Alternative/college rock, more eclectic than Overdrive	The newest venue at Saddleback, designed for post-college church goers ("adults ages 20s and 30s"). Its previous incarnation was called Fuse, but with the opening of the Refinery, Saddleback not only changed names and location (Fuse was in a permanent tent on campus), it also changed pastors. This demographic is notoriously difficult for churches to attract, and Saddleback was no different before Fuel. With Fuel, however, three services a weekend are all usually well-attended.

Terrace Cafe	Saddleback's outdoor coffee shop	Main service music is simulcast	Saddleback's most laid-back, casual venue. A coffee-cart and a patio on the top floor of building adjacent to the Worship Center, the Terrace Cafe is a place to eat, drink, and chat right in the middle of a sermon.
Traditions	A small room below the Terrace Cafe	Traditional hymns	An expectedly quiet and relatively solemn service compared to the Worship Center (let alone Overdrive). A pastor makes announcements along with some welcoming words throughout the first half hour of singing. Warren's sermon from the Worship Center is later simulcast through video feed.
Wildside	The Refinery Gym	Alternative (guitar-driven) rock	The junior-high-age service at Saddleback, programmed with many different elements such as music, games, skits, and interactive entertainment.
HSM	The Refinery Theater	Alternative (guitar-driven) rock	The high school service at Saddleback, programmed similarly to the junior high service.
Crave	The Refinery Theater	Alternative/college rock, more eclectic than Overdrive	The music is similar to Overdrive but the entire service is more participatory and interactive. The sermon is also given by Crave's own pastor and is typically not connected to Warren's weekend sermons. Crave's sermons are almost always on topics obviously relevant to college-age young adults. A typical sermon series might be on sex, dating, or friendship. Regardless of the topic and style of presentation, the sermons' core contents stay well within the bounds of conservative evangelical doctrine.
Regionals	Irvine, Corona, Laguna Hills, San Clemente	Adult-contemporary	Smaller scale reconstructions of the Lake Forest campus's Worship Center service.

also the church's cultural sensitivity to the surrounding community. Instead of being animated by the world-rejecting narratives of a historical conservative Protestantism, the differentiated venues of PDE churches like Saddleback signify a relaxed comfort with the world. From the music to the clothing to the aesthetics of the stage and signage, Saddleback venues work to fuse the cultural difference between "the world" and "the church."

The sermons in the venues, whether they are broadcast from the Worship Center, or performed directly by a pastor as in Fuel and Crave (the post-college-age and college-age venues), fit seamlessly into the larger performative harmony with the broader cultural environment that characterizes the weekend service. They fit because, according to Warren, they are designed with a crucial question in mind: "Would this message make sense to a totally unchurched person?" Warren and his pastoral staff begin with "the ground we have in common with unbelievers," that is, "our common needs, hurts, and interests as human beings."[13] This creative framework has produced thirty years of sermons that rely heavily on the background cultural symbolism of personal growth, intimate relationships, the nuclear family, emotional pain, stress, fulfillment, and happiness.

Much of the year, Warren and his staff sequence their sermons in series of three or four, with titles such as "One Month to Live," "Dangerous Surrender," "Forty Days of Love," or "Helping a Friend Through Tough Times." Sermon series are meant as hooks, drawing "the crowd" back for the following series' message. According to Warren, "Each message builds on the one before, creating a sense of anticipation."[14] And most importantly, if a compelling series topic is started on a heavily attended day like Easter, it motivates newcomers to return for the remainder of the series.

The individual sermons that make up the series are just as carefully designed. Typically no longer than forty-five minutes (often clocking in at a half hour), Saddleback sermons are performances crafted to maintain audience attention and retention. A sermon will sometimes have two pastors alternating every ten or fifteen minutes, or a single pastor might preach for fifteen minutes, giving way to the church band for a song or two before resuming. Sermons might be interlaced with video (sometimes from popular television shows like "*Everybody Loves Raymond*") or by short skits performed by staff or lay members. The overarching goal is to mix pacing to match what is perceived to be the frenetic attention span of "the crowd."

Another performative dimension of the weekend worship is Saddleback's expectation of the audience. They advertise on their website and through word-of-mouth that dress is very casual. Perhaps best known is Warren's personal proclivity for tropical isle couture. Since his rise to national and global fame in the mid-2000s, he has shifted to a jeans-and-stylish-collared-shirt look. Regardless, newcomers seem well aware of the relaxed dress code promoted by Warren and his staff. Additionally, Bibles are neither expected nor needed. In their place, weekend churchgoers are given one- or two-page handouts with the main points of the sermon outlined with blank spaces interspersed throughout. The audience is motivated to follow the message by filling in the blanks. This, for Warren, is a rudimentary form of note taking that socializes newcomers into mindfully attending to the sermon.

Each performative element of the weekend service serves one of two roles: it either draws individuals from "the community" into "the crowd" by fusing the church with the broader environment; or it draws individuals from "the crowd" into "the congregation."

The Congregation

As new believers move closer to the center of Warren's concentric rings of commitment, the more geographically diffuse they become. The first step for the new believer from "crowd" to "congregation"—the official membership of Saddleback Church—begins with joining a small group. Small groups are church-sponsored groups of six to twelve individuals who meet weekly in one of their homes (see chap. 5). And although they are dispersed in living rooms throughout southern California (in 136 municipalities, according to Steve Gladen, the senior pastor for small groups), they are seen as the foundation for everything else Saddleback Church does.

Typically, small groups at Saddleback are held on weeknights in the living room of a member's home. Some of these groups have been known to meet in coffee shops or in the break rooms of large corporations. One group, according to Gladen, even meets on the commuter train from south Orange County to Los Angeles. But a large majority meets in residential homes, which is a symbolically felicitous location for this type of gathering. They usually begin by casual mingling as people begin arriving. Some groups will even serve dinner before the meeting. Meetings usually begin with announcements: a sermon series is on the horizon, a church retreat is being planned, church volunteer opportunities are announced, new small-group study materials are available. Next, individuals in the group share about their week, typically regarding family stresses and joys, and work troubles and triumphs. This is followed in some groups by singing and in other groups by diving directly into the study material for the week. The latter is sometimes provided by Saddleback, especially if the church is currently in an important sermon series. In these cases, such as during the church's "Forty Days" campaigns, every small group is provided with books, workbooks, and DVDs, which complement the weekend sermon. Most other times, groups choose their own material, from simply studying a book of the Bible to reading a contemporary Christian novel like *The Shack*. Small groups almost always end with prayer time, though how this prayer time is conducted varies quite widely.

These groups are crucial for a large church like Saddleback because according to Warren, they close the "backdoor of the church."[15] They make

Table 4.3 "Relational" and "Medical" affinity groups at Saddleback Church

Relational Affinity Groups	Medical Affinity Groups
Transitioning in the Workplace: For Women	Bipolar Workshop
Post-Abortion Support Group	Diabetics in God
Hope for the Separated Man	Eating Disorder Support Group
Grief Support Workshop	Parents of Children with Special Needs
Career Coaching Ministry	Depression
Men on the Edge	Caring for Caregivers
Divorce Care	ADD Parents and Adults
Lose it for Life	Families & Friends of those with Mental Illness
Hope for Single Parents Workshop	Hepatitis C
Transitioning in the Workplace: For Men	Early Retired with MS
Hope for the Separated Wife	Cancer Support Group
Families with Incarcerated Loved Ones	Breast Cancer Support Group
Empty Arms	NAMI Family-to-Family Support Group
Ongoing Grief Support Group	Postpartum Support Group
	Young Adults with Asperger's
	Parkinson's Support Group
	Living with HIV/AIDS
	Alzheimer's Support Group
	Asperger's Syndrome/High Functioning Autism
	Chronic Pain/Illness Group
	Infertility Support Group
	MS with Christ

a big church feel small by nurturing intimate relationships in non-institutional, everyday places. The relational ties that grow through these small groups eventually bind individuals to the institution of Saddleback. Every new event, initiative, or program is tested, revised, and promoted through these groups.

A variation on the small group is the affinity group. These are weekly or monthly gatherings of Saddleback churchgoers, sometimes on campus, sometimes off, which are based on some shared characteristic between group members. There is a men's group (called "The Herd"), a women's group, a recovering addicts' group ("Celebrate Recovery"), a singles group, and dozens of smaller affinity groups separated into "relational" groups and "medical" groups (see table 4.3). The number, size, and frequency of meeting for these groups vary widely because they are mostly member initiated, organized, and maintained. Warren and his staff see affinity groups as "lay ministries," whereby lay members develop into "spiritual maturity" by helping others. The function of these groups, then, is not as much to create an intimate, personalized, and spatially diffuse religious practice as with small groups. The affinity group serves the dual purposes of socializing "the committed" and "core" members into a more serious evangelical practice while also providing specialized pastoral care (at a minimal cost) for "the congregation."

Because of their frequency, intimacy, and spatial reach, small groups and affinity groups are the most important programs for drawing "the crowd" into the narratives that provide durable frameworks of action for "the committed" and "the core." But the formal institutional ritual that marks the passage from "the crowd" into "the congregation," and later from "the congregation" into "the committed" and "the core," are the Saddleback Church membership classes.

Formally titled C.L.A.S.S. (Christian Life And Service Seminars; further evidence of Warren's abiding proclivity for acronyms), these daylong presentations/workshops are meant to standardize the Saddleback experience and provide a centripetal counterforce to the centrifugal trajectories of the programs, rituals, and narratives that characterize the transitions beyond "the congregation." They are divided into four separate classes:

- Class 101: Introduction to our church family
- Class 201: Introduction to spiritual maturity
- Class 301: Discovering my S.H.A.P.E. for ministry
- Class 401: Discovering my life mission

Only the first class is required for membership at Saddleback, although the entire series is strongly promoted by lay members, pastors, and staff. In Class 101, Warren (via recorded video, though many times live) and other pastors tell the history of Saddleback and explain the church's doctrine and structure. The narratives of Saddleback's history, of conservative evangelicalism, and of the "busy, scattered" lives of postsuburbanites are brought together into a single, coherent performative arc.

The Committed and the Core

This arc travels through the intimacy and personalization of one's "spiritual growth" through small groups, the main topic of Class 201. It then connects

Table 4.4 Specialized local ministries for the "committed"

Local Ministries	Church's Description
Elderly Outreach	Be a part of an outreach that seeks to minister to the elderly and disabled by offering them time spent in fellowship, prayer, and worship. Serving times can be scheduled around team availability.
Breakfast Together Outreach (Motel Ministry)	Come, make a difference for our neighbors in need by providing a pancake breakfast with cooking equipment that we provide on location. Help us as we share a time of worship, give an inspirational message, and pray with people looking for hope. Everyone says, "It's both spiritually rewarding, and fun!"
Angel Tree Christmas	Provide gifts for children whose parent/parents are incarcerated. Serve at patio table on weekends, help with processing or help with distribution.
Juvenile Hall	Demonstrate Christ's love to teenage boys at the Joplin Youth Center. Ways to get involved include weekly Sunday visitations, help with school work and help at game night.
After School Club in Santa Ana	Serve elementary students in Santa Ana by helping with homework assignments, readings skills, and other school projects.
Military/Camp Pendleton Outreach	Take advantage of the opportunity to minister to military families at Camp Pendleton through various avenues of service.
Mentoring on Purpose	Reach out to foster and at-risk youth in our community by spending one-on-one time with a young person for a year.
Purpose Driven Life in Recovery	Facilitate and lead Purpose Driven Life small group studies in rehab centers in Santa Ana.
Jail Ministry	Serve by reaching out to inmates in the local jails by providing them with a church service.
Urban Arts Outreach	Come to Santa Ana to build relationships, and learn more about the younger generation's creative interests.
Manna	Reach out to the community by providing a means for purchasing affordable food to meet physical needs and create opportunities to provide spiritual food through the love of Jesus.
Recycling for Bibles	Sort recyclables with your family or small group. The recycling money is used to purchase Bibles for those without, both locally and internationally.
Feed the Hungry	Provide a hot meal for those less fortunate. Listen, share and pray with those who visit.
Mexico Church Connection	Help educate and train the local churches to do missions in their own communities.
Mexico Rosario Church Partnership	Partner with churches in and around Rosarito to join their effort as they reach out to their communities.

one's deepening membership to the church to one's growing ability to give back in expressively individualized ways, the topic of Class 301. Finally, it ends in one's full fruition as a Christian—the achieved desire and ability to spread *evangelium*, the good word, which is the topic of Class 401. Its trajectory is always toward deeper commitment.

Such commitment is expressed through the socio-spatial logic of postsuburbia. Just as the center of postsuburbia is one's unique, personalized, and spatially diffuse residence, the center of commitment at Saddleback is one's unique, personalized, and spatially diffuse "ministry" (see table 4.4). (In chapter 6 I explain in more detail how individuals at Saddleback come to identify and cultivate a personalized ministry, what Warren refers to as one's "S.H.A.P.E.") It is important to note here, however, how Warren's narratives of "spiritual maturity," personal development, and deeper "commitment" to the church are shot through with the postsuburban logic of individual differentiation (the center) and spatial diffusion (the periphery). The ministries of "the committed" and "the core" are fundamentally evangelical excursions out into the world with pathways and destinations determined by the expressive individualism that subtends well-worn phrases like "God's plan for *my* life."

"What happens when people finally get to the core?" Warren asks in *The Purpose Driven Church*. "We move them back out into the community for ministry!"[16] However, this move "back out into the community" is a gradual one that begins as soon as one leaves "the crowd" for "the congregation." The journey of the postsuburban Christian is marked by this double move: toward and away from the geographical center of the church. This creates clear problems of institutional maintenance and message control for the central church bureaucracy. When there are over three thousand small groups meeting each week throughout the vast conurbation of southern California; when there are new affinity groups and ministries ending and beginning every month; when there are dozens of groups of short-term lay missionaries traveling around the globe at any given time; when the most committed members are also the most spatially dispersed, the church must be as flexible, pluralistic, and differentiated as its postsuburban environment.

5

Purpose Driven Places

Small Performances in Big Churches

To be known. To know and be known by the people you're calling
your "church family." Church family is a very intimate word. But if
you're just talking about the people you're sitting with in the pew
when you're all dressed up fancy then that's not a church family in
my mind anymore.
"Mary," Saddleback Church Small Group Member

To know Saddleback Church is to belong to a Saddleback small group. On a
warm early evening in August, I idled my car in front of a well-kept, classical
suburban "snout house." I was parked across the street, directly opposite the
house's three-car garage. The front door was tucked well behind the garage
and only slightly behind a modest living room window, curtains drawn. No
other cars were parked nearby, but I was sure this was the house where the
small group was hosted. It was 7:00 p.m., and the meeting should be starting
now.[1]

A little after seven a large Chevrolet Suburban pulled into the driveway
with a young mother and a daughter. They jumped out and headed inside. A
minute later a minivan pulled up and dropped off two teenage girls who hur-
ried into the house without a knock. Another minivan pulled into the driveway; a family poured out and rambled through the front door, again without
a knock. This must be the place.

I knocked on the front door. I heard several more people talking than I
saw come through this door—perhaps they live so close they can walk? Who

walks in sprawling south Orange County? I heard a dog bark, kids yelling. This must be the right place. But no one answered, so I knocked again and waited. Finally, a middle-aged man in a T-shirt opened the door: "You must be Justin. Come on in and don't bother knocking next time. No one knocks around here." Indeed. In an ideal PDE small group, everybody knows your name and no one ever knocks.

My first small group meeting was just like my last, nearly a year later. After entering, I dodged several running children, chatted with the families who arrived early for a shared dinner, greeted the latecomers as they also entered without knocking. By 7:15, the host (the "man of the house") herded everyone into the family room, adjacent to the kitchen. The meeting was called to order by the host who made a couple of announcements and then eagerly launched into the question, How was everyone's week? Each individual shared their "praises and prayers," their ups and downs of the last week. (Some weeks there are tears and encouraging cheers, and other weeks there are neither praises nor prayers, just exhaustion.) After going around the room, the host jumped right into "the material." On some occasions this could be a book in the Bible, chosen by the group for closer study, or it might be a small group workbook or DVD. On this occasion it was a Christian bestselling book they all had been wanting to read. Forty-five minutes to an hour was spent on discussing "the material," asking questions, veering off into other topics. Finally, the host asked us to form a circle, holding hands, and pray to close out the meeting. The prayers, always beginning with "Dear Lord" or "Dear Jesus," relate back to the "praises and prayers" at the beginning of the meeting, and tie them to the main themes of "the material." After "Amen," the group headed into the kitchen for dessert and small talk. Whatever serious theological issues raised in the formal meeting were dropped in favor of friendly chatter about family, food, sports, or some funny story. The kids rushed in. And slowly, after the milk and cake are gone, the group disintegrated into the Orange County night.

How to Make a Big Church Small

When Warren first published his "5 Circles of Commitment" model in *The Purpose Driven Church*, the concentric circles could have been developed spatially. The most committed members of the church, the "core," could have revolved around activities on the church campus, with the uncommitted, the "community," at the fringe in far-flung and disparate locations away from the campus. The goal might have been to draw the "community" centripetally to the "core" at the church campus. But no such geographic imagination lies at the heart of this model. While the Saddleback church campus is the site of a dizzying array of worship venues, hang-out spots, children's programs, community education events, and Bible study classes, church life at Saddleback is as geographically decentered and fragmented as its postsuburban environment.

One of the first things a new member at Saddleback learns is that "a Christian life is built on relationships" and that these relationships are best built and nurtured in small groups, typically consisting of between six and twelve individuals, that do not meet on the church campus but are dispersed to meet weekly in members' homes. And the next step for a committed new member at Saddleback after joining a small group (and thus spending more time per week in Saddleback-related activities outside of campus than on campus) is to join a short-term mission trip for lay members to Africa, Latin America, or South Asia. The more committed one is to Saddleback, the more geographically dispersed his or her religious life becomes. From the opposite perspective, Saddleback pastors design services and programs at the central campus explicitly to attract the unchurched "crowd." The concentric circles of commitment at Saddleback are spatially inverted in much the same way that postsuburban theorists have inverted the concentric ring model of the Chicago School (see chap. 3). As with postsuburbia, the center of Saddleback is no single center at all but rather an array of dispersed nodes, each one located in a member's heart and home, with its own unique periphery.

According to Steve Gladen, Saddleback's small groups pastor, more people attend Saddleback small groups in an average week than attend the weekend services. It is not hyperbole then when he and other pastors say that small groups are the foundation for everything else Saddleback does. From a sociological perspective, this makes sense. Small social groups can construct and maintain what Peter L. Berger calls "plausibility structures"—tightly bound, locally shared systems of meaning—easier than large groups, and thus the intense, intimate, and personal religious experiences that would tie disparate individuals together into a religious community would be best inculcated in small cell groups.[2] But such religious communalism only represents one side of the dynamic tension at the heart of evangelicalism. The other pole is characterized by a longing to reach out, connect with, and transform the outside world. This can be seen in the ideal religious so-called time budgets of many Saddleback members: one's week would consist of daily personal quiet time, a weekly small group meeting, and finally the weekend service. Sociologically, these can be placed on a spectrum from internal, pietistic, withdrawn religious experience to expressive, outgoing, evangelistic worship. Geographically, however, this evangelistic reaching out is a centripetal, communal pulling toward the spatial center of the church, while the inward, personal religious experience is spatially dispersed. The small group in this picture serves as an intermediary between the two socio-geographical poles of evangelical life at Saddleback. It is decentralized and fragmented, allowing for intimate and personal rehearsals of diverse religious narratives, while also drawing a small collection of individuals to a center, the host's home.

These small groups become performative events in which "the world" and "the church" are not separated and purified of each other, but are instead brought together under the symbolically integrating power of the residential home. Thus, small groups at PDE megachurches like Saddleback serve as sacred archipelagos in a sea of secularized postsuburban fragmentation, as they work to reintegrate some of the differentiated aspects of their members' lives.

The Small (Cell) Group in Postdenominational Evangelical Churches

In Roman Catholic and mainline Protestant churches it is taken for granted that the local religious community revolves geographically and socially around the physical location of the church. If not technically sacred places, these religious sites have served as centers for both religious practice and social connection. To belong to a church has meant belonging to a socio-spatial network that converged spatially, socially, and politically at the site of the physical church. For American Protestant churches, their materiality and spatial location often becomes synonymous with a local community.[3] And when a change in location and material structure is called for, it is commonly in conjunction with a revaluation of the local community.[4]

But for PDE churches focused primarily on growth, the local, socially centripetal worship site is inherently constraining because the churches' contemporary postsuburban constituencies (1) are too socially diverse to gather and appreciate one particular style of church service, and (2) seem to be looking for a variety of different solutions to the socio-spatial fragmentation experienced in advanced postsuburban places.[5] In other words, the local community church could meet a large number of people's desires but only minimally, or it could meet a small number of people's desires maximally, but it could not do both. This problem was highlighted by Peter Berger when he noted that religious belief in America was "polarized" between the bland deism of "God Bless America" and the intensely emotional and personally important practices and beliefs of "specific [private] enclaves." "Insofar as religion is common it lacks 'reality,'" he argued, "and insofar as it is 'real' it lacks commonality."[6]

Several recent studies of evangelical Protestantism have noted that this paradox has been addressed by weekend services that incorporate expressive individualism (evinced in the diverse styles of venues and accessibly therapeutic nature of many Sunday morning sermons), diverse social networks (versus the seemingly bureaucratic institutionalism of strict denominational congregations), and broadly familiar pop-cultural motifs (noticeable in the style of dress, music, and church architecture).[7] According to Saddleback pastors, however, these are secondary to the comprehensive—and fundamentally spatial—church-growth strategy of making a "large church feel small." This strategy locates the center of religious practice not in the megachurch auditorium, not on the dozen-acre church campus, but rather in the single-family home.

Evangelical Small Groups in the United States

Saddleback pastors locate the history of small groups in the early Christian church. They see small groups as being the most authentic expression of Christianity, though they have been lost for millennia through an excessive (and, in some views, deviously papist) concern with institutionalization. A similar narrative can be found in many popular evangelical books on small groups.[8] But although the small group's modern *institutional* history dates back only to the 1980s, an older and altogether different sort of small group held sway in American Protestantism from the late eighteenth century to the 1980s: the adult Sunday school. Originally an evangelical tool to educate poor and working-class children in both secular and sacred matters, by the late nineteenth century the Sunday school had narrowed its focus solely on religious material and expanded to include all classes and ages of churchgoers.[9] In its most common form it focused on the study of the Bible and was held before the main Sunday service. Later in the twentieth century, many Protestant churches began to hold such classes, then called "Bible studies" on a weeknight. But whether these proto-small groups were held on Sunday or Wednesday, they were almost always held on a church campus.[10] The goals were to "cultivate social life" in the congregation and also to do "spiritual work" by learning more about the Bible.[11] And the best way to do this was to give more opportunities to church members to interact in smaller settings. The spatial hegemony of the central church campus, however, was never questioned. Dozens of manuals written in the twentieth century on adult Sunday schools or Bible studies question the organizational structure and educational material of these groupings, but never their spatiality. It was taken for granted that the social life of the church would spatially revolve around the church campus.

The relentless evangelical strategizing for growth in membership, however, resulted in a pragmatic approach to church organization. In the early 1980s, reports of exponential growth in startlingly massive South Korean mega-churches—830,000 reported weekly attendees at Yoido Full Gospel Church in Seoul—began to reach evangelical circles.[12] One organizational innovation of these churches was the "home cell group" which was composed of five to fifteen church members who met regularly in one host's home. According to Joel Comiskey, an evangelical pastor and consultant in the "cell church movement," these original cell groups were structured around three principles: "worship" (Bible study, prayer), "fellowship" (casual and intimate social interaction), and "evangelism" (bringing non-Christians into the home cell group).[13] The cell groups were homogenous in design and tightly connected to an organizational structure, which tied them to various layers of pastoral accountability—all the way up to the head pastor. Weekly activities in each group revolved around reading materials provided by the church and connected to the Sunday sermon. The structure and interaction in the group, the "Pure Cell Model" as Comiskey labels it, was consistently focused on growing and multiplying the cells (evangelism), tying each member to a small, intimate social network (fellowship), and turning casual members into emotionally committed members (worship).[14]

As the cell model began to spread around the world (Comiskey finds it immediately spreading to Latin America through the work of Yoido Full Gospel's head pastor, David Yonggi Cho), American church growth consultants began to see its benefits. Various attempts were made to "import" this South Korean church growth method, as it was rebranded under various labels such as "the Metachurch," "the Serendipity model," and "the Covenant model."[15] American translations of cell groups were reconfigured in an American idiom so that they were much less homogenous, strictly hierarchical, and more focused on spontaneous interactions. The different models placed different levels of emphasis on each of the original Pure Cell model's stated goals. The Serendipity model, for example, was focused more on social interaction between church members (fellowship) while the Covenant model emphasized Bible study and prayer (worship).

As word of small-group success spread throughout the 1990s, PDE pastors began to add small home groups to their organizational structure. Currently, twenty-two of the largest thirty PDE megachurches have dedicated pastors for small groups in members' homes (See the appendix). The structure, style, and names of these small groups vary considerably. There are "community groups," "connect groups," "house churches," "victory cells," "life groups," "neighborhood cells," and "gateway groups." There is the ominous sounding "Governments of 12" at John Hagee's Cornerstone Church. And there is also the ideologically burdened name of "free market groups" at the postsuburban megachurch in Colorado Springs that was once pastored by Ted Haggard. One popular resource for pastors attempting to implement small groups lists ten basic types of small groups that are currently being used in the United States, from "sermon-based groups," which structure small group interaction as a formal extension of the Sunday service, to "organic small groups," which are designed to be spontaneous and flexible in both time, location, and subject matter. What all small groups have in common, though, is that they are geographically diffuse church gatherings held in members' homes in order to reach a fragmented constituency with various and multiple cultural backgrounds.

Home and the Small Group

Members' homes, then, are not just institutional nodes in a decentralized ecclesiastical organization. They are also places with a cultural history, which provide powerful symbolic resources that infuse small group programming in PDE churches. But the home has long been integral to daily evangelical life; for example, it was a vital resource in the rise of the American Christian Right in the last quarter of the twentieth century. The modern residential home, like the nuclear family, emerged in Western Europe and America alongside pietism, evangelicalism, and the bourgeoisie. And as each became imbricated with the others, they merged to form a self-referential way of life later to be known as "suburbia."[16] The nexus of home/family/salvation/middle-class-work came to full realization at least as early as the eighteenth century when the "Clapham Saints" emerged as evangelical exemplars in the far suburbs of London. Their concern with inculcating "personal and family piety" and "holiness in our domestic circles" was only trumped by their famous pursuit of the abolition of slavery.[17] For the Clapham suburbanites, the bourgeois residential home was the *axis mundi* around which all other spiritual and secular activities revolved. The apotheosis of domesticity at Clapham was not strictly evangelical in motivation, style, or effect. It was part of a broader rise of the bourgeois lifestyle wherein the single-family home came to represent an array of values and relationships that were becoming incompatible with the differentiated, specialized spheres of the state, market, and eventually civil society.[18] The domesticated home was separated from politics, work, and eventually education, and in the process became a haven

for public society's binary opposites: family bonds (vs. market-based relations), emotional interaction (vs. instrumental exploitation), personal fulfillment (vs. economic and legal exigency), and, of course, female/domestic
work (vs. male/public life).

The differentiation of the modern bourgeois home served at least three
purposes: (1) it provided for the more efficient reproduction of labor; (2) it
yielded more efficient worksites; and (3) it allowed the home to act as a refuge for all those values and institutions that served no immediate purpose in
public society.[19] The boundaries of the modern bourgeois home were sacral-
ized and reinforced in the legal codes of modern nation-states and therefore
served not only as the bases of order in liberal democracy but also as borders hypostasizing the separation of public from private, rational from irrational, reason from emotion, *gesellschaft* (society) from *gemeinschaft* (community), and practical action from personal belief.[20] Early evangelicals were
at least implicit accomplices in these separations as their focus on personal
salvation, individual and family piety, private Bible study, and eager disestab-
lishmentarianism led to an easy acceptance of the home as a personal and
spiritual refuge. Throughout the nineteenth century, evangelically inspired
domestic manuals such as Catherine Beecher and Harriet Beecher Stowe's
The American Woman's Home, along with temperance literature and artwork,
extolled the private home as the last best place for emotional and spiritual
fulfillment.[21]

It is no coincidence that the post–World War II rise of American evangelicalism was closely associated with organizations that sought to mobilize
the affective resources of the nuclear family and home life in order to ener-
gize a new generation of Christians. In the 1980s, organizations such as the
Moral Majority or Focus on the Family sought to launch peformative attacks
on the secularized spheres of local and national politics, institutional education, and mass-media from the secure stronghold of the family home. Issues
directly linked with this socio-spatial sphere of action—reproductive rights,
children's religious behavior in educational settings, and offensive media
content—garnered the broadest evangelical support.[22] This seemed like a
winning strategy: use the secure base of the home to win back lost symbolic
ground in secularized spheres of the market, state politics, and civil society. As a church growth strategy it at least did no harm to congregational
attendance, for it coincided with the growth of the congregations of culture
warriors' like Jerry Falwell (Thomas Road Baptist Church in Lynchburg, Virginia) and John Hagee (Cornerstone Church in San Antonio, Texas). But this
sort of church growth was also criticized by some evangelicals for mainly
drawing committed Christians from smaller churches instead of converting

new Christians. The message of the Religious Right, though commonly considered evangelical, was always already for the converted. It did not evangelize to the unchurched; it marked them as separate and profane.[23] The church-growth movement, out of which the PDE movement grew, was interested in drawing different boundaries. Lakewood Community Church's Joel Osteen, Calvary Chapel's Chuck Smith, Willow Creek's Bill Hybels, and Saddleback's Warren have expressly claimed to evangelize the "unchurched" rather than grow through "run-off" from other churches. These megachurches, then, have had little to do with these home-based culture wars, although they have had everything to do with home.

This focus on the home as the center of church life bespeaks a more generalized concern in contemporary evangelical churches with close, intimate social interaction, often referred to as "fellowship." When believers meet face to face in an intimate setting and focus their conversation on personal religious experience, they can be said to be "in fellowship." This interaction is seen by Saddleback pastors as the antidote to what Warren describes as the two fundamental facts of modern life: "transition and tension."[24] The intimacy and *gemeinschaftlich* or communal cohesion that is sought in fellowship has typically been the trademark of older, smaller, local churches, he describes as "family reunion churches."[25] But the goal of PDE churches is to make this socially integrating experience scaleable to a 2,000- or 20,000-member church. This is done primarily by structuring church life around small groups in residential homes. Described by another influential PDE pastor as the "backbone" of everything else that a church does, these small groups have become the "real church" to the more generalized, mass-marketed Sunday services.[26]

The Small Group Structure at Saddleback:
The Meanings for Pastors and Staff

Saddleback pastors consciously create and structure the church so that it mirrors its environment. Most pastors would reject this characterization because they do not perceive themselves—or Saddleback—to be mimicking "the world." Instead, they speak more in terms of "relevance." Clayton Coates, a former youth pastor at Saddleback (now a senior pastor in Texas), said, "Our job is not to be like the world, but to be relevant to the world. We need to show the world that what we are doing here directly relates to their lives."

What sort of lives, exactly? Steve Gladen describes the lives of Saddleback members in many of the same terms that Gottdiener, Fishman, and Knox use to describe postsuburbia. Members' lives are "fragmented," "diverse," and "disconnected." In describing the reality of this postsuburban condition, Saddleback pastors often refer to time pressures:

> The competition for time—I mean, I'm a pastor and I'm saying, "How do I juggle my 168 hours a week?" Because I've got kids in sports, I've got work, I've got culture that is forcing me into something else. So you structurally need to live in a sane environment, you know, where every spouse has their Day-Timers planned and you're just syncing up just to make sure that every kid is wherever they need to be. So that's what the church is competing against.[27]

Between work, school, shopping, family time, personal time, and the time it takes to commute in the car between all of these things, there is very little time for devoted church activities. Thus, the spatial fragmentation of postsuburban life is most often imagined in temporal terms. The spatially differentiated and dispersed lives of Saddleback members is felt most acutely through a severe lack of time. And Saddleback is structured around maximizing members' time, but this restructuring is done spatially.

The weekend services are split up not only into diverse demographic groups but also into eight different times over two days in eight different locations around south Orange County. Throughout the week, church activities take place both on and off campus, ranging from "community" events, such as the men's Bible study held in one of the large permanent tents on campus, to outreach programs held on high school and junior high campuses around south Orange County, or local P.E.A.C.E. trips conducted in south Los Angeles. In *The Purpose Driven Church*, Warren gives one rationale for structuring a church in such a diverse and differentiated manner. "Because human beings are so different," he explains, "no single church can possibly reach everyone. That's why we need all kinds of churches. Together we can accomplish what no single congregation, strategy, or style can accomplish by itself." Here he is writing to evangelical pastors, the large majority of whom lead or work at a church with a couple hundred members at most. He does not tell them that if one's church is large enough they can come close to reaching everyone (who wants to be reached), and that "all kinds of churches" can exist within one single *mega*-church.

The key for Saddleback in integrating such diversity is to think not only in terms of social differentiation (i.e., market niches, diverse weekend venues, relevant outreach programs) but also in terms of spatial differentiation. If Saddleback pastors accept that their church is an almost unwieldy diversity of believers, then it is a quick and relatively easy step to accept that the church ultimately will be spatially fragmented and decentralized. Just as Saddleback pastors can no longer speak of one type of member,[28] they can no longer speak of Saddleback church being in one central location. "Who is the church?" and "Where is the church?" are not questions that a Saddleback pastor wants to answer with any certainty. In attempting to mirror its postsuburban environment, Saddleback refuses to draw growth boundaries, locate a dominant multifunctional center of activity, and enact strict regulation on what can and can not take place in given zones.

Making Sense of Small Groups

The background cultural symbols and narratives that undergird Saddleback's polynucleated postsuburbanity have a relatively recent historicity and materiality (see chap. 3). But Saddleback pastors choose to frame their performances in a more distant but also more authoritative setting: that of the early Christian church as told in the book of Acts. Gladen, pointing to the world-historic nature of small groups, explains, "Throughout the book of Acts you have a framework that Saddleback follows, and that's from the temple courts and house to house. The temple courts would be their weekend services or Sunday services. House to house is where the gatherers took stuff deeper." In Acts 2:46–47 (NIV), the early Christians "continued to meet together in the temple courts. They broke bread in their homes [other translations: "house to house"] and ate together with glad and sincere hearts, praising God and enjoying the favor of all the people. And the Lord added to their number daily those who were being saved." This formula of "temple courts" and "house to house" provided a symbolic framework for nearly every pastor and small group host I interviewed. It became a way to choreograph the sociospatial differentiation of the vast decentralized network that is Saddleback Church. And it also became a way to script a balance between the centrifugal tendency of small groups, as we shall see, and the centripetal imperative of a central church location.

The framework of "temple courts" and "house to house" also serves to obscure the innovative nature of small groups in American evangelical churches. It locates the decentralization and diffusion of the church in ancient scripture, rather than in the contemporary church growth movement.[29] The innovative and constantly updated small group program at Saddleback, in which more than 20,000 people a week meet in locations scattered around southern California, is thus likened to the most authentic and ancient expression of Christianity that the church could undertake. "I would start [the story of small groups] in the New Testament," says Gladen. "For the first three hundred years they didn't have a formal church so that's all they had. When [small groups] went dormant is when we moved into church history when Christianity was made the religion with Constantine. And then you had a drift away from that [small group structure] because you had a more institutionalized church."

Other postsuburban evangelical churches have their own ways of organizing their spatial decentralization into a meaningful narrative. North Point Community Church in Alpharetta, Georgia, has categorized its differentiated church structure into what they call "the three kinds of environments . . . the foyer, the living room, and the kitchen." North Point claims over 17,000 weekly attendees and, like Saddleback, is in a paradigmatically postsuburban locale. The emotional salience of the home in postsuburbia is not lost on its lead pastor, Andy Stanley. He explains that his church consists of three different organizational structures, represented by these three different "environments" in the modern suburban home. Stanley explains, "Foyer environments are designed with the idea that guests may show up." This environment is manifested in the large weekend services or community outreach events. The second environment is the living room. "Living room environments are not simply about enjoying others but they're about meeting other people," Stanley explains. These are represented by more targeted, demographically narrower events held typically during the week but on the church campus. These are designed to break the church down into groups of 100 or 200. The last environment, "the kitchen or the kitchen table," is where

> the real deal happens. . . . When we have a family meeting we don't say, "Hey kids let's meet in the foyer." We don't even meet in the living room. It's a little bit formal. But where the pow-wows happen and we need to circle up the wagons and have a real intimate conversation, it happens at the kitchen table. It happens in the kitchen, and I imagine for your family it's pretty much the same. The kitchen, in our way of thinking, this is where life change happens. Because the kitchen isn't huge, it isn't medium, it's small. The kitchen is where we have our small groups. It's where our small group ministry happens. This is where you group up with a group of people and you're able to open God's word together. This is where you're able to share your life. This is where you get to say, "You gotta pray for us, we're struggling."[30]

Stanley, like Warren, envisions his church as a series of environments for the ever deeper expression of Christian devotion. Moving between these environments is imagined socially as a transition from a scattered, lost, peripheral crowd to a focused, centered, intimate core. Warren and his pastors narrate this through their interpretation of Acts and the early church's movement between the temple courts and early believers' houses. Stanley, however, zeroes directly in on the house. The church's goal, for Stanley, is to transition believers deeper into religious commitment by drawing them both figuratively and literally into the psycho-emotional and functional center of postsuburban life: the house as home.

Home figures in a slightly different way in another PDE megachurch's vision of small groups. Northridge Church, a PDE megachurch on the post-suburban fringe of Detroit claiming almost 14,000 weekly attendees, sees participation in a small group as an "unmasking," a revelation of one's true self. A promotional video, "Take Off Your Mask," on the front page of the church's website for small groups, shows scenes of mundane suburban life (set to a mawkish alternative rock melody): a mother grocery shopping, co-workers chatting next to an office cubicle, a man mowing his yard, a family eating supper, all of them wearing plastic children's animal masks (see figs. 5.1–5.3). Toward the end of the video, one masked suburbanite discards his mask beside the front door of his small group. As he enters we see others unmasked inside, smiling, chatting, welcoming. After the screen fades to black, it reads: "Take off your mask" (fade to black), "Be a part of something real" (fade to black), "Small groups."

One of the enduring cultural codes of suburbia is autonomy/heteronomy, and this trope of masks draws upon it.[31] The exigencies of public life, of work life, of social life, force us—so the video suggests—to act other than our true selves. The heteronomous influence of the world is perceived, as in the scene of a masked family at the dinner table, to invade even the home. Undoing this is not a task undertaken alone. Perhaps a new home and new extended family—a small group—is what is needed.

"Simple Systems, Not Complex Structures"

The original Korean megachurch model for small groups was highly structured, hierarchically embedded, and designed for rapid multiplication. Saddleback, like most PDE churches, has rejected this model for one that, in Gladen's words, is "structured for [personal] growth and not control," has a "flattened structure," and is focused more on fellowship than evangelism and multiplication. According to Gladen, American churches have not been particularly successful with small groups because they have

Figure 5.1 (above) and figure 5.2 (bellow) Scenes from a promotional video for small groups at Northridge Church, a PDE megachurch on the postsuburban fringe of Detroit, Michigan.

taken things that were culturally in one place and put them in America and try to force people into it. We've got books on it, we've got seminars on it, we do all this stuff. But in our culture, having done this for over 20 years, being in groups, you're just like, I can't force feed this because our culture rejects it.

In response to this rejection, Gladen has developed the motto, "simple systems, not complex structures." Small groups should not be organized into "hierarchical trees and org chart jungles . . . in order to build a big organization. In the end, you only want to help people get into groups that are healthy so they can experience life transformation."[32]

Figure 5.3 Another scene from a promotional video for small groups at Northridge Church, a PDE megachurch on the postsuburban fringe of Detroit, Michigan.

Another way to rephrase Gladen's restructuring of the Korean small group model is to ask, What sort of performative space would ring true to south Orange County individuals? What background cultural codes and scripts would have the possibility of fusing with the setting of the domestic home so that evangelical themes of loss, salvation, and praise might be seen as immediately relevant? From this perspective, the supposed simplicity of the Saddleback small group system is belied by a quietly sophisticated cultural performance.

The "eight key principles" Gladen has developed for organizing Saddleback small groups certainly tend toward simplicity:

1. *"Simple systems, not complex structures."* Gladen emphasizes that churches do not need large staffs and budgets to grow their small-group program. They need to learn how to "develop, guide, and encourage" lay members to take ownership of their small groups.
2. *"Purpose driven groups, not special interest groups."* Small groups work best when they are centered on "fellowship" and "worship" and the other purposes, rather than on an instrumental goal, such as a small group made up exclusively of church greeters.
3. *"Good enough, not perfection."* Gladen encourages his staff and lay leaders to try new things and make mistakes. The development of the small group program should be organic.
4. *"Relational, not multiplying."* Small groups should be focused on "building relationships," rather than growing other small groups.

5. *"Growth by campaigns, not disrupting community."* Small groups should continue to meet for as long as the host and the members agree to. New small groups grow not by splitting them up after a certain amount of time but by holding concerted campaigns every year to grow new groups.

6. *"Leadership potential, not proven leaders."* The most effective parts of a church's small group program are successful small-group hosts. They should be trained and encouraged to take on larger roles in "ministry."

7. *"Ratios, not size."* While some PDE churches have strict size limits for small groups, Saddleback small groups are allowed to grow to whatever size suits the host. Larger groups will often "subgroup," that is, break off into smaller groups and meet in different parts of the host's home.

8. *"Strategic care, not equal care."* Many groups need little pastoral care while others need quite a lot. Although some PDE churches mandate a certain amount of pastoral/staff interaction with small-group hosts, Saddleback "simplifies care management" by focusing mostly on hosts who need or want pastoral attention.[33]

These principles were developed for and presented to pastors from around the country who want to grow their own small-group programs, and to that end Gladen is seeking to give them practical, easily applicable advice. But these principles are more than conference one-liners. They are all geared toward creating a cultural scene in the small-group host's home where interpersonal interaction appears unstructured, natural, and intimate (rather than being structured by the imperatives of some bureaucratic institution); where one's personal narrative can be shared as an end-in-itself (rather than being ordered or suppressed for the sake of instrumental gain); and where personal fulfillment can be sought (instead of meeting institutional necessities in various public spheres). Recall the list of suburban cultural binary codes (chap. 3). Binaries such as family/public, female/male, family/work, faith/reason, emotion/rationality, home/world, community/society, freedom/restraint, autonomy/heteronomy, and ownership/servitude serve as powerful background culture structures that Saddleback pastors draw on. Words and phrases like "simplicity," "good enough, not perfection," "relational," "not disrupting community," and "natural group building" translate into an organizational model that keeps the organization—that is, the right-hand side of these suburban binaries—out of sight. The small-group home, then, becomes a real home. The organizational mission, Gladen writes, is to "help Small Group Leaders *relax* and use their *natural desire* to serve in ways that help their group grow *closer*" (italics added). Envisioning this, he continues: "When John and Mary walk in the front door of a small group, they're hoping that someone will be there who will greet them warmly, love them for who they are, pray for their challenges, encourage their growth in Christ, and praise their answered prayers. . . . Life on life takes time."[34]

The "Purpose Driven" Small Group

When I spoke with pastors, staff, and lay leaders, and consulted Saddleback small-group training materials, it became clear that the "Five Purposes"—a trademark of Warren's *Purpose Driven* writings—were seen to fundamentally organize the structure and action of small groups. These Five Purposes— "worship," "fellowship," "discipleship," "ministry," and "evangelism"—are Warren's interpretation of the Bible's answer to the age-old query: What is the purpose of life? The themes are simple and unsurprising, but they provide a very durable heuristic for Saddleback pastors when thinking through the practice and organizational structure of their Christianity. For Gladen, the Five Purposes didn't so much structure the small groups as much as the small groups provided a platform for practicing and understanding Warren's Five Purposes. Small groups, according to Gladen, are just one way to do this. So long as "you're going to produce in our culture people who are balancing the Five Purposes in their heart then I don't care what the delivery system you use as long as it works." The small-group hosts I interviewed emphasized the importance of the Five Purposes as well. When asked about weekly preparation for hosting, one host said, "I just think about the Five Purposes. As long as we focus on the Purposes we're OK."

But in my own observation of small groups, the Purposes rarely if ever served as more than a shibboleth. Hosts would portion time for "worship" or suggest community service events to give time to "ministry" and "evangelism," but what kept people coming back were deft, performative executions of the binary codes mentioned above: family (against public life and work), intimacy (against professionalism) and emotive caring (against public dispassion). Conversely, the small groups that dwindle and fail do so not because of an unsuccessful host, insufficient application of the Five Purposes, or a deficient execution of the Saddleback Small Group strategy, but rather because the small group performance of these binaries fell flat (as evinced in explanations such as "it felt cold," "they didn't seem to care," and "we just didn't click").

Despite the heavy emphasis pastors, staff and lay leaders put on the Five Purposes, the Saddleback Small Group strategy is, in fact, a recognition that small groups thrive because of close, intimate relationships. In terms of the Five Purposes, this is "fellowship." The Five Purposes are "worship," "fellowship," "discipleship," "ministry," and "evangelism." In different contexts Saddleback pastors will define these slightly differently, but they each have a basic meaning at Saddleback. Worship is most often connected with singing. The worship pastor, for example, is in charge of the music at Saddleback, and even leads the rock band in the main Sunday service. Discipleship is pastoral teaching. Ministry is serving others at church or in the world at large. And Evangelism is converting nonbelievers to conservative Protestant Christianity.

But in the concrete performative strategy of small groups, all of the "purposes" outside of fellowship become interpreted in such a way that they continually link back to fellowship. In the actual choreographing of Saddleback small groups, worshipping is reinterpreted as not just singing but also as showing happiness when another small group member shares a good experience. It could also be taking communion in small group or sharing in a spiritual practice like fasting. Discipleship is interpreted as focused conversation (in relation to a study guide or a Bible study) or interpersonal accountability. Ministry becomes the act of members serving one another, helping a member move, or bringing food to a postpartum family. And evangelism is seen as the group being open to new members.

In other words, the Five Purposes serve as a symbolic way to link the diffuse small groups back to the stated central mission of the church. But they are transformed in the process so that they take on meanings that cohere with the practices, symbols, and cultural histories of the suburban home. Worship, though it is almost completely associated with music and singing in Saddleback parlance, becomes a way of talking and sharing with others in the home. When a small group I observed decided to practice the untranslated version of worship—that is, to sing—it became awkward, stilted, and forced. And the same is the case for the other purposes. For example, some small groups will attempt to practice the purpose of ministry as it is formally understood on the Saddleback campus, and they will sign up as a group to serve in a community service project. But in speaking with community service coordinators at Saddleback, it appears that most small groups will participate once, maybe twice, but it is extremely rare for small groups to engage in service outside of group members' homes. (However, some individuals will continue to return separately on their own.) This is not because most people in small groups are self-centered suburbanites, but because these community service events make little sense within the larger narrative of small groups. Ministry becomes a coherent practice in the small group when it is reinterpreted to mean serving others within the group and within each others' homes.

The Place of the Small Group at Saddleback:
The Meanings for Members

This retranslation of the Five Purposes for small groups is the product of a
dialogue between the central campus of Saddleback (with its pastors, staff,
and lay leaders) and the small groups as they actually exist. At one end, there
is the central church with its organizational exigencies and its own meaning structures, and at the other end there are scattered, far-flung groups of
individuals with varying commitments to the central church, to the Saddleback mission, and even to conservative Protestantism. Obviously, this dialogue does not always produce consensus. The centripetal tendency of the
central church to maintain control over how small groups are symbolically
and structurally linked to the central campus and to the weekend service is
in an almost necessary tension with centrifugal tendencies of small groups to
ebb and flow and construct their own narratives and routines.

Fragmentation and Integration

Saddleback pastors are well aware of this tension. Saddleback's success in
growing and maintaining small groups is most likely due to pastors' high levels of tolerance for such tension. "Structure for growth, not control," was a
mantra I heard and read several times over the course of my time with Saddleback small groups. One of the ways in which Saddleback small groups are
structured for growth is by recognizing and accommodating postsuburban
fragmentation. During one of our interviews, Gladen told me,

> [A well-known evangelical church consultant] said that the church is going
> through a de-fragging time, you know, like when your computer defrags.
> Because it is fragmented. That's our society. We have groups meeting at
> 5:30 in the morning. I'm not a 5:30 in the morning type of guy. Again, we
> have groups in 136 cities now, every day of the week you can imagine, every
> time you can imagine because it's unique to people, it's organic.

Postsuburban fragmentation is experienced temporally, but it is also
experienced personally as a field of competing interests. Almost every small
group begins with members sharing about their week. During this sharing time members often talk about the friction between the differentiated
spheres/spaces of their lives: bosses demanding unreasonable sacrifice of
family time, an office culture that is perceived as "un-Christian," the difficulty of one's child adapting to a secular school, concern over the influence

of secular media on one's family, or the struggle within one's own family or extended family over the role and interpretation of evangelical Christianity in one's life. These and countless other topics are shared in small groups and thereby become objects for group interpretation and, later, reintegration back into one's personal narrative.

The act of telling stories of the tension between the differentiated spheres/spaces of one's life allows for new narratives to be crafted in which these spheres/spaces are reintegrated and sewn back together within the space of the small group home, under a larger narrative of Christian wholeness. An example of this fragmentation-integration process in the small group home can be seen in one small-group member's struggle with competing commitments to the sphere/space of family and that of religion. Sandra is married with three children and only started attending church when she became pregnant with their first child.[35] Her husband had never attended church, agreed to give it a chance, but eventually lost interest and stopped going. Sandra joined a small group shortly after she began attending Saddleback. And during much of her time with the group her husband's absence and perceived recalcitrance regarding religion at home was a source of discomfort and anxiety for her, and she shared this in the group. The group members, however, had no discomfort and anxiety about it. They were, by all appearances, sympathetic and saw Sandra's situation as a painful one with no immediate resolution. Divorce was absolutely out of the question, and "accepting Christ" must be done completely of one's own will. No scheming or pressuring would help. Group members, instead of offering solutions, gave new readings to her situation: God works in his own way at his own pace. God softens our hearts at the right time, not on our time. Evangelism is not about forcing doctrine on anyone, it is rather the act of letting Jesus live through you.

These were the words and sentiments of group members, week after week. They were often tossed out as worn pieces of wisdom that everyone knows, as nothing special. But as time went on, Sandra's reading of the fragmentation in her life became part of a larger narrative of how God works in the world. In an interview outside of small group, Sandra said that she appreciated the way Saddleback allows people to

> go at their own pace. I think that everybody has a timing in their life and their walk with God. And I feel like God speaks to you and softens your heart and tells you this is when you're ready and here's how I want it to happen. Sometimes when you're forced into that scenario or people are pressuring you . . . [pause] It's just hard for me to hear these hardcore

evangelists standing on the corner condemning people and it's like, oh no. I don't think most people are going to be receptive to that. They need a good friend or a family member or somebody that they trust or know to show them, hey this is how my life has changed. Or maybe you seem different to them. Or how do you handle that so well? I think that's how real people are impacted.

These realizations were the result of performances in the small group home where Sandra's and the group's actions were interpreted and reinterpreted by each other over months and years. The symbolic resources of the home, the family room, shared meals, and of course, the explicit textual materials that were the object of study, worked not to fix but to re-frame key narratives of Sandra's life. The fact that this symbolic work was done in the context of a family setting in the warmth of a home made it seem as if she had possessed this narrative all along. The effectiveness of the small group performance—as with any performance—is that it is never seen as a performance at all.

Another example is Chris, who works in a high-pressure, commission-only sales job. Although he is successful and happy with the amount of time the job allows him to devote to church-related activities, he sees his co-workers as rude, spiteful, and thoroughly un-Christian. Despite repeated attempts to reach out to them as a Christian and as a friend, he feels that he has been betrayed and ostracized. If he were not a Christian, Chris often relates, then this situation would not trouble him as much. He would just do his work and ignore the rest. But because he goes to work every day and feels a strong aversion toward his co-workers, he feels as though he is less of a Christian. This does not affect just his work and his faith, but also his family. After a day at work, he feels that he often comes home and is less than Christian to his family. These experiences are common objects of reflection for him both in casual sharing time at the beginning of small group meetings and his more formal, focused quiet time. Most topics, for Chris, relate back to this tension in his life between the sphere/space of his personal religious practice, that of his secular work environment, and that of his family and home.

During the year I spent observing Chris's small group, I saw how the story of his work environment changed. As he related various events from work to the group, they often responded by prodding Chris for a larger context. What was God doing with Chris by putting him in that workplace? What did God want Chris to learn from his work environment? The responses rarely dealt with work itself. Instead they revolved around reinterpreting Chris's work environment in the context of an omniscient, omnipotent God who has laid out a plan for Chris's life. By the end of my time with Chris's group, I saw his stories of work change. Work became a testing ground, a site for intentional religious practice, without which Chris would see himself as a less-mature Christian.

Group Over Church

The crafting and reshaping of personal life narratives are long processes: "Life on life takes time," as Gladen stated. It also takes the right kind of space. The weekly living room chat between committed small group members can take on the sort of energy and heat that Gladen alluded to when speaking of the ideal Saddleback small group: "Iron on iron has to happen many times in order for both to be sharpened." The problem this presents for the church is that this cannot possibly be replicated on the central campus. The stories, symbols, and routines of the small group became the center of Christian practice for most of the subjects I interviewed—pastors, staff, and lay members alike. At any given small-group meeting, it is likely that at least a quarter of the members did not attend the main service the previous weekend. It was common to meet small-group members who only rarely attend the weekend service. I even met several small-group members who did not attend Saddleback Church at all.

I learned this was common when I interviewed one pastor and mentioned this observation. I told him how struck I was by the devotion of people to small groups. They were so committed to their small group that they saw the weekend service, and the central campus itself, as almost superfluous. He straightened up. "Well, you have to be careful that the small group doesn't just turn into a clique. It's not just a hangout group. It's meant to connect you to the worship service here and to ministry and evangelism." He reiterated the Acts model of reciprocity between the "temple" and "house to house." But beyond this mild frustration, it does not appear that Saddleback pastors, staff, and lay leaders have structured small groups or put pressure on hosts to strengthen the links between the weekend service and weeknight small groups. In fact, Saddleback claims, proudly, that there is "110% participation" in their small group program, meaning that there are necessarily small-group members who are not members of the church and likely do not attend weekend services.

Small groups have become larger as a whole, and for many members more important, than the weekend service at the central campus. In any case, small groups and the central weekend service are seen to serve two completely different purposes. Sandra still attends the weekend service in the same manner as when she first began over four years ago. She chooses the venue depending on time and her mood, and sits toward the back, rarely talking with anyone and almost never seeing anyone she knows. This is fine, however, because she is not attending for *fellowship*. She is attending to "get refreshed," to listen to music and sermons that "inspire" her. The anonymity of the weekend service becomes part of the draw. The ability to find a quiet seat, sit back, listen, and relax is what makes it so attractive.

Flexibility

From the sociological perspective of the religious market model, small groups contribute to the popularity of the PDE megachurch because "small fellowships" lead to "high commitment," which, in turn, leads to greater satisfaction with the religious product.[36] But while small group fellowship appears to lead to high commitment, it is a commitment to the small group. Invariably, the small group members I observed and interviewed expressed devotion to their small group and also to Rick Warren. But Saddleback, the institution on the central campus, was seen more instrumentally. It was a central site for resources, but it was not a central site in most of the personal spiritual narratives I heard.

The home (see chap. 3) is the center of most Saddleback members' spiritual lives, while the church campus becomes one of many peripheral sites at which Christianity is practiced. This is not to say that the campus is unimportant or is not a significant locale for Saddleback members. For many, the church campus is a site not only for worship services but for training seminars, membership classes, occasional worship events, affinity group meetings, youth programs, and various counseling resources. The church campus is an extremely significant site. It is, however, a site that can be accessed in very different ways, by varying intensities, in fits and starts.

The key to Saddleback's success through small groups, then, is not the high commitment that is the supposed product of small fellowships. Instead, it is flexible commitment. Small groups allow for an intense and centered spiritual practice that is nevertheless free of the seemingly burdensome demands of sacred space and time. The space and time of the Saddleback Church campus, in relation to the home, is secularized; it is made to bend to the exigencies of secular time budgets, spatial aesthetics, and practices. The central church campus is opened up and made porous so that it can be accessed, used, and reinterpreted according to the fragmented and variegated daily lives of its postsuburban constituency. The church, however, does not come apart under these centrifugal forces because it is not, and does not demand to be, the center. This role lies with the residential home of the small group.

Conclusion

Small groups are the sine qua non of postsuburban sacred archipelagos. From the perspective of an older sociology of secularization, these groups provide the stability for the development of "plausibility structures" whereby the tension between a religious worldview and a largely secularized lifestyle is lowered. And from the perspective of the religious market model, they lead to high commitment and thus greater satisfaction with the religious product. Neither of these views, however, capture the sort of spatialized meaning-work these groups afford.

Small groups recapitulate the fragmented, decentralized, and diverse nature of postsuburbia through performances that allow a realization of postsuburbia's binary other: integration, centralization, and uniformity. By inverting the logic of the urban-spatial center-periphery, the organizational center of the church becomes a distant performative backdrop to the central site of religious practice, the home. A precarious balance is struck in these groups between hewing closely to the programs, narrative arcs, and performances of the central church, and nurturing a unique, individualized, and intimate atmosphere in the small-group home. This balance produces an amazing variety of small groups because, as Gladen points out, they are "structured for growth not control." One example of this can be seen in the political ideologies nurtured in some small groups, even though electoral politics are nearly irrelevant to Saddleback's programs, sermons, and communications (see chap. 7). Strong political ideologies can be nurtured, completely unmotivated by the central church, in these small groups. The right-wing Christian politics that are generally avoided by Warren and his staff can flourish in the small-group atmosphere where like-minded individuals can develop and strengthen their sense of political common sense. But on another hand it is the same small group structure that allows for politically progressive groups to form, or for some groups to harbor openly gay and lesbian members, or, more commonly, members with relatively heterodox religious views.

Ultimately, the fragmentation and diversity of the Saddleback small-group structure is what builds dense and durable networks of interpersonal meaning within each small group. The general diversity allows for easy movement in and out of any particular group and, in the end, for any single group to be built entirely on elective affinities. Just as highly differentiated postsuburbia contains a multitude of political and culture dispositions but a strong homogeneity within subgroups, so small groups at Saddleback are an equal display of variation and uniformity.[37]

It is in these internally uniform groups that similar worldly problems, hopes, fears, and dreams are transmuted into religiously relevant ones. This work of reinterpreting "the world" through the meaning structures of "the church" resonates so powerfully with small-group members because the symbols, scripts, and narratives employed in any given group are highly individualized and strongly linked to the safety and authenticity of the home. An effective act of translation in a small group of young families in, say, Rancho Santa Margarita, will look very different in a group of middle-age couples in Laguna Hills.

The specificity of individualization and the cultural power of the home are the twin engines for the durable relevance of evangelical Christianity among Saddleback churchgoers. The rapidly fading large-scale "plausibility structures"[38] or widespread "religious authority"[39] that subtended the "sacred canopy" of older models of Protestant church-building are distilled into the small group. In this way, the narratives of classical evangelicalism seamlessly structure the narratives of everyday, postsuburban life. But the answer does not lie simply in smaller social aggregates. It is also in small groups based on the spatiality and materiality of the single-family home. Not only does this place-strategy draw on the historical origin of the early church (as in Warren's easy use of Acts 2), it also mobilizes secularized but traditional narratives based on the nuclear family in the home. It not only provides church members with "serious relationships" but also provides them with a place where at least some of their differentiated, fragmented, and delocalized social roles can be reintegrated. Only now, the reintegration is not under a "sacred canopy" but rather the much smaller and more fragile roof of the evangelical postsuburban home.

6

Purpose Driven Planet

The Globalization of Evangelical Postsuburbia

The evangelical performance of postsuburban space is tied to the materiality and symbolism of the home, the individual body, the mall, the office park, the freeway, and the patchwork, differentiated postsuburban landscape. But it is also tied to the symbolic materialities that undergird identity-boundary distinctions such as us/them, suburb/city, south (Orange) county/north (Orange) county, America/the world, and First-World/Third-World. Each of these binary distinctions are commonplace heuristics for Saddleback members to locate themselves within the Los Angeles metropolitan region and the world as a whole.[1]

In the various Saddleback performances of postsuburbia (in sermons, programs, literature, church websites, training courses, and small groups), these cultural-spatial binaries linked up to other binaries such as safe/dangerous, clean/unclean, wealth/poverty, healthy/sick, and, above all, saved/unsaved. These links form a constellation of binaries that make up a spatio-cultural structure by which evangelicals at Saddleback are able to make sense of burgeoning global processes and effects that are more commonly ignored in postsuburban life. Many Saddleback members are involved daily with such global processes. Irvine, just a fifteen-minute drive from the Saddleback campus, is an important node in the transnational operation of dozens of domestic and foreign-based corporations. Downtown Los Angeles and Long Beach, important transnational nodes in their own right, are within commuting distance, and several military and military-industrial sites (such as Camp Pendleton, or Lockheed Martin, and Northrop Grumman) have been professional points of origin for many current south Orange County residents. In the small groups I observed, there were middle managers for transnational food suppliers, multinational environmental engineering firms, global travel-related businesses, and global recruiting firms. Several members had foreign experience through the military in Iraq, Japan, and Germany.

While many of them were actively engaged in the local, embodied production of globalization, their conceptual tools for conceiving of south Orange County's place within these global forces and processes were almost completely drawn from the constellation of binary distinctions produced by Saddleback Church performances. This constellation was not just the basis for easy dispositions toward "the Other," a sort of micropolitics of withdrawn, anticosmopolitanism.[2] It is true that because the suburbs and postsuburbs are marked by an increasing isolation and withdrawal into the privacy of the residential home, this anticosmopolitanism is what has characterized the paranoid, xenophobic style of the previous generation of more fundamentalist evangelicals such as Jerry Falwell, Pat Robertson, John Hagee, and Tim LaHaye.[3] This same domestic inwardness, however, has formed the symbolic scaffolding for a robust and energetic mobilization of thousands of Saddleback members in what might be regarded as a new evangelical cosmopolitanism.

Launching P.E.A.C.E.

In a sermon in fall 2003, Rick Warren launched what he called "a new phase in the history of Saddleback Church." Warren declared, "We're going global. We want to now help the whole world." Through what he called the Global P.E.A.C.E. Plan, Saddleback Church would train and send out small groups of lay members throughout the world to fight "spiritual lostness" (later changed to "spiritual emptiness"), "corrupt leadership," "poverty," "disease," and "ignorance." This vision would become more focused over the following year and a half until it was ready for an official public launch at Angel Stadium in Anaheim, California, during Saddleback's twenty-fifth-year anniversary celebration. In front of 40,000 attendees, Warren relaunched the P.E.A.C.E. Plan, announcing his ambition to "mobilize one billion foot soldiers for the Kingdom of God." In Warren's words, this would be nothing short of a "new Reformation."

This global project did not just mark a new era for Saddleback's transnational evangelism (it had earlier been piecemeal and largely dependent on missionary work through the Southern Baptist Convention), it was also resonant with a more general shift in American evangelical transnationalism. Of course, as one writer in the evangelical serial *Christianity Today* put it, "Christians have been transnational since the Pentecost."[4] But in this new phase, transnational evangelicalism has shifted away from a quasi-professional missionary elite, dependent on churches, denominations, and para-church organizations for maintaining long-term, often permanent missions. The new direction is toward small-groups of lay members, briefly trained and coordinated through their local, often nondenominational church, who embark on one- to three-week trips abroad. The trips are often arranged with foreign local churches and usually consist of volunteer work (building churches and other infrastructure projects), evangelism, and collective worship and fellowship.

Short-term missions are clearly growing in popularity among U.S. churches of all stripes. In one recent study, 44 percent of congregations surveyed reported sending small groups of lay members abroad for short periods of time.[5] In the same study, participants were asked if they had previously gone on short-term missions abroad. Of those who were teenagers in 1950s, 1960s, or 1970s, only 2 percent had previously gone. Five percent of those who had been teenagers in the 1990s, and 12 percent who had been teenagers since the 1990s had participated. Another study reported that each year U.S. churches send 1.6 million lay members on short-term missions.[6] These trips are almost always self-funded, and at a minimum of a $1,000 trip, the total yearly travel expenditures for short-term missions is at least $1.6 billion.[7]

Despite their growing popularity, short-term missions have an uneasy place within the culture structure of American evangelicalism. Historically, missionary work has been kept at arm's length from the average congregant. Often organized by denominations and para-church organizations, missions have involved lay members almost solely as funding sources. In Warren's words, professional missionary organizations have asked individual churches to "pay, pray, and stay out of the way." And because American evangelicalism has thrived on a religious practice centered on domesticity, close interpersonal relationships, and individual improvement, such divisions of labor were hardly problematic. In fact, the recent dissolution of this division does not appear to come from a grassroots desire for more hands-on transnational evangelism. Many Saddleback members had not considered missionary work at all until it was promoted through the P.E.A.C.E. Plan. And even then, most members choose not to go, and those that do often struggle with the decision. How, then, are short-term missions incorporated into the larger evangelical performances of postsuburbia at Saddleback? How are these transnational excursions—weeks long, in often difficult conditions, to parts of the world few Orange County residents consider vacation destinations—made into meaningful performances in their own right? In what ways does short-term missionary work fuse (or not) with personal and collective narratives of an evangelical homeland in postsuburbia?

These questions were not important for every intended audience of Warren's P.E.A.C.E. Plan. He was not just attempting to mobilize his own church members. He needed churches from around the world with which to partner, and mass-mediatic attention to lend his vision credibility. For the former, Warren used national and international church conferences (held mainly at the Saddleback campus) to promote the P.E.A.C.E. Plan as a calling from God. To pastors and church staff, he spoke of Christian churches as "the hope of the world." Referring to what evangelicals call the "Great Commission," Warren told an auditorium of church conference-goers in 2008, "'Even as the Father has sent me, so I send you,' Jesus said. That's why this mission is to the entire world." What is the nature of this mission? "Our mission is the global glory of God." And this mission is undertaken by spreading Christianity and its seemingly adjunct benefits of health, prosperity, social order, and education.

To each audience—Saddleback members, national and international church leaders, and the media—Warren laid out the elements of his P.E.A.C.E. Plan by first outlining the problems it would address (see table 6.1). He calls these "the five global giants." They have undergone minor but

Table 6.1 The "Five Global Giants" and the P.E.A.C.E. Plan counterparts

Five Global Giants	The P.E.A.C.E. Plan
Spiritual Emptiness/Spiritual Lostness	Partnering with other churches/Promote reconciliation/Plant churches
Self-centered Leadership/Corrupt Leadership	Equip servant leaders
Poverty	Assist the poor
Disease	Care for the sick
Lack of education/Ignorance	Educate the next generation

telling changes since they were first presented in 2003, and the changes depend on the audience in question. The first and foremost "global giant" Warren seeks to confront is "spiritual emptiness." At an international church conference held at Saddleback in 2008, Warren got straight to the point: There are 6,000 unreached "people groups" in the world who "don't know that God has a purpose for their lives, that God loves them and sent Christ to die for them."[8] All other ills flow from this lack of salvation, what Warren euphemistically calls a "broken relationship." To church leaders, Warren is clear: a lack of evangelical salvation is *the* global giant. The following four "giants" are just variations on this theme.

The second global giant is "selfish leadership" or "corrupt leadership." "We have the wrong kind of people in leadership," Warren says. "Many leaders are self-serving. They're not like Jesus Christ." We need "servant leaders," people who have "moral bases" and who are "wise." The evidence of this problem, for Warren, is that 90 percent of all pastors in the developing world have no formal training.

The third global giant is poverty. To Christian audiences, Warren drives this point home in a different way from the previous two. The first two global giants are obvious problems to evangelicals who are defined in part by their commitment to conversionary expansion. But social ills like poverty, and the fourth and fifth giants, disease and a lack of formal education, have long been viewed in the American evangelical world as epiphenomenal to matters of salvation or, worse, corrupting distractions from more fundamental spiritual issues.[9] To a conference of pastors he acknowledges that many think this is somebody else's problem and, at any rate, "we need to solve our problems first." But, Warren argues, "we have no idea of the problems over there." He launches into statistics—three billion people in the world live on less than two dollars a day—and descriptions—girls sold into prostitution because their families are so poor—in an effort to justify expanding his global giants to include social issues. In his first sermon on the P.E.A.C.E. Plan in 2003, Warren spoke directly to his postsuburban constituency:

> We get in a bubble here in Orange County and we think the rest of the world lives like we do. We just go about our daily lives forgetting the way that most of the world lives. And when we do that we tend to judge people for being poor. Job 12:5 says, "A person who has an easy life," and that would be you, that would be me, "has no appreciation for misfortune. He thinks it's the fate of those who slip up." Tell that to the parents of 2 million little girls who have been sold into prostitution in southeast Asia.[10]

Warren took a similar tack in presenting the giants of disease and a lack of education.

These global "Goliaths," in the eyes of Warren, have a "David" capable of defeating them and this David is none other than "the Church." The millions of Protestant Christian churches around the world, he argues, make up a diffuse, networked, and global institution. When seen from this perspective, he continues, the global church has the widest distribution network, the most volunteers, the most widely accepted moral authority, and—"our ace in the hole"—it has supernatural abilities granted by God.

All of this leads seamlessly to the first solution to the global giants—the first P of P.E.A.C.E., originally formulated in 2003 as "Plant new churches." It has since undergone two changes, one as "Partnering with other churches," the other as "Promote reconciliation." While each of these means very different things in its commonsense usage, they all get to the heart of the P.E.A.C.E. Plan's evangelistic logic: there are problems in the world and they can be solved only through the saving grace of Jesus Christ. The first iteration of this in 2003 was the purest expression. The first and most important global problem was "spiritual lostness" (more direct than the later "emptiness" but still more politic than "lack of salvation"), and P stood for planting new churches around the globe where unbelievers could be saved and "grow in Christ."

As the first P.E.A.C.E. groups began to implement the plan, Saddleback leaders quickly discovered that planting churches—hardly an innovative idea in the field of evangelistic missions—was too much to ask of lay members traveling for two to three weeks at a time. Thus, "partnering" with existing churches came to be seen as the best mode for evangelism. Between 2003 and 2005 Warren and his staff began seeing their mission as one of helping churches around the world, rather than building new ones. With the Purpose Driven church-management system they had been promoting since the 1990s, Warren and Saddleback saw themselves as the Microsoft of global Christianity. If the local church is a personal computer, then "the Purpose Driven paradigm is the . . . Windows system for the 21st-century church."[11]

But in 2007, after two years of promoting the P.E.A.C.E. plan around the world, Warren decided to "re-launch" the plan in a new version: "P.E.A.C.E. Plan 2.0." One key difference in this plan would be a further change to the first P, from *Partnering with other churches* to *Promote reconciliation.* This change would broaden the plan on two fronts. First, it would give governments, NGOs, and para-church organizations a role; the key units would no longer only be churches and lay members. Second, "Promote reconciliation" has a very elastic meaning, from implying political reconciliation through civil societal structures to its use by Saddleback pastors as a code phrase for evangelistic conversion ("helping people get reconciled with God," as Mike Constantz, the head pastor for the P.E.A.C.E. Plan at Saddleback, put it). It also allowed the plan to undergo a stylistic secularization. Already, the other four letters in the acronym stood for goals few non-Christians would argue with: leadership and management training, poverty assistance, expanding basic health care, and supporting formal education. But this first P, whether as *Planting churches* or *Partnering with churches*, was unabashedly religious in its goal and methods. With *Promote reconciliation*, however, Warren could subtly secularize his plan. In a 2009 talk sponsored by the Pew Forum on Religion and Public Life, Warren gave as an example of reconciliation the political actions of Paul Kagame, president of Rwanda. Individuals getting "reconciled with God" was never mentioned. But Warren, especially in front of Christian audiences, is clear that reconciliation is above all an initiation of a full (and classically evangelical) personal relationship with Jesus Christ/ God. "The most important thing in life," Warren preached at the launching of P.E.A.C.E. 2.0, "is that the war is over between you and God and [therefore] between you and other people." Planting and partnering with other churches, however, is still very much a part of the plan. Only now it has become a key method of P.E.A.C.E., rather than an end in itself.

Telling a Story of P.E.A.C.E.

At every introduction and retelling of the P.E.A.C.E. Plan, Warren hews to the same general format: he presents the global giants and then their antidotes in P.E.A.C.E., followed by an argument that churches are the best "delivery system" for the antidotes. But the particular narratives he weaves around this format depend on the audience. With church leaders, the story of the P.E.A.C.E. Plan is a scriptural one. At the P.E.A.C.E. 2.0 launch, in front of hundreds of pastors, Warren began by referencing verses that indicate God's global ambitions. "God wants to expand your vision," Warren argued. "Most churches think only about their own church and their own community, but our mission is the global glory of God." And the global glory of God comes through evangelism and planting churches. Thus, the overarching story he tells for pastors is typically one of obeying God's will as interpreted through scripture. Christianity must have a global reach, nonbelievers must be exposed to *evangelium,* and churches must be globally networked because it is commanded by God.

To secular media outlets, the story of the P.E.A.C.E. Plan is one of a revolution in American evangelicalism. When addressing conferences held by the Pew Forum or TED (Technology, Entertainment, Design) or speaking to journalists from BBC or *Time* magazine, Warren emphasizes the global giants differently. It is poverty, disease, and illiteracy, alongside a vague "spiritual emptiness" that trouble the world. Warren argues that churches, because they are so ubiquitous, and Christians, because they are virtuous (insofar as they are "saved," and obey God's will), can help defeat these global giants. And even when the virtuousness of Christians is called into question and the plan is seen as the product of naïveté, it is still interpreted by secular observers in the media as an essentially humanitarian mission. For example, a reporter for *Time* introduced the plan as a church-based initiative to provide "local health care, literacy, and economic development, leadership training and spiritual growth" to the developing world.[12] After seeing Warren present his plan to the Aspen Institute, the sociologist Alan Wolfe, writing for the *Wall Street Journal,* declared that "Historians are likely to pinpoint Mr. Warren's trip to Rwanda as the moment when conservative evangelical Protestantism made questions of social justice central to its concerns."[13] And on her ecumenical program on contemporary spirituality on American Public Media, Krista Tippett introduced Warren and his wife as channeling "their visibility and wealth into global projects to fight AIDS and poverty."[14]

In the midst of secular media representatives Warren is careful to downplay the same selling points used for pastors. The mission is not the "global glory of God" through evangelism and church planting, but the global alleviation of poverty, disease, and illiteracy. Warren's story of how this becomes the new passion for an otherwise conservative evangelical megachurch pastor is one that leans heavily on the classic evangelical themes of conversion and *reversion*. In different tellings, Warren underwent a personal conversion where he began to see that God cared deeply about social issues such as poverty and disease, and God wanted Christians to care about these issues as well. It was a story of reversion in the sense that this personal conversion led Warren to recover an important element in Christian tradition, that is, social justice. He saw himself, he told reporters, as uniting the two competing strains in historical American Protestantism—the liberal, mainline "social gospel" and the conservative, evangelical focus on personal behavior and salvation—into the "total gospel."[15] The P.E.A.C.E. Plan, for Warren, is the logical outcome of such a synthesis.

The story, however, changes once again when it is told to Saddleback members. To begin with, for Saddleback members there is not simply a "Global P.E.A.C.E. Plan." Rather, there is a multiscalar P.E.A.C.E. Plan with a geographical vision, which begins with the atomized individual in what Warren calls "Personal P.E.A.C.E." It scales up to "Local P.E.A.C.E." where one's "local community," never geographically defined by Warren, is the target of one's missionary work, and finally expands to a fully "Global P.E.A.C.E." In Class 401, one of Saddleback's four membership classes, Constantz, who teaches the portion pertaining to the P.E.A.C.E. Plan, lays out what he calls a "New Testament pattern" for missions. Based on Acts 1:8, where the resurrected Jesus tells his disciples that they will "be my witnesses in Jerusalem, in all Judea and Samaria, and to the ends of the earth" (NRSV), Warren and Constantz lay out a geographical vision for individual missionary work.[16] "Now what does this mean, Jerusalem, Judea and Samaria?" asks Constantz in Class 401.

> Well, when this was written, Jerusalem was right where they were at. It means their friends, their co-workers, it meant right there, right where you're at. That you will be my witnesses. . . . So you are already a witness at your home, at your work, at school, when you're shopping, when you're driving. . . . Now Judea was the larger place beyond Jerusalem, kind of like a county or a state, just a little bit broader than that. And he said, you'll be witnessing beyond just Jerusalem. It doesn't just stay here forever. And then he says, "in Samaria" which means, these are the people who live among you but they're different because the Samarians were culturally different than the people he was talking to in Acts. They live among you but they're different. Do we have people like that in Orange County? Yes we do. We are very diverse. . . . And then he says, "to the ends of the earth."

From Acts 1:8, Saddleback pastors have constructed a multiscalar narrative of missionary work that begins with "Personal P.E.A.C.E." where "you are already a witness in your home, at your work, at school, when you're shopping, when you're driving," and ends with "Global P.E.A.C.E.," where God has commanded the religious conversion of the entire earth. It should be noted here how emblematic this type of translative work is at Saddleback and in contemporary evangelicalism in America. That the author of Acts had a specific geographic vision in mind when invoking the place-names of Jerusalem, Judea, Samaria, and the ends of the earth is either unnoticed or considered to be irrelevant for evangelicals. The core doctrine of Christian conversionism (articulated in "The Great Commission" [Matt. 28:19] and through the appropriation of the Latin *evangelium*) is used to create a new geographic vision of God's plan for the world, one where Jerusalem, Judea, and Samaria are not historical-geographical places but are flexible spatial-narrative frameworks, which structure contemporary evangelical religious practice.

By telling the story of the P.E.A.C.E. Plan through the book of Acts rather than through the narrative of the twentieth-century fracturing of American

Protestantism (as he does in popular media interviews), Warren appears to recognize the sort of culture-structural problems he faces in weaving social-humanitarian aspects of the P.E.A.C.E. Plan into the larger postsuburban narratives of Saddleback. The latter narratives, centered as they are around socio-spatially differentiated individualism, were the context of the poor initial response by Saddleback members to the plan. When Constantz first arrived as the director of the P.E.A.C.E. Plan, Warren had already presented it at least twice in different weekend sermons.

> I'd be walking up and down the campus meeting people and I'd ask them, "Hey did you hear pastor Rick teach on the P.E.A.C.E. Plan?" And almost everybody had heard the P.E.A.C.E. Plan and I'd ask them what they thought of it. And this was a typical answer: "Yes, I've heard of it. Love Rick. Love the P.E.A.C.E. Plan. Not going to do it."

Members gave several different reasons why they were hesitant, but one member summed it up best: "This is great but somebody else can do it. I do all the other four purposes just great. I don't need to go to Africa to do the fifth. . . . This [P.E.A.C.E. Plan] doesn't have anything to do with me."

But like any good performer Warren relied on a slow build and over time adapted his performance to answer responses like these. It took him a year and a half to originally unveil the full plan to his congregation, and in this time he took several different angles in his presentation. In the fall of 2003, in the first sermon in which the plan was mentioned, Warren began with an argument reminiscent of the Rawlsian "natural lottery,"[17] though obviously with a heavy evangelical undertone. "You could have been born in another time," he told a packed house on that fall Sunday morning.

> You could have been born in the Middle Ages when they had no indoor plumbing. Or you could have been born today and you could have been born in Sudan where they're in the middle of a civil war. But of all of the places that God could have put you to live your life he put you here in this area to be a part of this church at this particular time. Now, how many of you would say, "Based on what I know about the rest of the world, I consider my life to be unusually blessed." Yeah, I would say so too. We have all been blessed by God in an unusual way.

Instead of one's socio-geographic status upon birth being a matter of luck (and hence, for Rawls, a key element for impartial ethical judgment), here it is a spiritual burden. Warren goes on to explain that there are "four laws of God's blessing" that, together, form a bargain between God and the faithful.

> God told Abraham in Genesis 12, "I will bless you and you will be a bless-
> ing to others." God doesn't bless my life just so I can feel good. . . . No. He
> blesses me to be a blessing to other people. . . . When we bless others, God
> promises to take care of our needs. In fact, there's almost nothing that God
> won't do for the purpose of the person who really wants to help other peo-
> ple. . . . God says, "When you care about helping other people, I assume
> responsibility for your problems, for your difficulties, for the things you're
> going through."

This bargain of blessing is one of the crucial elements in the self-narra-tives of many Orange County evangelicals. Wealth, safety, cleanliness, order, and even an attractive climate are all seen as gifts from God. They are justly received, however, so long as God's will is followed. For many, God appears to be most concerned with domestic issues and personal conduct. And herein lies both the opportunity and challenge for Warren. The opportunity lies in an opening to reinterpret this bargain so that God's concerns appear to be both geographically and socially broader, even global. The challenge is that the uninterpreted bargain story appears to resonate precisely because it is part of a larger set of narratives in American postsuburban evangelicalism that is inward-looking, domestic, and local.

The key to molding a more expansive and outward-looking narrative of the bargain of blessing—one that fits more seamlessly with the other narra-tives that structure meaning at Saddleback—is to link the bargain narrative not directly to God's will but rather indirectly through the tropes of personal spiritual growth, development, and self-improvement. These are key tropes in all aspects of Saddleback Church's religious practice (see chap. 4). The individual is the key relevant unit in Saddleback discourse, from the indi-vidual's own discrete emotional and spiritual shortcomings to each person's unique developmental pathway toward salvation and "spiritual maturity." Nearly all socio-religious action at Saddleback is justified by its effects on the individual, and the P.E.A.C.E. program's transnational evangelism is no different.

Saddleback's discursive use of the individual is not monotone nor is it explicit. It is often woven into language and practice that suggest a religious collectivism (as in the oft-repeated phrase "church family" or the focus on small groups) or a classical asceticism (as in the opening sentence of *Purpose Driven Life* (PDL): "It's not about you"). But in most every case, apparently collectivist or ascetic language and practice camouflage direct appeals to the perceived desires of the discrete individual. A key cultural binary that supports related narratives of suburban and postsuburban life is autonomy/ heteronomy. The tensions between self-directedness and other-directedness, personal freedom and collective tyranny, and actively making one's self and passively accepting a given self are all ubiquitous elements in cultural representations, aesthetic design rationales, and empirical studies of suburbia and postsuburbia (see chap. 3).[18]

Saddleback uses such tensions in specific ways. It is not individualism *simpliciter* that Saddleback uses as both ends and means but rather specific types of individualism. The easiest type to employ and perhaps the most effective is the least subtle and most widely derided, that is, *acquisitive individualism*. Closely connected with Weber's *Protestant Ethic* and what Robert Bellah. describes as "utilitarian individualism,"[19] acquisitive individualism describes a self-understanding that sees one's material possessions as objective representations of one's intrinsic self-worth.[20] At Saddleback, acquisitive individualism is the engine of the bargain of blessing: the more one gives to God, the more God gives back. The upshot for the faithful is that, as Warren often remarks, "You cannot out-give God." But this type of individualism is also turned on its head when Saddleback pastors imply that the average member's high-level of material well-being stands as a debt to be repaid to God. The bargain of blessing runs two ways. In the original 2003 P.E.A.C.E. sermon, after outlining the bargain of blessing, Warren explains to his congregation:

> We've been given material and physical and spiritual abundance that a lot of people around the world don't have. Now think this through with me. If I have been blessed more than the rest of the world, then would it stand to reason that God would want me to care about the rest of the world? Does that make sense? That if I have been blessed more than others then I would be expected to care about those other people?

This acquisitive individualism, then, surprisingly has within it the resources for its own negation.

A subtler form of individualism, *expressive individualism*, is also employed in the promotion of P.E.A.C.E. Expressive individualism indicates a worldview that sees each individual as sui generis and in need of the freedom and support to fully realize (or express) her unique potential.[21] This type of individualism lies at the heart of Saddleback's membership training program (see chap. 4). It allows such Saddleback mission statements as "Every member is a minister," "Every ministry is important," and "Ministry is the expression of my SHAPE," to be easily interpreted as statements of Saddleback's commitment to the distinctive nature of each individual. The church, far from repressively requiring conformity, appears to openly celebrate (within sometimes obvious and sometimes not-so-obvious boundaries) the special uniqueness of each individual soul. And once one discovers her S.H.A.P.E. (Spiritual gifts, Heart, Abilities, Personality and Experiences) it is incumbent on her to nurture and express this individuality through service to God (i.e., through "ministry").

This is most evident in Saddleback's Class 401, subtitled "Discovering my life mission." It is a subtly misleading subtitle because at Saddleback and in American evangelicalism, one does not have a personalized mission to discover. The mission is religious conversion. What Saddleback has done is to create an institutional narrative and infrastructure that centers on the personalization of achieving this mission. In fact, this personalization—the expression of one's individuality in the service of God—is raised to the level of spiritual imperative. "You are unique, wonderfully complex, a composite of many different factors," Warren writes in explaining the importance of an individual churchgoer's S.H.A.P.E. He continues:

> What God made you to be determines what he intends for you to do. Your ministry is determined by your makeup. If you don't understand your shape, you end up doing things that God never intended or designed you to do. . . . By identifying and understanding the five SHAPE factors, we can discover God's will for our lives—the *unique* way he intends for each of us to serve him. . . . Instead of trying to reshape yourself to be like someone else, you should celebrate the shape God has given you.[22]

In Class 401, members are encouraged to develop their own "Personal P.E.A.C.E. Plan" that draws on one's own "unique, wonderfully complex" individual makeup. How one "lives out" her own "Personal P.E.A.C.E." in her daily life is an entirely personal decision. But Saddleback pastors circumscribe this expressive individuality by giving it definite ends. Expressive individualism is so important to Saddleback programs and especially P.E.A.C.E. because it provides maximum flexibility in matters of style and method. The ends of religious action, however, are, as with any American conservative Protestant church, completely non-negotiable.[23]

Nevertheless, individual style and method are not wholly contingent. Members are encouraged toward "growth and maturity," in the words of Pastor Constantz. And these qualities can only be nurtured by pushing oneself to serve God in an ever more expansive role. The "New Testament pattern," mentioned earlier, is intended to draw members along this trajectory of spiritual growth from their personal "Jerusalem" to "the ends of the earth." This framework draws on a third type of individualism, *developmental individualism*. The latter could be connected to the liberalism of John Stuart Mill or the democratic philosophy of John Dewey, but is more commonly experienced in terms of self-help, self-transformation, and individual potential.[24] As the sociologist Micki McGee argues, developmental individualism (or "self-improvement culture") is historically interwoven with American evangelicalism, from the proto-evangelicalism of Cotton Mather's "Two Callings" to the Houston megachurch pastor Joel Osteen's *Your Best Life Now*.[25] When, in Class 401, the teaching pastor announces that "living on mission" (i.e., living a life that embodies evangelism or religious conversion) is "founded in growth and maturity," and "God has us on a continuum of growth," it resonates on many different levels.

The power of developmental individualism lies in its real usefulness for navigating one's movement through the most important spheres of modern life. For Ulrich Beck, "In the individualized society the individual must therefore learn, on pain of permanent disadvantage, to conceive of himself or herself as the center of action, as the planning office with respect to his/ her own biography, abilities, orientations, relationships, and so on."[26] As John Archer has pointed out, this imperative of individuality has not just a history but also a geography. The early British and American suburbs were intentional "instruments for fashioning personal identity" within the context of an emergent bourgeois individualization of society. Suburbia, Archer writes:

> was part of a framework of a nationalist politics that equated self-made men with the strength of a republican state. To facilitate that politics meant facilitating that housing, specifically housing of a suburban character: detached dwellings in which individual men and their families lived separately on their own plots of land, able to articulate identity by means of dwelling type, style, plan, interior furnishings, and even gender relations.[27]

Saddleback Church, perfectly situated amid the historical and geographical forces of developmental individualization highlighted by Beck, McGee, Archer, and others, is thus able to mobilize a domestic, local, and inward-looking religious practice by reinterpreting the primacy of the individual within a narrative that binds self-improvement to geographically expansive evangelism.

This narrative begins with the smallest, most local actions for spiritual self-improvement. "Maybe the first step is to walk across the street and get to know your neighbor," Constantz tells Class 401. "Maybe it's to ask the person at work or at school, 'I want to hear your story.'" But "once you start taking those steps, guess what God does? He starts taking you to the next place and then to the next place." The Global P.E.A.C.E. Plan, therefore, is revealed as the ultimate self-improvement project. The post-suburban believer begins by "witnessing" to her neighbor but eventually, through the support of her small group and others at the church, grows to tackling the global giants highlighted by Saddleback pastors. This is not the domestic, inward-looking evangelicalism of the small group or the market-differentiated consumption of Saddleback's venues and weekly programs. Yet P.E.A.C.E. leaders subtly draw on both of these when they appeal to the potential for personal growth that lies in participating in P.E.A.C.E. missions. "At some point in your spiritual growth," Warren told his congregation in 2003, "you have to stop receiving and you have to start giving out. . . . You can't just keep taking it in and taking it in and continue to grow."

It should not be surprising that the most expansive, humanitarian, and politically progressive program at Saddleback is tied so closely to the language of individualism. The socio-spatial affinity between postdenominational evangelicalism and postsuburbia is built on socially differentiated individuation. From the suburban single-family home as a performative technology for realizing a self-made personal identity to the evangelical emphasis placed on an intimate personal relationship with Jesus Christ, the postsuburban megachurch works deftly with many different modes of individualism. And while the P.E.A.C.E. Plan is no different in its heavy reliance on the deployment of various individualisms, some types are appropriated in practice more than others. Developmental individualism was a consistent theme in members' retelling of P.E.A.C.E. trips and their consideration of future participation. The following section further explores how the different narratives used by Warren and his pastors became a part of members' experiences on these short-term missions.

P.E.A.C.E. as Personal Growth

When Warren talks about the plan as an opportunity for growth, he sometimes adds that it is *necessary* for growth. Without participating in these short-term missions, he told his congregation in 2004, a Saddleback Christian "cannot continue to grow." As he laid out the major global problems he saw facing humanity in 2003, he asked "So what is God's plan for this?" He answered in a matter of fact tone: "God's plan is you. You are the only plan that God has to take care of the disease and suffering in the world. God has no other plan."

These sorts of calls to action resonate with members in no small part because they can be seamlessly incorporated into secular concerns of personal authenticity, self-differentiation, and a narrowing worldview where, as Anthony Giddens stated, the individual "becomes the centre-point of reflection and concern."[28] For many members of Saddleback, P.E.A.C.E. trips became a stage on which they constructed different elements of their identities as Christians. In the following vignettes, two P.E.A.C.E. trip experiences are presented, one perceived as unsuccessful and the other as very successful. The differences between the two were not in how each perceived their efficacy in the mission field or the ease and comfort of the trip itself. Rather, they differed in how easily the trip could be incorporated into each member's narrative of personal growth. The question for these members and many others who shared their experiences with me was not What did I do on the mission trip? It was instead, What did the mission trip do to me?

Jill and Mary

Jill belonged to one of the several thousand small groups at Saddleback that meet weekly in homes around southern California. She, like many other members, initially thought the P.E.A.C.E. Plan was "a perfectly good idea" but was far beyond anything she wanted to do herself. She had not felt "personally moved" to go, and besides, she had two young children and a less than supportive husband. Nevertheless, in 2005 and 2006, the church began encouraging individual members and small groups—through a redesigned Class 401 and announcements in sermons and newsletters—to become involved in the P.E.A.C.E. Plan. Jill's small-group leader was one of the first lay members to go on a P.E.A.C.E. trip at Saddleback (he went with other small-group leaders as part of an institutional push by the church to get their members involved.) When he came back he was "on fire about this thing." He felt that he had been transformed by the experience, that it gave him a deeper sense of his own Christianity, and he was encouraging the rest of the group to do the same. Jill was impressed by her leader's story, but she still didn't consider going because "there was just too much going on in my life at that time."

The leader's wife, Mary, had planned on going with her husband on his trip but had to stay behind at the last minute because childcare plans fell through. After his return, however, she began to plan a trip of her own. She went to different P.E.A.C.E. meetings at the church for trips to Rwanda, but she didn't feel a personal connection to the programs in which the groups would be engaged, and besides, none of the trips "meshed" with her schedule as a school teacher. Walking out of one of the meetings for a Rwanda trip, she grabbed a schedule with all of the upcoming P.E.A.C.E. trips. "I had highlighted the ones that would work for me, what would work in my schedule for God's work [laughing]. Honestly! And then I took it out to the parking lot and I prayed, 'Ok, God, where should I go? Which direction do I need head toward?' And I think there were three or four that worked with my schedule and I totally felt pulled to go to the Thailand one and I did." The trip was to Pattaya and Bangkok to assist several para-church organizations that work to lead girls and women out of the sex trade. Mary had recently been reading an article on sex trafficking and this, along with other things she had read and heard about, "flashed into my head at that moment. And I felt like OK, this makes sense." She attended the Thailand trip meeting and immediately called Jill, her friend and fellow small-group member. "I called Jill and said, 'Hey, you have to come with me! This will be so great for us!'"

Although Mary felt "personally called" to "serve" on this trip, Jill was unsure and hesitant:

> In [the spring], Mary called me and told me that she was thinking about going on a trip to Thailand and I had mentioned before that I was interested and what did I think? And I was like, "Thailand?!" And it was kind of a shock but she had gone to the Global P.E.A.C.E. things they have at the church every month. And so she went to the Rwanda one and sat in on whatever their pitch was and didn't feel led there. She went to the Thailand one and met some people and felt drawn there.

Jill was no less unsure about going than before not only for practical reasons (such as family matters) but because she did not feel the same personal calling:

> So I thought, "Why don't I just go to this meeting and get a feel for this and kind of learn more about this." And that's how it started. So I went and I learned that the mission was to work with women in the sex trade, mostly in Pattaya but also in Bangkok. So that's how it started, and I prayed about it. I wasn't sure but I just felt like I just need to show up and see how things went. And if God closed the door then this just wasn't the right time for me. And everything just kept progressing and before I knew it was time to go and I had raised the money. So we went.

Jill's telling of her trip's initiation was unusual because many members I talked with looked for divine signals when deciding if, when, and where to go on a P.E.A.C.E. trip. Many members spoke of God "opening doors." Jill went along with her friend and waited for the door she was being pulled through to close.

What happened on the trip was fairly typical for short-term missions, but especially for Saddleback P.E.A.C.E. trips. The trip was often disorganized and the group's efforts were diffuse. Jill said she was frustrated during the trip because there was so much to do with so many different groups and not nearly enough time:

> What we did was we spent five or six days in Pattaya, but we worked with [an anti-sex-trade NGO], we worked with an orphanage, and every day we worked with somebody else. So I would meet a girl and I would start talking to her and I would be like, "Good luck to you," because that's all I could do. . . . I just felt like we were a total fly-by. But there were definitely things that were impactful, but then again, I couldn't do anything about them. So I kept feeling like I'm missing something, like I don't feel like I'm doing anything here.

Her friend Mary, however, had a very different experience even as she and Jill rarely left each other's side during the trip. For Mary:

> The trip was fabulous. . . . It was really great because all of the things in Matthew 25, you know, did you feed me? Did you clothe me? Did you care for me when I was sick? I was able to do all those things because it was such a potpourri trip. It was such a blessing to me. And totally, again, opened my eyes to stuff that I had no idea that existed in the world. And it gives me a new way to be specific in my prayer now that I'm back home.

Just as for Jill, the trip was a major disappointment:

> So, for me it's really hard because even now that I'm back and everyone says, "How was your trip?" And I'm like, "It was really good" [in an unsure tone]. I mean, I feel like I learned a lot but I feel like I kind of missed out. And I kind of feel like it was more Mary's passion, the sex trade.

In the multiple interviews I conducted with each woman, neither expressed immediate interest in returning on a P.E.A.C.E. trip, let alone to Pattaya and Bangkok. The logistics of family life was the primary reason, but each woman expressed this in a different way. Mary wanted the next mission trip to be a joint adventure with her daughter when she is old enough. She hoped that in the future she and her daughter could share a passion for a particular geographic location and type of service. Jill also was interested in returning on a mission trip when her children are older. But she wanted the next one to be her own trip, her own personal calling.

Sandra

Sandra did not initiate her P.E.A.C.E. trip through her small group but rather signed up with Saddleback's P.E.A.C.E. team when the plan was initially launched in 2005. She wanted to go right away. She attended one of the P.E.A.C.E. events the church held where there were more than a dozen tables set up outside the main worship center. At each table was a different country with different initiatives P.E.A.C.E. groups would work on. Sandra told me:

> One night I went to the tables and somehow I ended up with Rwanda. I'm not exactly sure how but I went to all the tables and that seemed the best to me. And I understand now why for a certain reason . . . I was raised in part by a black nanny. And there was a lot of stuff still from being raised in a black place, because I was farmed out there. I was molested in a black neighborhood. And God needed me to be fully healed. And I went to Rwanda and embraced everyone there. . . . I received my healing, my final healing in that.

For Sandra, when God opened the door for her to Rwanda, he was opening a door for her own personal healing. She had agonized over which trip to go on and chose the Rwanda trip for a series of practical reasons. But it was after the trip, when she was attempting to incorporate it into her domestic life that it became clear why God sent her on *that* trip. She needed personal healing, a "final healing," and a small church on the outskirts of Kigali could be the medium for it.

In this interpretation, the efficacy of the P.E.A.C.E. trip becomes nearly irrelevant. In fact, Sandra's trip was even more mismanaged than Jill's and Mary's, and included more difficult living conditions, group in-fighting, and several cases of serious illness:

> It was the experience from hell. . . . We got to Rwanda, we went out to Kigali. This church had been praying for four years for somebody to come. We got there and they drive us out way outside of Kigali. We have no leader, no one from Saddleback who can tell us what we're supposed to do.

I'm the devotional [prayer] leader, I give the meditation in the morning and we pray: "Lord help us, we don't know what we're doing."

What followed was a chaotic week of working and worshipping with this small church on the periphery of Kigali. Most of the time was spent in marathon church services, five hours in the morning and evening of singing, praying, and preaching. In fact, Sandra gave the first sermon of her life, through an interpreter, on the group's first day at the church. No one else in the group was eager to try their hand at preaching, so they decided they would each give his or her "testimony" (a personal story of how one came to be a Christian).

So through the course of time we all give our testimony: divorced women, drug addicts, alcohol. They're looking at us, going, "Ugh!" You could hear them gasp! "I was married, my husband beat me." "Gasp!" You know? And, "We got divorced." Gasp! You know because in their Nazarene church, this didn't fly.

That their personal testimonies might be perceived as offensive and might ultimately alienate them from the small church was not considered. Instead, such events were seen as opportunities to "grow in the Lord." Thus, at each step (or misstep) in this mission trip Sandra interpreted difficulties, rejections, failures, and group in-fighting as preludes to spiritual growth. The church's marathon services gave her the opportunity to preach for the first time, something that at Saddleback, as a woman, she would never be allowed to do. The group's infighting led to a deeper bonds both within the group and between the group and the church. The general disorganization of the trip opened up unexpected opportunities to start up small businesses with church members.

Sandra's sense of a personal calling, of this trip's central importance to her own spiritual growth, acted as a guiding narrative framework that allowed for every event to be interpreted as personally transformative. And indeed, Sandra came away feeling "transformed." She told me that others who choose not to go or go and come back disappointed "thought of it as a trip perhaps to a far away, scary place but I saw it as an opportunity for me to grow."

An Evangelical Cosmopolitanism?

As tempting as it might be to see the P.E.A.C.E. Plan and its mission trips as thinly disguised Christian-cultural imperialism, its real effects both in the targeted communities and in the lives of the postsuburban "short-termers" is much more complicated. The goal of this chapter was not to focus on the former; questions pertaining to the effects of short-term missions are urgently important but are outside the scope of this project. Instead, my goal shows how the P.E.A.C.E. Plan worked through key postsuburban tropes, framing these short-term missions as performances of differentiated individuality. In previous generations of American evangelicalism such individuality was anathema, seen as the proximate cause of liberal selfishness and secular relativism. While the core individualism of evangelicalism (e.g., salvation as a personal act, holiness as individual spiritual development) was always present, it was, in these previous generations, circumscribed by and channeled into the family and the division of labor within the tightly knit family church. In this environment, missionary work was seen as one specialized function among many within this division of labor. It was no more incumbent on members to go on missions than it was for them to become pastors. But in the new postdenominational evangelical megachurch, missionary work is becoming transformed from a differentiated and necessary function of church maintenance to yet another church program for interpreting and reinterpreting the "transitions and tensions," as Warren says, of the postsuburban environment.

7

Purpose Driven Politics

The Saddleback Civil Forum and the New Civility of Evangelism

Given that the previous generation of American megachurch leaders included some famously political firebrands like Jerry Falwell and John Hagee, it is curious that Warren's cohort is largely apolitical. The names Joel Osteen, Bill Hybels, and Andy Stanley have no resonance in American politics, yet are household names in American evangelicalism. How is it that, despite the nearly unbreakable bond between American political conservatism and American evangelicalism, PDE churches are so relatively unpoliticized?

The answer can be found by looking into recent forays into American politics by Warren and Saddleback Church. What we find is not the older religious politics of the Religious Right, but a new more flexible appropriation of politics for religious, and more precisely, evangelical, ends. The goal of the PDE church is not societal change, but societal relevance.

On August 16, 2008, Rick Warren convened the "Saddleback Civil Forum on the Presidency" where presidential candidates Barack Obama and John McCain appeared together for the first time in the 2008 campaign. Observers in the United States and around the world questioned the motives of Warren and the wisdom of the candidates for engaging in a church-sponsored event that was both public and political. The debate over the forum's legitimacy seemed to hinge on the proper allocation of Saddleback and Warren within a set of cultural binaries that typically cohere: public/private, state/church, political/cultural, reason/faith, and civil/uncivil. Was this "civil" forum an aspect of private discourse concerning public governance? Or was it public deliberation being distorted by private commitments? Was it an instance of church incursion on state procedures? Or was the religious environment simply an inconsequential background to secularized discourse over state matters? Was faith simply seeking a seat at reason's table? Or was faith polluting the entire scene?[1]

Warren's choice of "Civil Forum" for the title for this event suggested that he was looking to construct himself, Saddleback, and evangelicalism as existing within the valorized side of the binary codes above. By alluding to the concept of civil society, Warren seemed to be situating this event between state politics and private, personal concern. By all appearances the performance in south Orange County on August 16 looked to be an effort at constructing a distinctly postsuburban civil society in which evangelicals were full participants. As he stated countless times before, during, and after the event, "We believe in the separation of church and state, *but we do not believe in the separation of faith and politics*, because faith is just a worldview, and everybody has some kind of world view."[2] By this, Warren was claiming religiosity's rightful place in the American civil society.

The event, then, could be seen by outsiders as an uncivil and illegitimate incursion by particularist actors into a universalist and cooperative sphere of communication. From this viewpoint, the Civil Forum was a project of deprivatization and desecularization—a crypto-theocratic effort aimed at reintegrating church and state. I argue to the contrary, that certain instances of public religion, like the evangelically sponsored Civil Forum, are misunderstood if seen through the placeless lens of macrosociological concepts like desecularization and deprivatization. This is because at the cultural core of contemporary American evangelicalism lies a deep commitment to an expansive, conversionary spreading of one's faith, face-to-face, individual-to-individual, heart-to-heart in a local context.[3] Even the "mass" medium of television broadcasting, when transmitting evangelical and evangelistic performances, becomes intimate and "parapersonal."[4] Sometimes referred to as "sharing" one's "testimony," this commitment is formally expressed as an adherence to "the Great Commission," that is, to spreading *evangelium*— the "good news" of salvation through a personal relationship with Jesus Christ. Others call this proselytism. But by any name, this core mission is understood by Warren and Saddleback pastors—and across mainstream American evangelicalism—as a distinctly local, contextual undertaking.

The rhetoric and action of Rick Warren, the discourse among Saddleback congregants, and the institutional actions of Saddleback suggest that the Civil Forum was a local, place-based strategy for evangelism, not for a Falwellian union of conservative Christianity and American government. From its inception through to its current incarnation, the forum has been crafted and used as a local evangelical tool by which "the church" can regain respectability and normalcy in the eyes of "the community."[5] Such respectability and normalcy, rather than bases for a "micropolitics" that might later authorize theocratic desecularization, are instead continually used as instrumentally necessary conditions for a locally emplaced evangelism.[6] What this means is that public religious action does not always mobilize individuals to political action or even political dispositions; sometimes it is the reverse: political action can mobilize individuals to religious action. It is possible, in other words, that culture can have its own ends.

By looking back at the first Civil Forum, held four months prior to the Obama-McCain forum, I show how these events were originally conceived and thereby how they have changed. I then inspect the implicit claim in the title of these events: that they are sites of participation in civil society. After asking what the Civil Forum's claim on the spheres of state politics and civil society might be, I explain that the act of civility and the attempted construction of a civil-societal place at the campus of Saddleback Church has little to do with political deliberation and political judgment—the sine qua non of democratic state politics and civil society—but is rather just another performative recasting of Saddleback and evangelicalism as an integrated part of the local, postsuburban environment. In other words, politics is the *means*, but a local, apolitical, and intimate evangelicalism is the *end*.

. . . On the Way to the Forum

The Saddleback Civil Forum on the Presidency was not the first program of this kind the church held. It is not always acknowledged in the news accounts and blog discussions of the event that it was part of a series of "civil" fora that Warren and other senior pastors had started planning less than a year prior. In April 2008, Warren quietly launched this series with the goal of "reaching out to the local community."[7] The first event would bring several Holocaust survivors to Saddleback to "share their life-changing stories," with the goal of getting "the community to come together on issues that we all care about." The official name of the first event was the "Saddleback Civil

Forum on Holocaust Survivors" though it was originally called the Saddle-back Community Forum when it was first announced to congregants. By the time of the event, on April 18, Warren and his senior pastor Tom Holladay were alternating between calling it a community forum and a civil forum. Like many of Warren's ideas, the Civil Forum would start off as a grand but vague idea and quickly coalesce into a focused initiative.

Very little advertising was done for this first event. A mass email was sent out, a banner advertisement appeared on the church's website, and it was mentioned in the weekend service. Individualized requests were made to local politicians and religious leaders, but there was no media blitz. It did not even make the events calendar of the *Orange County Register*. It was held on a Monday night, and the turn-out filled almost two-thirds of the 3,000-seat main auditorium. Holladay began the event with a brief introduction:

> This is the beginning of what we're calling community forums here at Sad-dleback. This is one of the visions of Pastor Rick Warren where we have events just for the community where we bring people in that you would like to meet, that you would like to interact with. Sometimes it might be just one person. Other times like tonight it would be a number of people.

Warren couldn't make the event because of illness, but he introduced the guests of the event through a taped video feed:

> Hello everybody and welcome to the very first Saddleback Civil Forum. I can't tell you how much I regret not being with you tonight because I've planned and dreamed and prayed for this day for at least a year and a half. About a year and a half ago I started thinking about—could we not just start a series of community forums, of civil forums where we invite the community to join with us together on a week night to hear, to discuss, to talk about topics that involve everybody in the commu-nity or would be of an inspirational nature, regardless of their religious background, political affiliation, age, economic status or whatever. [This is] a time for the community to come together on issues that we all care about. I have been planning this community forum with Pastor Tom for a long, long time.

The transition between "community" and "civil" in this introduction was evidence that Warren's definition of community was fluid. "[T]opics that involve everybody in the community," were not necessarily topics that involve *only* "the community." Indeed, the subject of this first event was not a matter just for the Saddleback Valley community in south Orange County. Not only is the Holocaust obviously of supralocal concern, the Holocaust survivors that were invited to share their stories were not all from southern Orange County but were contacted through the national Shoah Foundation Institute at the University of Southern California. Therefore, it was not clear that the gathering that night on April 18 was indeed a *community* gathering. The Holocaust survivor panel was made up of nonpracticing and liberal Jews,[8] while the audience appeared to consist overwhelmingly of Saddleback Church members, that is, conservative evangelicals. Despite the stated goals of Holladay and Warren, the event did not bring "the community" together but rather brought two separate communities together.

For much of the night these communities appeared to coexist in harmony. The accounts given by each panelist were riveting, and the audience appeared to be rapt. The stories of brutal oppression, sheer terror, and miraculous rescues seemed to resonate with the audience. But the necessary impasses or aporias in these narratives stood in stark contrast to the clear morales and teleological resolutions of Saddleback sermons. These contradictions were obscured for most of the night as the stories unfolded into unique biographies that told of individual strength and endurance, characteristics that are understood as high virtues both at Saddleback Church and in southern Orange County in general.

As the night drew to a close, Holladay invited Erik Rees, pastor of community and communications at Saddleback, to tell the audience "about a card that's in front of you and to tell you about more [fora] just like this." Rees quickly strode on stage, his first words being, "How many of you have been blessed by this evening? I sure have." By signaling the unique evangelical nature of this event—its capacity to "bless" those in attendance—Rees implicitly acknowledged the evangelical majority in the audience while also signaling to the non-evangelicals that despite what they had seen for the last two hours, Saddleback indeed is an evangelical church, not simply a community gathering place. "The original name of this church is Saddleback Community Church," Rees continued,

> and that's why we did this tonight and that's why we have many more of these planned. So if you'd like to be in touch with us and have us notify you when the next community forum is, there's a little green card on the seat rack in front of you. Just give us your name and your phone number, your visa number, and everything's fine. (laughter) Just kidding. No, just give us some information so that we can notify you of the next one we have so we can continue to do these things so we can help learn and educate together

about wonderful topics like tonight. So thank you for being here. It's a wonderful blessing that you're here and a blessing to have our guests here.

Months later, Rees described to me the logic of that little green card. The goal of gathering the information is to be able to invite "the community," that is, nonbelievers, back to the same type of community event so that they eventually might feel comfortable enough to make the next step of attending a weekend service. "Other churches would call some of what I do assimilation," Rees told me. "How do we move people from community to campus, from campus to church, church to Christ—which is faith—and then to [membership classes] which is our developmental adult process. So these [community and membership classes] are our bookends."

Fortunately for Rees and Saddleback, contacting those that filled out the little green cards would be unnecessary for the next Civil Forum. On July 21, 2008, CNN, MSNBC, NPR, and Fox News reported that an unprecedented agreement had been reached between the presidential candidates Obama and McCain to appear together at a megachurch in Orange County called Saddleback Valley Community Church. The next day, the story was in the *New York Times* and *USA Today* with stories following in the weeks ahead in the *Washington Post, Newsweek, TIME,* the *New Yorker,* and the *Wall Street Journal.* The narrative that quickly developed was summed up in the headline of an op-ed in the *Washington Post*: "Megachurch and State." Rick Warren's and Saddleback's new role in presidential politics represented a troubling sign to many that the old Religious Right battle lines would soon be drawn again. Warren spent much of his time in the weeks between the announcement and the forum in interviews explaining that he intended no such thing. Rather, the goal of the event, Warren contended, was simply to have a "civil" discussion "without the buzzers and the rebuttals and the sound bites, and [I thought] maybe if I just sat down and invited them to Saddleback Church, I could put together a panel, and let them just ask the questions, and let everybody hear it."[9]

The Saddleback Civil Forum on the Presidency (originally called the Saddleback Civil Forum on Leadership and Compassion) would look nothing like the original Civil Forum. With the Secret Service, dozens of national and international media outlets, and hundreds of protesters, this forum would be no simple outreach to "the community." By the time it was announced to the media, there could be no shifting back and forth between "community" and "civil" fora. As the original press release from Warren's public relations agent told it, McCain and Obama would appear together at a "Saddleback Civil Forum" with a "civil . . . format," where the candidates would engage in "civil discourse," and the church would model "civility."[10] "The Saddleback Civil Forum," it was stated in the press release, "was established to promote civil discourse and the common good of all." But what was the import of "civil" and "civility" for Warren and Saddleback? Why make the shift from community to civil? And what of the shift from the earlier purpose of getting "the community together on issues that we all care about" to the new purpose of "civil discourse" and the "common good of all"? Warren had made a crucial shift in his own understanding of the civil. He transitioned from the first forum, where civil was used almost as a synonym for "polite," to the second where it began to stand alongside "the common good." It appeared that Warren was beginning to connect "civil" not to mundane "community" but to something much grander: American civil society.

But if the Civil Forum is not a public-religious incursion into the non-religious spheres of state and civil society, then what was Warren doing with the concepts of "civil discourse," and "common good"? His frequent allusions to the civil sphere through the use of these terms, not to mention the frequent use of "civil" as an adjective more generally, requires us to take seriously the role that the non-religious sphere of civil society plays in Warren's and Saddleback Church members' understanding of their position vis-à-vis American political life.

Evangelicalism and Civil Society

When Warren stated countless times before, during, and after the event that he and his church "believe in the separation of church and state," but "do not believe in the separation of faith and politics," he seemed to work toward resetting the terms of American religion's public relationship to state politics and civil society.[11] These terms have been the object of discursive, political, and legal battles in the United States for much of the twentieth century. Out of these battles a coherent narrative of Christianity in twentieth-century America, remarkably similar to simple declensionist secularization narratives (see chap. 2), has emerged in conservative Christian circles over the past thirty years. America, so many conservative Christians believe, was birthed a Christian nation, matured as a Christian nation, and sometime in the 1960s turned its back on God. Subsequently, committed Christians have been barred from active participation not only in political life but in public life in general. From Francis Shaefer to Richard J. Neuhaus to Jerry Falwell, the narrators of this story tell of a forceful clearing of America's civil sphere. In this account, the civil transformation demanded of religion has been its utter denuding. It is high time, so they believe, that conservative Christians re-enter public life.[12]

This narrative has authorized (and has been authorized by) the emergence of what has come to be known as the Religious Right. Associated with organizations like Falwell's Moral Majority, Pat Robertson's Christian Coalition, James Dobson's Focus on the Family, and the Family Research Council, the new Christian conservative movement of the 1980s and 1990s saw civil society as a battleground. But unlike the civil society narratives emerging at the same time that saw discursive battles in the civil sphere as clashes between solidary compatriots,[13] the narrative of the Religious Right framed this communicative arena as a battle between particular interests. In this view, civil society was a field of discursive battle in which Christians had been defeated and exiled. This meant that the price of admission back into the civil sphere—the civil transformation that required public religious actors to suspend non-universalist commitments and communication—stripped them of the very characteristics that defined them as participants. Their participation in civil society meant nothing if they could not participate as partisan religionists.

The high-water mark of this movement was likely 2004 with George W. Bush's reelection, and further gains for Republicans in the House of Representatives and the Senate. It was during that election that Warren made his first foray, after nearly twenty-five years as a pastor, into national politics. Saddleback had set up voter registration booths during the campaign season outside the main auditorium, a new but nonpartisan step for the church. But a week before the election, Warren sent out a mass email to his members and other pastors around the United States in which he urged his fellow Christians to vote according to a conservative evangelical interpretation of certain Bible passages regarding "abortion, gay marriages, human cloning, harvesting babies for stem-cell research, [and] euthanasia." In this email, with the subject heading "The Most Important Election," Warren acknowledged that as a pastor he was not allowed to endorse a candidate and, in any case, there could be an acceptable diversity of political views within the church on matters such as social welfare and war. "But," writes Warren:

> for those of us who accept the Bible as God's Word and know that God has a unique, sovereign purpose for every life, I believe there are five issues that are non-negotiable. To me, they're not even debatable because God's Word is clear on these issues. In order to live a purpose-driven life—to affirm what God has clearly stated about his purpose for every person he creates—we must take a stand by finding out what the candidates believe

PURPOSE DRIVEN POLITICS >> 143

about these five issues, and then vote accordingly. Here are five questions to ask when considering who to vote for in this election:

1. What does each candidate believe about abortion and protecting the lives of unborn children?
2. What does each candidate believe about using unborn babies for stem-cell harvesting?
3. What does each candidate believe about homosexual marriage?
4. What does each candidate believe about human cloning?
5. What does each candidate believe about euthanasia—the killing of elderly and invalids?

As if there might still be lingering doubt about the perfect harmony between one's religious and political commitments, Warren ends the email:

Please, please do not forfeit your responsibility on these crucial issues! This election REALLY counts more than most others have. Be sure to vote, and be sure to encourage every Christian you know to vote on Tuesday. If you are able to vote early, do so. Then ask all your Christian friends on Tuesday "Have you voted yet?" and pray for godly leaders to be elected.[14]

But as the 2004 election was indeed a high-water mark for conservative Republicans, so was it for Warren and Saddleback's partisan politicking.

The email was just one of hundreds that Warren sends out every year to pastors around the world and members of his congregation. Most of them are about a new weekend series being planned or a new type of venue opening on the Saddleback campus. And like all these, the 2004 election email faded to be replaced by the next email about some new Saddleback Church program. It did not appear to cause a stir within the church. Of all the members of Saddleback I interviewed who attended the church in 2004 none claims to have remembered the email. When told about it, none thought it odd or out of place. For them, Christians have a right and a duty to engage in politics because to not do so would be "letting non-Christians set the country's agenda," said one member. Warren's email reiterates this idea by arguing, "If the members of our congregation fail to vote on Tuesday, we are actually surrendering our responsibility to choose the direction of our country." The background script for the performative act of this email was clearly the "naked public square" narrative in which *civil* and *uncivil* in late twentieth- and early twenty-first-century America is seen to be a thin disguise for *secular* and *religious*.[15] In this script, the civil requirements for participation are equal to religious surrender.

The email, as all of Warren's communicative efforts at Saddleback, appeared to fit seamlessly within the congregation's understanding of itself and its relation to American political life. But the genius of Warren and the contemporary evangelical movement he represents is that predominant scripts are generally open for revision. Immediately after the 2004 election he was interviewed by NPR and PBS, and asked about the political role of conservative evangelicalism in general and his "five non-negotiable issues" letter in particular. Warren was mildly combative in these interviews, saying, "I think religious people for years have had their faith and values just made fun of and attacked in the name of tolerance," and the 2004 election was about gaining "a seat at the table" for these people. Those on the other side of his non-negotiable issues were "in a bubble."[16] The picture he painted of the 2004 election was one in which a vast heartland of so-called religious-value voters exercised their democratic majority will over an arrogant, elitist, but small, urban minority. The 2004 election was, for Warren, a "cultural shift."[17]

But the background script that authorized this sort of narrative was in the process of revision. In the same interviews, Warren for the first time in a national media context began to talk about social versus personal values, which for Warren coincide with "liberal" and "conservative" values:

> The Bible talks about lots of values, and there are social values, which have to do with justice and poverty and equality and things like that, and then there are personal values, which have to do with personal morality. And, historically, liberals have championed the social values, and conservatives have championed the personal morality values. Well, the truth is the Bible talks about both of them, and if ever there was a candidate that really espoused both he'd probably get 80, 90 percent of the vote.[18]

And by the end of November 2004, Warren seemed to be performing from a different script entirely. From an interview in late November with Larry King:

> KING: Let's talk about the—are you concerned about the evangelical right, which is very politically motivated?
>
> WARREN: Yeah.
>
> KING: One example we might give of it, Bob Jones's letter to President Bush after the election. "God has graciously granted America, though she doesn't deserve it, a reprieve from the agenda of paganism. You owe

the liberals nothing. They despise you because they despise your Christ." Isn't that bad for the nation?

WARREN: Yeah, there's a lot of things that are said in the name of Christianity, not just in the past but right now, that *I'd like to totally disavow.* And I would just say, that's not me. In the first place, a lot of the people don't understand, there's *a difference between the Religious Right and evangelicals.* And between evangelicals and main-line believers and Catholics. In this election, Catholics and evangelicals found that they had a lot more in common than not in common. And a lot of those are the things about, they don't want the society going vulgarized, you know, where it's getting coarser and coarser.[19] (Italics added)

Warren's attempt here to distance himself from the Religious Right, to draw evangelicals into broader coalitions, and to secularize the motivation and result of his politics (by coding them as antithetical, in civil discursive terms, to action that is "vulgar" and "coarse") was the beginning of a new strategy to *civilize* conservative evangelicalism. It coincided with a personal transition into national and international stardom.

In 2004 Warren was a superstar of American evangelicalism, with one of the largest churches in the United States and the author of a *New York Times* best seller and an extremely popular church-growth book and training system. The BBC interviewed him in a series called "Who Runs America?" as one of "America's key decision-makers." But none of this compared to 2005 when his best-selling book *Purpose Driven Life* (PDL) hit historic record sales, his "Global P.E.A.C.E. Plan" was launched at Angel Stadium in front of 30,000 attendees, *Time* and the *Nation* both called him "America's Pastor," and Oprah and other pop media outlets discovered him through a bizarre hostage situation in Atlanta in which PDL saved the day.

As he rose to megastardom in 2005, Warren avoided politics of any sort. In interviews with *Time* magazine, CNN, ABC, and Fox News and at the Pew Forum on Religion and Public Life (in which his respondents were the likes of David Brooks of the *New York Times*, E. J. Dionne of the *Washington Post*, Jeffrey Goldberg of the *New Yorker*, Juan Williams of NPR, and reporters for the major networks), Warren actively eschewed any involvement in politics or policy advocacy. Most of the media appearances were about the smashing success of his book and its role in such current events as the Terry Schiavo controversy and the Atlanta hostage situation, mentioned earlier, in which a woman was held hostage by a rampaging gunman but persuaded him to surrender to police by reading him PDL (and also giving him crystal meth). But when questions about his political intentions arose, he batted them away, saying that politics are unimportant and "one of the things that evangelicals have is a true view of the limitations of politics."[20] In a mid-2005 profile of Warren in the *Nation*, a politically left-leaning magazine, Wendy Kaminer wrote that Warren "has shunned the political stage and claims he wants to be a pastor, not a 'policymaker.' . . . Warren's desire to avoid discussions of issues like abortion, stem cell research and gay rights seems genuine."[21]

The story of Rick Warren as "America's Pastor" that emerged in 2005 was one in which a new style of evangelical leader, less concerned with divisive cultural issues, forged a new path for conservative Christians into the communicative arena of civil society. "Unlike some of his high-profile peers, Warren steers clear of politics," wrote one reporter for the *Boston Globe*.[22] A *Slate* magazine feature on "new evangelical politics" in 2006 declared:

> Once we had Pat Robertson's apocalyptic visions to look forward to every election. Now we have Rick Warren, pastor of Saddleback Church in California and author of *The Purpose Driven Life*, who roams around Washington quietly in his Hawaiian shirt making alliances with progressive pastors to save the environment. So mainstream is he that Starbucks loaned him their grande cups as his personal billboard: "You were made by God and for God, and until you understand that, life will never make sense." So mainstream is he that he's practically invisible.[23]

In other words, Warren had become so civilly acceptable that he was no longer an outsider, no longer an uncivil religionist, but rather a civil participant whose methods and ends were universally intelligible.

Placing the Civil/Uncivil Forum

This potential opening up of civil society to the "new evangelicals" did not include any desecularizing or deprivatizing changes in civil society itself. The proclamations of a "softer" "more progressive" Saddleback-style evangelicalism were meant to note the proper civil transformation of conservative Christians, not the transformation of civil society. But it was for this reason that the Saddleback Civil Forum was immediately seen as a particularist incursion on the civil sphere. Warren, it appeared, was finally calling for the civil sphere's transformation. It did not take long after the announcement of the event on July 21 for the usual critics to emerge. Americans United for Separation of Church and State and other secularist groups issued press releases calling the civil forum "an implicit endorsement of Evangelical political clout," and "a sad indicator of the diminished tradition of the separation of church and state," and "a Sunday school Bible drill."[24] But critiques of the event that cast it as uncivil ranged the political and theological spectrum. One would expect more liberal op-ed columnists such as DeWayne Wickham of the *USA Today* or Frank Rich of the *New York Times* to describe the forum as showy nonsense that masked an "ecclesiastical probing" of the candidates.[25] And, of course, politically Left websites and blogs were ablaze.[26] But from the political Right, Kathleen Parker of the *Washington Post* flatly called it an uncivil "religious test." "The winner, of course, was Warren," wrote Parker.[27] "The loser was America." The conservative provocateur Michelle Malkin called it a "waste of time" to inject religious "blather" into the political arena.[28] The religiously mainline president of the Interfaith Alliance, Welton Gady, agreed: "I did not see a clear winner but I did see a clear loser—it was [moderates] like us. While I appreciate Pastor Rick Warren's civility, I believe questions like: 'What does it mean to trust in Christ?' have no place in a political forum."[29] The moderate, church-going religion editor at *Newsweek*, John Meacham, said there "is a whiff of the theocratic about it."[30]

Many of these critics saw a double-particularism at work in the forum because of the long-standing affinity between conservative evangelicals and political conservatives. The Civil Forum was both politically and religiously partisan in their eyes. Issues of ticket distribution, ticket price, audience partisanship, forum questions, and follow-up responses, and of course the "cone of silence" controversy were all evidence of this particularist incivility in the eyes of critics.[31] Warren's handling of the "cone of silence" controversy and even his efforts at maintaining nonpartisanship led to further scrutiny.

The inevitable expressions of Warren's and Saddleback's commitments to evangelicalism and conservative political and social issues easily led critics to cast the Civil Forum not only as uncivil but also as Falwellian and crypto-theocratic. This view appears perfectly reasonable within a placeless perspective of competing social spheres. How else could one view the effects of holding "civil discourse" (i.e., political discourse) in an explicitly religious building, moderated by a religious leader, with the overwhelming majority of the audience being committed religionists, and with explicitly religious topics as the subject of the discourse? How could such discourse *not* impinge upon the autonomy of the spheres of state and civil society? And how could the claims for the civility of such discourse be seen as anything other than an effort to recast the "civil"? Thus, the placeless macrosociological perspective necessarily leads to the conclusion that the public religious acts of Saddleback and Warren are desecularizing and deprivatizing challenges. But this perspective cannot shed light on how or why Saddleback and PDE churches have changed since 2004; how Warren could go from being a typical culture warrior who complains of being mocked and demands respect to being a "new evangelical leader" who has reached out to Democrats and at least attempted good-faith nonpartisanship during the 2008 campaign; and how Saddleback and evangelical congregations like it have sought to balance their own civil transformation with their long-standing desire to transform civil society.

These transformations come into focus when they are embedded within the cultural geography of south Orange County and the peculiarly local networks of religious meaning within evangelical congregations. By seeing the Civil Forum not as a systemically antagonistic act of public religion but rather as a place-based performance of evangelism, a picture comes into focus in which the forum can be seen as an evangelical intervention in ongoing transitions in one particular locale: postsuburban Orange County. I found that the Civil Forum was made to work on a number of different levels.

1. Demographic and Political Transitions

Like all initiatives at Saddleback, the Civil Forum on the Presidency was part of a larger effort to reach out to the local Orange County "community." As we have read (chaps. 1 and 4), the community for Saddleback pastors has a very specific meaning: "The community," writes Warren in *The Purpose Driven Church*, "is the pool of lost people that live within driving distance of your church that have made no commitment at all to either Jesus Christ or your church.[32] They are the unchurched that you want to reach." This is the bedrock for nearly everything else that evangelical churches like Saddleback do. Sensitivity to the cultural, political, and economic change in the "community" is seen to be paramount to the health of evangelical megachurches. Saddleback pastors hold focus groups, gather data from campus events and the church website, and liberally mine their own daily experiences in order to maintain sensitivity to "felt-needs of the community." This means that while Warren can challenge and stretch the membership of Saddleback[33]—what he calls the "congregation" in his "5 circles of commitment" (see fig. 1)—he can not get too far out in front of the community lest he alienate potential converts.

While most "white people in Orange County," as the sociologist R. Stephen Warner argues, "can be oblivious to the fact that they live in one of the most diverse communities,"[34] Warren and the Saddleback staff are eager to detect and respond to the county's changing diversity. At the Pew Forum in 2005, Warren explained:

> You only build a church on the people who are wherever you are. So for instance, probably 25 percent of my church is Asian. Why? Because the

University of California–Irvine is 80 percent Asian. So I've got a church full of Asians. We've got less than 1 percent black where I live in my part of the county but 100 percent of them attend Saddleback church. They all go to Saddleback. . . . . One-third of Orange County is Spanish-speaking. Saddleback has started 21 Spanish-speaking churches and we have a Spanish-speaking congregation in our church. We actually have 22 different services in our church appealing to all different kinds of ages, styles of music. If you were to come this Sunday, you could come and you could hear me speak, but you could choose whether you're going to go to the reggae service—we actually have reggae music, or you can go to the jazz service or you can go to the black gospel service. You can go to the unplugged service. You say, why do you do that? I can't even get my own family to agree on music, much less 22,000 people. What's wrong with that? You know, we all like different styles of music, so we have different styles of music in our services—it allows people to choose. But I would say our church accurately reflects the demographics of the community. We're Asian, we're Spanish, we're a few blacks, and we're white.[35]

Unsurprisingly, Warren has his finger on the demographic pulse of Orange County. Census data show that Asian and Hispanic/Latino residents have been increasing relative to white residents in Orange County for several decades (see fig. 7.1). And the changes are not only ethnic but are also in family composition. Orange County, and the Saddleback area especially, has long been an enclave for young families. Warren knew early on that young families would be the cornerstone of his budding church. One of his first acts as a new pastor in 1979 was to comb garage sales in south Orange County for nursery equipment for the church. More to the point, he goes to great lengths to stress the importance of quality childcare in the early success of his church.[36] But one of the striking demographic shifts in Orange County has been its aging. As the young families of the early 1980s age, it appears that new young families have not replaced them in equal numbers. At any rate, this increase in Orange County demographic diversity is not, as Warren implied at the Pew Forum event, simply the harbinger of an expanded array of music tastes. It has also brought with it an increase in political diversity—especially notable in the famously conservative stronghold of Orange County. Since the 2000 general election there has been a steady moderation in Orange County politics, with an increasing number of voters registering and voting Democrat (see figs. 7.2–7.5).

These cultural transitions in Orange County have been acknowledged by Saddleback in several different ways. In an institutional way, the small

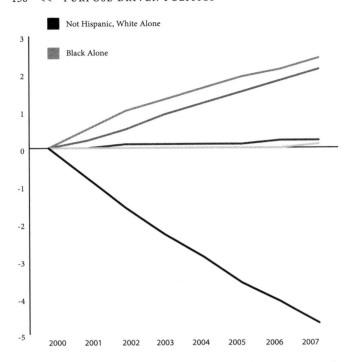

Figure 7.1 Percent change in self-reported ethnicity of residents from 2000, Orange County, CA (Source: Department of Finance, State of California, http://www.dof.ca.gov/ research/demographic/reports/estimates/e-3/by_year_2000-04/).

groups, the multitude of church venues and service times, and new satellite campuses have been a direct response to such diversity. These initiatives have all come about through the leadership at Saddleback recognizing that the "pool of lost people within driving distance" is growing increasingly diverse.[37]

2. Local Evangelism

"What this says to millions of people is the church is not kook," Warren told his staff the week before the Civil Forum on the Presidency. "They're not quacks, they're not nuts." In this emotional staff meeting just days before their church would be the center of international media attention, Warren stressed the point that this event above all else was an evangel*istic*—not evangel*ical*—moment. In other words, the Civil Forum would be an opportunity to lead individuals to Christ. Warren went on to tell his staff the story of a recent AIDS conference, which he and eleven staff members attended in Mexico City. Some of the conference was "OK" and "inspiring," other parts

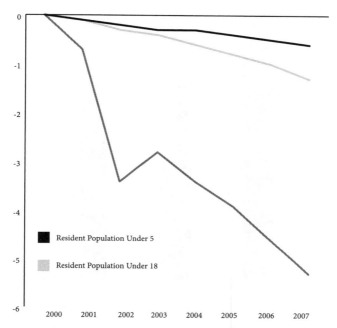

Figure 7.2 Percent change from 2000, Orange County, CA (Source: Department of Finance, State of California, http://www.dof.ca.gov/research/demographic/state_census_data_center/products-services/documents/age-sex-Race.xls).

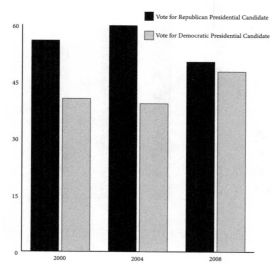

Figure 7.3 Percentage of Orange County votes in U.S. presidential elections.

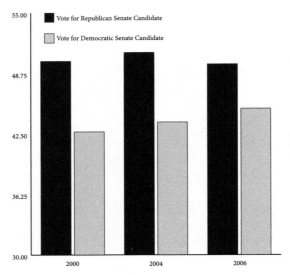

Figure 7.4 Percentage of Orange County votes in U.S. senatorial elections.

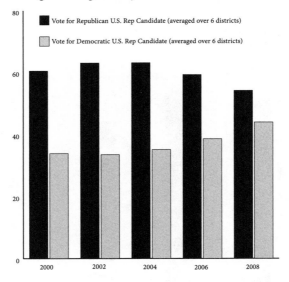

Figure 7.5 Percentage of Orange County votes in U.S. congressional elections,.

"lewd," "anti-Christian," and "evil." "So why did [I] go?" he asked rhetorically. "Because that's where the church needs to be. In the center of the cesspool saying we're not going to let you go to hell." The purpose of the civil forum then was not to engage in politics—perhaps not any more than the purpose of attending the AIDS conference was to eradicate AIDS. The purpose was to be in the center of U.S. politics—a cesspool, perhaps, from an evangelical perspective[38]—in order to lead individuals, one by one, to Christ. The entire weekend, then, would be an important evangelistic moment, as the spectacle of Saturday's forum would lead local nonbelievers onto the church campus the following day for Sunday service.

"The Bible says, be as wise as serpents, yet harmless as doves," Warren said in the meeting. The church needed to use this event wisely "as a bridge for evangelism." If the local community could see that "that's the place where they believe in the good word and the common good" then they might just give Saddleback a try. The following day's service was advertised at the Civil Forum and in national broadcast and newspaper reports. Saddleback made every effort at employing "market synergy" between the Saturday and Sunday events, and it paid dividends. The title of the Sunday sermon, which had the largest single day draw in 2008 outside of Easter and Christmas, and doubled the attendance of a normal August weekend, was "The Kind of Leader America Needs."[39] The titillating title suggested that Warren might come clean and at least implicitly back one of the candidates, the way he did in 2004. The title was sure to pique maximum interest less than twenty-four hours after the big event. But instead of the culture warrior substance of his 2004 intervention, the post–Civil Forum sermon went beyond being a model of nonpartisanship; it was almost completely apolitical. The first song at the 9:00 a.m. service was an upbeat R&B number with a saxophone and electric guitar solo.

The lyrics that followed told of the freedom, love, and mercy that are "available" at all times from God. After the first song, Warren strode on stage in his casual way, with an easy smile. The crowd burst loudly into a standing ovation, a departure from the typical warm but polite applause at a normal weekend service. Warren jokingly began:

> You know last night I was bored and didn't have anything to do so I thought I'd hang out with a couple of friends of mine named Barack and John. Actually it was a very great privilege to interview the candidates for the future president of the United States. Today we're going to talk about leadership, the kind of leadership that America needs. Now I'm not an expert. I'm no authority of politics. But I do know about leadership.

Warren then launched into a classic Saddleback sermon, structured around themes that relate directly and easily to the postsuburban individuals in the audience. While Warren made some effort at linking his three qualities of leadership America should be looking for in a presidential leader—integrity, humility, and generosity—to politics, he quickly segued into relating these qualities to the everyday lives of the individuals in his audience. It turned out that these characteristics of leadership were not primarily criteria by which a citizen could normatively judge a potential democratic representative; they were instead codes that could explain ennui, emptiness, ineffectiveness, and loneliness.

The first characteristic, integrity, began, in the course of Warren's telling, as a standard by which citizens could judge political leaders. Politicians, he argued, should be the same people privately that they are publicly, and that this authentic consistency is what defines integrity. But it quickly turned into an argument that it is his *audience* that should be worrying about its own integrity:

> People say, "Well it doesn't matter what a leader does in his private life."
> But it matters if you want God's blessing. The truth is, what you do in your
> private life always affects your public life. And in fact that's the definition
> of integrity: that your public and private life are the same. Any time you
> segment your life into public and private, you lack integrity. In fact, any-
> time you segment it in any way—when you say, "This is my school life,
> this is my work life, this is my family life, this is my sex life, this is my fun
> life, this is what-I-do-with-my-buddies-life, and on and on," then you lack
> integrity.

He continued:

> [Integrity means] the way you treat your wife and the way you treat your
> children is not different than the way you show up at church. And the way
> you talk at work is not different than the way you talk in small groups.
> Integrity means, what you see is what you get. It means you're not wearing
> a mask, you're not a phony, you're not a fake. It doesn't mean you're per-
> fect. It means you're not a fake.

Warren went through the same process with the second of the two remaining qualities of leadership. He began by briefly relating them to political leadership—and then only in the most general and innocuous way.[40] The political relevance of the first two qualities quickly gave way to their immediate relevance for Saddleback members' lives. On humility, Warren, as he consistently does in his sermons, loosely drew on contextually unrelated Bible verses (a common practice among conservative evangelicals, in the hermeneutic tradition of systematic theology). He put up on the jumbo video screens a verse from the New Testament, James 4:6 (NIV), "God opposes the proud but gives grace to the humble," and from the Old Testament, Proverbs 11:2 (New Living Translation), "Pride leads to disgrace, but with humility comes wisdom." He then told his audience to circle the terms "grace" and "disgrace" in their handouts, and then asked, "Which of these do you want in your life?" He did not ask how these verses might help them make normative political judgments or interpret policy proposals; instead he wanted the individuals in the audience to use these verses to evaluate their own private lives. To this end, he gave the audience practical advice on humility:

> What do we know about humility? We know a number of things. First, humility is a choice. You are to humble yourself. You know not once does it say in the bible, pray for God to humble you. Now it is not your job to humble other people. Your husband, your wife or anybody else. Humility is something you do to yourself. . . . Second, humility is not thinking less of yourself, it's thinking less about yourself.

Warren did not even attempt to draw the link between these personal strategies of engendering humility and the ostensible political task at hand.

Finally, the section of his sermon devoted to generosity had nothing at all to do with political leadership, but everything to do with an evangelistic understanding of personal religiosity. Generosity is important, Warren said, because "everything you have is because of the generosity of God," and when we are generous to others, "it makes us more like him." Warren spent the next several minutes explaining the virtues of giving money and time to others in need, and also practical advice on doing it. "Do your giving while you're living, so you're knowin' where it's goin'," he told his audience. The obvious connections between politico-economic generosity in one's personal attitudes on taxes or civic participation were left unstated. Instead, generosity in individual leadership was not political but personal. How one gave personally to those around one is what God cares about.

Warren concluded the message by finally getting straight to the point:

> All leadership is, if you want to summarize it, is influence. I can take you to a playground and in fifteen minutes you can see who the leader is. It's the kid every other kid is following. He or she didn't have to be elected. They

just have influence. And you have influence—over neighbors, friends, relatives at the office, at school, so you are a leader.

In other words, the three qualities Christians should look for in a political leader are, in fact, three qualities Christians must cultivate in themselves and others, through evangelism. "The kind of leadership American needs," then, is not going to come from political leaders but rather from the hard-working, normal, Christian individuals who transform there lives, one by one, day by day, in "fellowship" and "worship" with other Christians.

On this level, Saddleback staff and members saw the Civil Forum as an ideal opportunity for evangelism. It was an opportunity for the church, in the words of Warren, to appear "mainstream." This mainstreaming of conservative evangelicalism is as much about reaching out to the "unchurched" and "underchurched" as it is about reassuring the thousands of weekly attendees for whom Saddleback is their first (at least post-adolescent) church. In other words, local evangelism for Saddleback is as much about reaching new members as it is retaining the ones already there.

3. Postsuburban Civil Society

The Civil Forum was not only a "bridge to evangelism" situated within the demographic transitions of Orange County in the early twenty-first century, it was an acknowledgment of, and response to, a peculiarly postsuburban political consciousness. Insofar as postsuburbia's hallmarks are fragmentation and decentralization, postsuburban politics are seen by both researchers and postsuburbanites to be a series of quasi-private negotiations between powerful interests.[41] Questions of a Rousseauian general will or Warren's "common good" make little sense within the material realities of "splintering urbanism"[42]—privatized roads, parks, schools, gathering places and HOAs—and classic suburban narratives of self-reliance, individualism, and privacy. And not surprisingly the very political structure of postsuburbia mirrors its material and cultural realities. As the edited collection *Postsuburban California* shows, when collective politics are considered by voters in Orange County, it is done so through the prism of economic growth (job creation through corporate tax breaks and deregulation) and individual tax rates.[43] Public ceremonies in Orange County have a long history of being held on private property and funded by corporate interests, while the parameters of political deliberation have traditionally been set by "growth networks"—public-private linkages between pro-growth, conservative politicians, real estate interests, and multinational corporations.[44]

In this context, a postsuburban civil society is nearly an oxymoron. The terms "private," "privacy," and "privatization" are central to most analyses of modern suburbs and postsuburbs. Histories of modern suburban form and the single-family home almost always narrow in on the condensing of the nuclear family, the rise of private family space as the locus of personal identity formation, and the attendant denuding of public space as defining characteristics of low-density residential space.[45] Studies of postsuburban politics show that the political discourse of economic growth and low taxes, fractured local political structures (there are thirty-four municipalities within Orange County, not including the quasi-public community associations in unincorporated developments in south Orange County), a long-standing escapist suburban civic culture,[46] and a passionate desire for privacy all contribute to the reformulation of "citizen" as "taxpayer."[47] It was no coincidence, then, that although Warren had to forgo "a lot of the questions I wanted to have answered" in the forum—questions on AIDS, climate change, and poverty—he was able to subtly ask about Obama's new income tax increase threshold of $250,000.[48] One pastor casually mentioned to me that that was one of his favorite questions of the night because, "$250,000 is not rich in Orange County."

Although a postsuburban civil society may yet be an oxymoron, the Saddleback Civil Forum offered a platform for the materialization and visualization of the socio-political connections obscured by the decentralization and fragmentation of postsuburbia. "How cool was it," one Saddleback member asked me, "that the church was the center of the [American] political world for a day?" She went on to say that although she watched it from home, she felt "really tied" to the presidential campaign in a way that she hadn't before. Other members I talked to about the forum expressed similar feelings. No one had changed his or her mind about the candidates through the event, and none expressed any greater appreciation for alternative political views. But there was a near unanimous sense of closeness to the American political process that this event brought. "I didn't pay attention to politics at all until I heard about [the Civil Forum on the Presidency]," another member told me. "But afterwards I was reading up on everything, and I got really into it."

For individuals whose political engagement rarely extends beyond the local homeowners' association, the Civil Forum served as a welcome respite from the deracinating postsuburban politics that distills individuals interests down to their personal property. In this way, Warren's addition of the "common good" to the "good news" provided space a for a political vision where a national civil society could be seen as real, and the fate of all Americans could be seen as more than the result of private wills and

158 << PURPOSE DRIVEN POLITICS

private virtue. Far from being an act of encouraging political engagement, however, the incorporation of Saddleback into the American political process was seen by Warren as a way to legitimize the church, not sacralize politics. The forum was not followed by voter registration drives at the church, as in the past. Nor was it followed by a politically relevant sermon or church campaign. In fact, three weeks after the Civil Forum, Saddleback launched the "Forty Days of Love" campaign, which consisted of a series of sermons and small-group study guides centered on Pastor Holladay's new book about relating with Christlike love to those close to you. It could not have been more apolitical.

The Future of the Civil Forum

Less than a month after the 2008 presidential election, Saddleback Church held its third Civil Forum titled "The Civil Forum on Global Health." In lieu of the church's "Global Summit on AIDS and the Church," held annually on World AIDS Day, Warren decided to "honor" the outgoing president George W. Bush by awarding him the first "International Medal of PEACE" at a dedicated civil forum event.[49] However, this one was not held on the Saddleback campus; it was not even held in Southern California. It was held in Washington, DC, at the Newseum (a nonpartisan, non-religious museum of news and freedom of the press), and its focus and only guests were George W. Bush and Laura Bush.

In addition to a short press release, it was briefly announced at the previous weekend's services at Saddleback and broadcast on the Lake Forest campus. And barely anyone noticed. None of the major news networks picked up the story, and its screening on the Saddleback campus was sparsely attended. An email went out the night of the event from Tom Holladay. Lacking the normal stylized flair of most Saddleback emails, it was simply "a quick reminder of two things." First, "Join us for the Civil Forum on AIDS from Washington DC, being broadcast at the worship center at 7 p.m. tonight." And second, Holladay reminded church members to download the new ten-minute podcasts the church produces each week called "DriveTime Devotion."

The forum in Washington had none of the frisson of the August one, and thus none of the evangelistic potential. As a platform for Bush to focus on his relatively uncontroversial global AIDS policy as well as his Christian faith, Warren described it as a "celebration," an "honor," a "chat." It was held in a small theater with tickets distributed on an invitation-only basis. Its format, marketing, and organization suggested that Warren was neither concerned with reaching out to the "community" nor involving himself in national politics. Well after the event, some staff at the church remembered it as a favor by Warren to Bush more than a "real" civil forum event.

But the logic of the fora as a local evangelistic tool continued to work. Saddleback has since held civil fora on "Reconciliation" (September 25, 2009), featuring the Rwandan president Paul Kagame; "Orphans and Adoption" (May 10, 2010), featuring local and national health and social services professionals; "Peace in a Globalized Society" (March 6, 2011), featuring former British prime minister Tony Blair; and "Service and Leadership" (November 29, 2010), with George W. Bush once again. These events were publicized much more strongly and broadly than the first forum with Bush, and following the local evangelistic logic of the original fora, they were marketed as events "for the community." Tickets were free and open to the public, members were encouraged to bring their friends or watch the events as small groups in their homes, and the email announcements were in color, with pictures and video. For example, Bush's second forum was billed as a part of Saddleback's "Christmas Countdown To Your Decade of Destiny" (capitalization in the original).

While the topics of the fora since they began in early 2008 are ostensibly political and of formally civil interest, it is clear that their marketing, format, and intention is local, organizational, and evangelistic. They show how politics and the civil sphere are not always the ends of religio-political action, but in some circumstances they can be the means to pietistic, religious ends. By drawing on the universalistic nature of the civil sphere, Saddleback's civil fora appear to concern everyone, that is, the entire "community." From this angle, the universalism of civil society is not threatened by the particularistic intrusion of Warren and his megachurch; rather, this universalism is but one more strategy for local, intimate, evangelistic conversion.

Conclusion

"Dear Lord, May the Credibility of the Church Be Increased."
—Rick Warren, in a prayer with Saddleback staff members the
week before the Civil Forum on the Presidency, August 12, 2008

Warren could have named this event and the series of which it was a part any number of things. He could have kept the original name, Community Forum, or left the event virtually nameless with something like the Saddleback Presidential Forum. Or still he could have called it a Religious Forum, as did one Canadian journalist.[50] His injection, however, of the term "civil" into this event fit seamlessly into the updated secularization narrative of evangelicalism: religion in general and conservative Protestant Christianity in particular have been exiled not just from political life but from public life, understood essentially as civil society. As one Saddleback pastor said, "These Civil Forums are about the church being a part of regular, public life."

This implies, of course, a perception that "the church" has not been "part of regular, public life." In this sense, then, the Civil Forum is a response to a perceived marginalization of Christianity—a double secularization experienced culturally in a variety ways (see chap. 2) and geographically through socio-spatial differentiation (see chap. 3). But it is not a *political* response; that is, it is not a response of de-secularization. Far from a continuation of Falwellian politics, the evangelicalism represented by Saddleback accepts a secular federal government, secular public schools, and a diverse mass media almost with glee. Its sights are instead set on evangelizing to local, embodied individuals. And one strategy to achieve this is to bring evangelicalism—the material institutions and immaterial discourse—into the fragmented and fluid culture of its post-suburban environment.

It might be argued that the grand mediatic dimensions of the forum are, in fact, evidence of the supralocal ambition of Warren and Saddleback. Why would they go to all the trouble just to grow their local church? Might there be some larger network that would stand to gain from this event? While there is clearly a vibrant nondenominational network of evangelical churches in the United States and throughout the world, it played no role in the Civil Forum on the Presidency, let alone the civil forum series in general.[51] There were no coordinated sermons on "the kind of leader America needs," nor was there participation in the event, before or after.[52] Yet it seems incredible that Warren and Saddleback staff would put in so much effort to produce a national and global media event for such a geographically limited purpose. The appearance of a significant incongruity between effort and payoff here is the product of a perspective that equates religious action with instrumental action, and public religious action with political action. If religious action is seen as localized cultural action, then the motivation and ends of such action appear very differently.

This act of public religion was not an effort to challenge the autonomous logic of the state, civil society, or the market. It was not even, to paraphrase Casanova, a refusal to accept the assigned marginal place of religious action within the privatized sphere of religion. It was public evangelism. And it was meant to work precisely within the privatized sphere of religion. Warren's effort at legitimizing the church was not a prelude to further public action, but was one isolated initiative among many at Saddleback (what pastors there call "hooks in the water") to "reach out to the community" with the goal of evangelism. Far from an act of deprivatization and desecularization, the public religion of Saddleback-style evangelicalism is, in essence, a strategy for saving one local, private soul at a time.

8

Conclusion

Assembling Places of Fusion, De-fusion, and
Diffusion in the Postsuburban Landscape

My research project began with the assumption that the modern world has
been undergoing a process of secularization for some time and that vibrant,
growing and non-immigrant religious communities were bucking the trend
by accessing some religious/affective energies that shrinking or stagnant
religious communities could not or would not access. This is both implicitly and explicitly argued in several excellent recent analyses of American
evangelicalism.[1] But as a geographer I wondered if this unique store of religious energy (produced, some argue, through a confluence of discursive and
material practices) was connected to the spaces and places ordered, built,
and occupied by these evangelicals. It seemed plausible that the physical and
cultural environment of the megachurch was a generator of sorts for these
affective energies. The megachurch with its architectural pastiche of the holy
and the profane might serve as a uniquely open and accessible sacred space
in a sea of secular banality.

This cultural geography made sense to me at the beginning of this project
and makes sense to me now, though in a much different way. As the title

of chapter 2 suggests, the island imagery of sacred archipelagos in a sea of secularity fuels much of the book's analysis. However, it became obvious to me through the course of my time with church members at Saddleback that these sacred archipelagos were not simply tight-knit communities that shared the same "plausibility structure," in the words of Peter L. Berger. The shrinking and spatializing of Berger's "sacred canopy" works for the local, suburban, and urban family church where there is a central affective-spatial site around which a distinct community coalesces. In this sense, archipelago imagery works quite well.

But postsuburban PDE churches like Saddleback are not sacred islands, nor even chains of islands. This spatial imagery needs to be suspended in order to more fully capture the other spatialities of religious life at Saddleback. How can we account for the differentiated affective investments of Saddleback members, the flexible and fluid communal frisson that emerges in very different ways in very different spaces, the dialectic of socio-spatial fragmentation and self-transformative integration through various church programs? Archipelago imagery flattens out the variegated performative energies produced at the weekend sermon, the affinity group, the small group, the daily quiet time, or the global mission field.

Each of these spaces function in the network of Saddleback church not because they reproduce a single, unified affective-communal energy—"performative fusion" in the cultural pragmatics of Jeffrey Alexander. They work because each space distinctly fuses together different narratives, different actors, and different spaces—none of which can possibly be fused altogether at once. This is precisely because postsuburbia is an environment of radical socio-spatial fragmentation. The flows of information, symbols, capital, individuals, and materiality that make up postsuburbia are inherently contradictory. No one institution could symbolically integrate them. But the postsuburban PDE church comes close because it is itself structured as fragmented and contradictory.

Each institutional node at Saddleback becomes a space of discrete, finely scaled fusion. As the site of small groups, daily quiet time, family prayer, and domestic dramas that later take on cosmic significance, the home for Saddleback churchgoers is the affective center around which all other religiously significant activity turns. The performances that emanate from the central church are not so much about practical religious activity—worshipping, prayer, contemplation—as about establishing the very grounds for religion's relevance. The centralized, communal performances work insofar as they recast the spatial scales of evangelicalism in the image of the disparate spaces of postsuburbia—the office cubicle, the living room, the freeway, the backyard. The expansive, world-conquering image of conversionary evangel-icalism is re-scaled into the individual narratives of postsuburbia so that the witnessing Jerusalem of Acts 1 becomes one's master-planned, tract neighbor-hood. Thus, spiritual action is seen to properly take place in the personalized settings of one's own life: in the small group, in the personalized short-term mission trip, at work, or in the grocery store. By mobilizing the elements of one's mundane domestic life—the unruly teenage child, a loveless marriage, even mortgage debt—for religious action, one is performing and thereby underwriting the irreducible relevance of evangelical Christianity.

Sacred Subdivisions as Sacred Space?

But even as differentiated, fragmented, and partial affective spaces, I still hesitate to call the spaces of fusion in postdenominational evangelicalism, "sacred." Even in its most structural-functional sense, "sacred" is too strong a word for the affective energy that surrounds these spaces in the PDE church. Insofar as the term implies a strict bounding of sacred things and actions from those profane, a communal site for collective expressions of social energy, and a construction and policing of in- and outgroups, spaces of fusion at Saddleback are not sacred. They blend the sacred and profane, channel collective effervescence into both enlarging and dividing the congre-gation, and seek to bridge the divide between in- and out-groups.

One reason for this spatial-material ambiguity in Saddleback's practices is the foundational evangelical ambivalence to ritual and materialized sacral-ity. The *evangelium* (good news) of evangelicalism is premised on a sharp dichotomy between faith, grace, and felt experience on one side, and seem-ingly idolatrous and legalistic rituals on the other. American evangelical-ism, even in its contemporary, postdenominational form, remains heavily indebted to the centuries-old Protestant critiques of Roman Catholicism, in which the reality of Christ and eternal salvation was obscured and debased by a superstitious focus on traditional and irrational ritualistic practices. In cultural pragmatic terms, the Roman Catholic liturgy became a de-fused cultural performance whereby Protestants—as both performers and audi-ence—lost cathexis with the liturgical tradition and were alienated from the performances of the clergy. The attempt to recover an "authentic" Christian practice purified of superstitious and clergy-driven ritual constituted the self-understanding of Protestant and later evangelical projects.

Of course, evangelicalism and countless other Protestant varieties of reli-gious practice are shot through with ritualistic practices.[2] From the ubiq-uitous evangelical practices of adult baptism and communion to the more unevenly practiced revival meetings and altar calls, the evangelical critique of ritual is belied by evangelicalism's enduring dependence on practices that "focus attention," "structure schematically qualified environments," "create ritualized actors," and thereby give new order to space and time.[3] The Protestant critique of ritual, then, becomes a serious problem for evangelicals who are vigilant against violating the prohibition against it. Practices that appear ritualistic, and thus are in danger of becoming de-fused, are recast as authentic statements of internal, spiritual states. For example, baptism at Saddleback Church—as in most every form of Protestantism—is explicitly understood as a symbolic representation and not as having any ritualistic efficacy in itself. In the first membership class, newcomers learn that "Baptism doesn't make you a believer—it shows that you already believe. Baptism does not 'save' you, only your faith in Christ does that. Baptism is like a wedding ring—it's the outward symbol of the commitment you make in your heart." The ritualistic practice of baptism is thus de-mystified for its practitioners; it does not *do* anything but rather illustrates, shows, and symbolizes, something else, something that is seen to be real, authentic, and non-ritualistic: the individual act of initiating and committing to a personal relationship with Jesus Christ.

In cultural pragmatic terms, Protestant critiques have de-fused traditional Christian rituals, rendering them as plainly cultural performances. Foundational ritualistic performances such as baptism and communion are recovered in evangelicalism by appropriating their now obvious culturally constructed nature—"Baptism doesn't save you"—in service of performances that are still seen as non-cultural, authentic, and holy—"only your faith in Christ does that." The challenge for PDE churches is to craft and proliferate practices that can still produce ritualistic effects on attention, environment, and identity-formation without appearing to be ritualistic. In other words, they need performances that do not *appear* to be performances. Therefore, effective ritualistic performances must appear to arise naturally from daily life, free of artifice and self-consciousness. Baptism and communion cannot possibly do this and so are relegated to self-conscious social acts that can only symbolize and awkwardly represent the "real," apparently unperformed spiritual state of believers. This kind of spirituality is cultivated most obviously in acts of prayer and singing but more subtly in the joining and maintenance of a small group, volunteering at church services, attending church meetings, and traveling as part of a short-term mission. All of these acts are sacred in the formal sense of being set apart from mundane life. But their sacrality is dependent upon them being woven into mundane, everyday life so as not to appear ritualistic, artificial, and inauthentic. This means that postsuburban evangelicalism is in the midst of creating a distinctly *postsuburban sacrality* because evangelical sacred action is bound tightly to the everyday materiality of postsuburban space.

The most effective space for this evangelical binding of sacred and mundane is the home. Home as the spatial center of postsuburbia and as the cultural refuge of the self from the demands and vagaries of society is clearly already laden with secular affective potential. Nevertheless, its power in PDE performances lies precisely in the qualities that differentiate it from classical sacred space. Instead of binding, demarcating, and policing borders, the home in PDE performances acts as an integrating and hybridizing force; instead of centripetally drawing a community to its center, it serves as a diffuse, individualized, and endlessly adaptable tool for working on the self. But most importantly, the home is an ideal setting for evangelical performances because it is a foundational environment for postsuburban identity and thus one for authentic, intentional action. In the postsuburban home, prayer becomes more intimate, singing becomes more authentic, fellowship becomes more emotional, and scripture becomes more relevant. The central church campus comes to symbolize and illustrate the "real" changes that take place in the home in exactly the same way that ritualistic baptism does for "real" saving faith.

Diffusion against De-fusion

This image of the postsuburban megachurch cuts against the grain of much of the current literature on American evangelicalism that sees it at least partially as a "micro-politics" of imperialism, "cowboy capitalism," and politically reactionary.[4] Although it is a well-established fact that American evangelicals skew strongly rightward in their politics and that conservative politicians shape their electoral strategies accordingly, both pastors and lay members at Saddleback consistently view state politics as largely irrelevant. This is not to say that they are quietist homebodies; rather, the apparent scale of PDE institutions—the megabuildings, the megabudgets, the megacrowds, and sometimes the megaperformances in these megachurches—far exceeds the scale of PDE narratives and practices. When megachurch pastors like Warren or Bill Hybels say that their institutional goals include making "a big church feel small," they are attempting to translate between the exigencies of large institutions and the cultural energy of postsuburban domestic life.

In chapter 2, when we looked at the reality of the *longue durée* of secularization-as-structural-differentiation in liberal Western societies, we also viewed the primacy of this local, domestic life for religious actors. Because advanced, modern societies are structurally differentiated, religion is seen to be confined to its own sphere of action. This does not mean that religious actors remain confined to the sphere of religion; it means that their "intersystemic" action is almost always seen as in need of justification and translation into secular terms. Thus, when Warren briefly entered into state politics in the presidential campaign of 2004 through mass email (see chap. 7), he quickly struck a conciliatory, nonpartisan tone when interviewed in national media outlets in the following months. When asked about that email in 2008 Warren responded, "I don't have much faith in government solutions. . . . None of my values have changed from four years ago, but my agenda has definitely changed."[5] The years following the 2004 election were spent by Warren on initiatives that he saw as growing his church spiritually and materially. And his foray into national politics in 2008 was more a vehicle for local evangelism, while his engagement in California state politics with Proposition 8 was brief, extremely late in the campaign season, and ultimately retracted.[6]

If the real effects of secularization are not kept in view, then Warren's politics appear to be the thin edge of a larger "assemblage" of theocratic-capitalist interests.[7] But seen as part of a place-specific performance, the politics of the megachurch becomes another way of imbricating the intimate domesticity of the home with the institutional and social demands of the central church. This relationship between the individual and family and the larger institution of the megachurch is fragile and contingent. Sometimes the cultural energy generated by connecting the personal to the political patches over other failures in institutional performativity. But most often PDE churches perform with deft precision and have little need for the unstable heat produced by bellicose political rhetoric. In the case of Saddleback, any sustained political engagement, such as the month-long preparation for the Civil Forum on the Presidency, merely sets the table for further performances of diffuse, local, embodied postsuburban evangelicalism.

These performances are fundamentally spatial. The spatiality of the PDE megachurch is expressed most clearly in the dialectic between the weekly communal gathering at the central church campus and the diffusion of small groups in members' homes throughout the church's metropolitan region. This dialectic of the centripetal and centrifugal socio-spatial forces of postsuburbia is recapitulated in the weekend service as well. On Sunday (and Saturday in the largest congregations), when the congregation is dispersed in different venues and different service times, every weekend performance is a stylistic variation on the week's central message.

This dialectic allows for a maximum flexibility on the part of churches and churchgoers alike. Saddleback can adjust its messages, formats, musical styles, and even its institutional structure on the fly because a change in one venue, ministry, or initiative will have little or no effect on the differentiated, diffuse parts that make up the PDE megachurch. In fact, this level of differentiated flexibility means that it is anachronistic to speak of the PDE megachurch as a single institution. Its genius—both institutionally and culturally—is that it allows for an infinitely specialized experience of conservative evangelicalism. Sin, resurrection, atonement, grace, biblical infallibility, evangelism—these touchstones of conservative evangelicalism are all woven inseparably into the fabric of PDE church life. But their presentation and practice vary endlessly because there is no circumscribed jurisdiction for legitimate rehearsals and performances in the PDE church. Because such rehearsals and performances occur daily throughout these churches' metropolitan regions—in homes, offices, parks, and coffee shops—even the core doctrine of conservative evangelicalism can be altered.

For instance, the difference between grace and law—between salvation and grace freely given through the blood of Jesus Christ on one hand, and the divine laws of the Holy Father on the other (a long-vexing problem for Protestants of all stripes)—is negotiated and re-negotiated in a thousand small ways every week in PDE church small groups. There are small groups with openly gay members, while other groups mirror the demographic and dispositional makeup of the Tea Party movement (that is, heterosexual, white, older, and middle class). Some groups are made up of traditional, conservative families with stay-at-home mothers and working fathers; other groups are a collection of divorced parents, working mothers, and stay-at-home fathers. The same diversity could be tracked along a number of socio-cultural indicators. Particular scriptural interpretations of sin, law, and grace in any single group will carry sufficient weight to enforce a level of communal homogeneity. But between groups, these interpretations can vary significantly.

Despite its roots in the conservative Southern Baptist Convention, Saddleback subtly encourages this fragmented diversity. In Class 101, the day-long, introductory membership unit for Saddleback, Warren follows an introduction to his church's doctrinal creeds with an oft-quoted (and diversely attributed) call for ecumenicalism: "In essentials, unity; in nonessentials, liberty; in all things, charity." In the background scripts for Saddleback performances, this statement is a guide for constructing and enacting a wide variety of postsuburban narratives. The brilliance of these performances is that they are constructed and enacted simultaneously within different scales and in different locales. And by this fragmented variety, classical evangelical themes become thoroughly infused with the spatialities, materialities, and culture structures of the individualized, intimate worlds of their postsuburban audience. In this way, postsuburban places become "purpose driven" places.

APPENDIX A

Largest 100 megachurches according to a continuously updated database managed by Scott Thumma at the Hartford Center for Religion Research. The average weekly attendance numbers are gathered from denomination reports, self-reporting by churches, and research visits. Churches that are primarily multicampus churches have been excluded. The database is available online at http://hirr. hartsem.edu/megachurch/database.html (last accessed on June 7, 2011). Small group data was gathered through Internet research and phone interviews. Urban location was determined qualitatively by determining relative proximity to an urban core and peripheral freeway interchanges, age of the church campus, and the surrounding built environment, and in some cases through phone interviews (to determine if the church served multiple urban nodes).

NAME	CITY	STATE	AVG. ATTEND.	DENOMINATION	SMALL GROUPS?	URBAN LOCATION	METROPOLITAN STATISTICAL AREA
Lakewood Church	Houston	TX	43500	PDE/NONDENOM	Yes: "Life Groups"	Commercial Cluster	Houston
LifeChurch	Edmond	OK	26776	PDE/EC	Yes: "Life Groups"	Postsuburbia	Oklahoma City
Fellowship Church	Grapevine	TX	24000	PDE/SBC	Yes: "HomeTeams"	Postsuburbia	Dallas
Willow Creek Community Church	South Barrington	IL	23400	PDE/NONDENOM	Yes: "Neighborhood Life"	Postsuburbia	Chicago
North Point Community Church	Alpharetta	GA	23377	PDE/NONDENOM	Yes: "Community Groups"	Postsuburbia	Atlanta
Second Baptist Church	Houston	TX	22723	SBC	No: Bible Study	Suburbia	Houston
Saddleback Valley Community Church	Lake Forest	CA	22418	PDE/SBC	Yes: Small Groups	Postsuburbia	Los Angeles
West Angeles Church of God in Christ	Los Angeles	CA	20000	COGIC	No: Bible Study	Urban	Los Angeles
Southeast Christian Church	Louisville	KY	17261	PDE/NONDENOM	Yes" "Community groups"	Postsuburbia	Louisville
Fellowship of the Woodlands	Conroe	TX	17142	PDE/NONDENOM	Yes: Small Groups	Postsuburbia	Houston
The Potter's House	Dallas	TX	17000	PDE/NONDENOM	No: Bible Study	Postsuburbia	Dallas
Hopewell Missionary Baptist	Norcross	GA	16000	BAPT	No: Bible Study	Old Industrial Suburb	Atlanta
Phoenix First Assembly of God	Phoenix	AZ	16000	PDE/AG	No: Bible Study	Postsuburbia	Phoenix
Calvary Chapel	Ft. Lauderdale	FL	15921	PDE/CAL	Yes" "Community groups"	Postsuburbia	South Florida
Central Christian Church	Henderson	NV	15081	PDE/NONDENOM	Yes: Small Groups	Postsuburbia	Las Vegas
First Baptist Church	Hammond	IN	15059	IFB	No: Bible Study	Old Commercial Cluster	Chicago
Harvest Christian Fellowship	Riverside	CA	15000	PDE/CAL	Yes: Home Bible Studies	Postsuburbia	Los Angeles
World Changers Ministries	College Park	GA	15000	PDE/NONDENOM	No: Bible Study	Postsuburbia	Atlanta
Prestonwood Baptist Church	Plano	TX	14975	SBC	No: "Bible Fellowship Classes"	Postsuburbia	Dallas
New Light Christian Center	Houston	TX	13500	PDE/NONDENOM	No	Old Suburb	Houston
Thomas Road Baptist Church	Lynchburg	VA	13100	SBC	No: Bible Study	Small city center	Lynchburg
New Birth Missionary Baptist	Lithonia	GA	13000	BAPT	No: Bible Study	Postsuburbia	Atlanta
Christian Life Centre - Christian Cultural Center	Brooklyn	NY	13000	PDE/NONDENOM	No: Bible Study and Affinity Groups	Urban	New York
Calvary Chapel	Albuquerque	NM	13000	PDE/CAL	Yes: "Home Fellowships"	Old industrial Suburb	Albuquerque
Community Bible Church	San Antonio	TX	12646	PDE/NONDENOM	Yes: "Life Groups"	Postsuburbia	San Antonio
Palm Beach Gardens Christ Fellowship	Palm Beach Gardens	FL	12399	PDE/NONDENOM	Yes: "Life Groups"	Postsuburbia	South Florida

	NAME	CITY	STATE	AVG. ATTEND.	DENOMINATION	SMALL GROUPS?	URBAN LOCATION	METROPOLITAN STATISTICAL AREA
27	Rock Church	San Diego	CA	12129	PDE/NONDENOM	Yes: Small Groups	Postsuburbia	San Diego
28	Christ's Church of the Valley	Peoria	AZ	12013	PDE/NONDENOM	Yes: "Neighborhood Groups"	Postsuburbia	Phoenix
29	Faith Community Church	West Covina	CA	12000	PDE/NONDENOM	Yes: Small Groups	Postsuburbia	Los Angeles
30	Eagle Brook Church	White Bear Lake	MN	11591	PDE/BGC	Yes: Groups	Postsuburbia	Minneapolis
31	Mclean Bible Church	Vienna	VA	11512	PDE/NONDENOM	Yes: Small Groups	Postsuburbia	Washington-Arlington
32	Crossroads Community Church	Cincinnati	OH	11469	PDE/NONDENOM	Yes: Small Groups and Community Groups	Old Suburb	Cincinnati
33	Calvary Community Church	Phoenix	AZ	11433	PDE/CAL	Yes: "Home Bible Studies"	Postsuburbia	Phoenix
34	Gateway Church	Southlake	TX	11295	PDE/NONDENOM	Yes: "Gateway Groups"	Postsuburbia	Dallas
35	Kensington Community Church	Troy	MI	11099	PDE/NONDENOM	Yes: Small Groups	Postsuburbia	Detroit
36	Brentwood Baptist	Houston	TX	11000	SBC	No: Bible Study	Postsuburbia	Houston
37	Church On The Move	Tulsa	OK	11000	PDE/NONDENOM	No: Bible Study and Affinity Groups	Postsuburbia	Tulsa
38	Word of Faith International Christian Center	Southfield	MI	11000	WOF	No: Bible Study	Urban Cluster	Detroit
39	Calvary Chapel South Bay	Gardena	CA	10800	PDE/CAL	No: Programs	Old Commercial Cluster	Los Angeles
40	Mariners Church	Irvine	CA	10700	PDE/NONDENOM	Yes: Small Groups	Postsuburbia	Los Angeles
41	Lake Pointe Baptist	Rockwall	TX	10571	PDE/SBC	No: "Bible Fellowship Classes"	Postsuburbia	Dallas
42	Redemption World Outreach Center	Greenville	SC	10550	IPHC	No: Bible Study and Support Groups	Urban Cluster	Greenville
43	Calvary Temple	Modesto	CA	10515	AG	No: Bible Study	Older Suburb	Modesto
44	Valley Bible Fellowship	Bakersfield	CA	10500	PDE/NONDENOM	No: Bible Study and Support Groups	Postsuburbia	Bakersfield
45	The Rock And World Outreach Center	San Bernardino	CA	10454	PDE/NONDENOM	Yes: Small Groups	Postsuburbia	Riverside
46	First Baptist Church	Springdale	AR	10382	SBC	No: Bible Study	Older Suburb	Fayetteville
47	Calvary Chapel of Philadelphia	Philadelphia	PA	10000	PDE/CAL	Yes: Small Groups	Postsuburbia	Philadelphia
48	City of Refuge Church	Gardena	CA	10000	PAW	No: Bible Study	Old Suburb	Los Angeles
49	Cornerstone Church	San Antonio	TX	10000	PDE/NONDENOM	Yes: Government of 12	Postsuburbia	San Antonio
50	Ebenezer AME	Ft. Washington	MD	10000	AME	No: Bible Study	Postsuburbia	Washington-Arlington
51	First African Methodist Episcopal Church	Los Angeles	CA	10000	AME	No: Bible Study	Urban	Los Angeles
52	Free Chapel Worship Center	Gainesville	GA	10000	PDE/NONDENOM	Yes: Small Groups	Postsuburbia	Atlanta
53	Greater Saint Stephen Full Gospel Baptist	New Orleans	LA	10000	BAPT	No: Bible Study	Urban	New Orleans
54	Jubilee Christian Center	San Jose	CA	10000	PDE/NONDENOM	Yes: "Life Groups"	Postsuburbia	San Francisco
55	Mars Hill Bible Church	Grandville	MI	10000	PDE/NONDENOM	Yes: "House Churches"	Postsuburbia	Grand Rapids
56	Temple of Deliverance	Memphis	TN	10000	COGIC	No: Bible Study	Urban	Memphis
57	Bayside Covenant Church	Roseville	CA	9983	PDE/EC	Yes: Small Groups	Postsuburbia	Sacramento
58	Church On The Way	Van Nuys	CA	9869	4SQ	Yes: Small Groups	Postsuburbia	Los Angeles
59	Salem Baptist Church	Chicago	IL	9800	BAPT	No: Bible Study	Urban	Chicago
60	Covenant Church	Carrollton	TX	9765	PDE/NONDENOM	Yes: Small Groups	Postsuburbia	Dallas
61	Abundant Living Faith Center	El Paso	TX	9750	PDE/NONDENOM	Yes: Small Groups	Postsuburbia	El Paso

NAME	CITY	STATE	AVG. ATTEND.	DENOMINATION	SMALL GROUPS?	URBAN LOCATION	METROPOLITAN STATISTICAL AREA
Church of the Resurrection	Leawood	KS	9607	UMC	No: Bible Study	Postsuburbia	Kansas City
Calvary Chapel of Costa Mesa	Santa Ana	CA	9500	PDE/CAL	No: Bible Study	Postsuburbia	Los Angeles
Northridge Church	Plymouth	MI	9445	PDE/NONDENOM	Yes: Small Groups	Postsuburbia	Detroit
Ben Hill United Methodist	Atlanta	GA	9414	UMC	No	Urban	Atlanta
New Spring Community Church	Anderson	SC	9326	PDE/SBC	Yes: Small Groups	Postsuburbia	Anderson
Victory Christian Center	Tulsa	OK	9255	PDE/NONDENOM	Yes: Victory Cells	Postsuburbia	Tulsa
Bethel Baptist Institut'l Church	Jacksonville	FL	9250	BAPT	No	Urban	Jacksonville
New York City Church of Christ	Englewood Cliffs	NJ	9213	COC	No	Urban	New York
Southland Christian Church	Nicholasville	KY	9148	PDE/NONDENOM	Yes: "Life Groups"	Postsuburbia	Lexington
Glide Memorial United Methodist	San Francisco	CA	9016	UMC	No	Urban	San Francisco
Detroit World Outreach Center	Redford	MI	9000	AG	No	Urban	Detroit
Family Christian Center	Munster	IN	9000	PDE/NONDENOM	Yes: Cell Groups	Postsuburbia	Chicago
Mount Zion Baptist Church	Whites Creek	TN	9000	BAPT	No: Programs	Postsuburbia	Nashville
New Birth Baptist Church	Miami	FL	9000	BAPT	No: Bible Study	Urban	South Florida
Shepherd of the Hills	Porter Ranch	CA	8922	CHRISTIAN	Yes: Small Groups	Postsuburbia	Los Angeles
James River Assembly	Ozark	MO	8780	PDE/AG	Yes: "Life Groups"	Postsuburbia	Springfield
New Life Church	Colorado Springs	CO	8600	PDE/NONDENOM	Yes: "New Life Groups"	Postsuburbia	Colorado Springs
Sa-Rang Community Church	Anaheim	CA	8600	NONDENOM	No: Bible Study	Urban Cluster	Los Angeles
New Hope Christian Fellowship	Honolulu	HI	8556	4SQ	Yes: Small Groups	Industrial cluster	Honolulu
Flamingo Road Baptist Church	Cooper City	FL	8500	PDE/SBC	Yes: Connect Groups	Postsuburbia	South Florida
Real Life Ministries	Post Falls	ID	8500	PDE/NONDENOM	Yes: "Home Groups"	Postsuburbia	Spokane, WA/ Coeur D'Alene, ID
Oak Hills Church	San Antonio	TX	8356	PDE/NONDENOM	Yes: Small Groups	Postsuburbia	San Antonio
Flatirons Community Church	Lafayette	CO	8286	PDE/NONDENOM	Yes: "Community Groups"	Postsuburbia	Denver
Lancaster County Bible Church	Manheim	PA	8216	PDE/NONDENOM	Yes: "Life Groups"	Postsuburbia	Lancaster
Bethany World Prayer Center	Baker	LA	8000	PDE/NONDENOM	Yes: Small Groups	Postsuburbia	Baton Rouge
Brooklyn Tabernacle	Brooklyn	NY	8000	NONDENOM	No	Urban	New York
Calvary Chapel Melbourne	Melbourne	FL	8000	PDE/CAL	Yes: "Home Groups"	Postsuburbia	South Florida
Calvary Chapel Tucson	Tucson	AZ	8000	PDE/CAL	Yes: "Home Fellowships"	Postsuburbia	Tucson
Central Church of God	Charlotte	NC	8000	COG	Yes: House to House Groups	Postsuburbia	Charlotte
Friendship West Baptist Church	Dallas	TX	8000	BAPT	No: Bible Study and Support Groups	Postsuburbia	Dallas
High Desert Church	Victorville	CA	8000	PDE/BAPT	Yes: "Life Groups"	Postsuburbia	Los Angeles
Living Word Christian Center	Brooklyn Park	MN	8000	PDE/NONDENOM	Yes: Small Groups	Postsuburbia	Minneapolis
Saint Stephens Baptist Church	Louisville	KY	8000	BAPT	Yes: Life Groups	Urban	Louisville
Shoreline Christian Center	Austin	TX	8000	PDE/NONDENOM	Yes: Connect Groups	Postsuburbia	Austin
The Chapel	Akron	OH	8000	PDE/NONDENOM	Yes: Small Groups	Downtown Akron	Akron
Times Square Church	New York City	NY	8000	NONDENOM	No: Bible Study	Urban	New York
Mt. Paran Church of God	Atlanta	GA	7850	COG	No: Bible Study	Postsuburbia	Atlanta
Victory Christian Center	Oklahoma City	OK	7800	PDE/NONDENOM	Yes: Small Groups	Postsuburbia	Oklahoma City
First United Methodist Church— Marietta	Marietta	GA	7776	UMC	No: Bible Study and Support Groups	Old Suburb	Atlanta

' OF DENOMINATION
REVIATIONS
?: Four Square
. Assemblies of God
E: African Methodist
piscopal
'T: Baptist (unspecified)

BGC: Baptist General Conference
CAL: Calvary Churches
CHRISTIAN: Christian (unspecified)
COC: Church of Christ
COGIC: Church of God in Christ
EC: Evangelical Covenant

IFB: Independent Fundamentalist Baptist
IPHC: International Pentecostal Holiness Church
NONDENOM: Nondenominational

PAW: Pentecostal Assemblies of the World
PDE: Postdenominational Evangelical
SBC: Southern Baptist Convention
UMC: United Methodist Church
WOF: Word of Faith

NOTES TO CHAPTER 1

1. "Faith Matters: A Purpose Driven Strife," *Nightline*, ABC News (March 7, 2007); Rich Karlgaard, "Purpose Driven," *Forbes.com* (2004) available online at http://www.forbes.com/forbes/2004/0216/039.html. "BIO: Rick Warren," Pastor Rick and Kay Warren Online Newsroom (2011) available online at http://www.rickwarrennews.com/bio_rwarren.htm

2. For academic representations see Roger Finke and Rodney Stark, *The Churching of America, 1776–2005: Winners and Losers in Our Religious Economy* (New Brunswick, NJ: Rutgers University Press, 2005); Wade Clark Roof, *Spiritual Marketplace: Baby Boomers and the Remaking of American Religion* (Princeton, NJ: Princeton University Press, 1999); Robert Wuthnow, *After Heaven: Spirituality in America Since the 1950s* (Berkeley: University of California Press, 1998). For popular media attention see the recent documentaries *Jesus Camp* (2006) and *Friends of God* (2007) and the *Newsweek–Washington Post* online collaboration "On Faith" (accessible at http://newsweek.washingtonpost.com/onfaith/) where religion is seen as "the most pervasive yet least understood topic in global life."

3. "U.S. Religious Landscape Survey," Pew Forum on Religion and Public Life (2008), available online at http://religions.pewforum.org/ (last accessed April 15, 2010).

4. "Losing Faith in Modern America," *New Zealand Herald* (2008), A1; Duke Helfand, "More People Say They Have No Religion," *Los Angeles Times* (2009), A13; Cathy Lynn Grossman, "Almost All Denominations Losing Ground, Survey Finds: Faith Is Shifting, Drifting or Vanishing Outright," *USA Today* (2009), 1A; Jon Meacham, "The End of Christian America," *Newsweek* (2009), 34–38.

5. Quoted in Meacham, "End of Christian American," 34.

6. Sacred space/place is discussed further in the conclusion. The traditional sociological concept of sacred space/place can be found in Emile Durkheim, *The Elementary Forms of Religious Life* (New York: Oxford University Press, 2001), 228–229; Mircea Eliade, *The Sacred and the Profane: The Nature of Religion* (New York: Harcourt, Brace and World, 1959). See also David Chidester and Edward Tabor Linenthal, "introduction" to *American Sacred Space,* ed. David Chidester and Edward Tabor Linenthal (Bloomington: Indiana University Press, 1995), 1–42.

7. See especially, R. Stephen Warner, "Work in Progress Toward a New Paradigm for the Sociological Study of Religion in the United States," *American Journal of Sociology* 98, no. 5 (1993): 1044–1093; Rodney Stark and Roger Finke, *Acts of Faith: Explaining the Human Side of Religion* (Berkeley: University of California Press, 2000); Shayne Lee and Phillip Luke Sinitiere, *Holy Mavericks: Evangelical Innovators and the Spiritual Marketplace* (New York: New York University Press, 2009).

8. R. Stephen Warner, 2004, "Enlisting Smelser's Theory of Ambivalence to Maintain Progress in Sociology of Religion's New Paradigm," in *Self, Social Structure, and Beliefs: Explorations in Sociology,* ed. Jeffrey C. Alexander, Gary T. Marx, and Christine L. Williams (Berkeley: University of California Press), 105.

9. For a brief overview of the market explanation of megachurch popularity, see Stephen Ellingson, "The Rise of the Megachurches and Changes in Religious Culture: Review Article," *Sociology Compass* 3, no. 1 (2009): 21.

10. Lee and Sinitiere, *Holy Mavericks,* 3, 23, 176. For a definitive statement on supernatural goods, see Stark and Finke, *Acts of Faith,* 88–91.

11. The religious market model has been formulated in a weak and a strong version. The weak version can be found in R. Stephen Warner's "New Paradigm," where economic concepts are used to highlight the advantages to religious organizations of a disestablished, pluralistic, and diverse socio-religious environment. The egoistic, instrumental rationality that the language of economic markets implies is not, in this weak version, put to any analytic work. Instead, the weak version relies on historical-cultural explanations that benefit little from the market terminology. The strong version can be found in the rational-choice framework of Rodney Stark and Roger Finke (2000; 2005) in which potential consumers are marketed supernatural goods by religious firms.

12. James Wood, "God in the Quad," *New Yorker* (August 31, 2009), 75.

13. This premise is now hard-won common sense in cultural geography. See J. Nicholas Entrikin, *The Betweenness of Place: Towards a Geography of Modernity* (Baltimore: Johns Hopkins University Press, 1991), 53–59; Tim Cresswell, *Place: A Short Introduction* (Malden, MA: Wiley-Blackwell, 2004), 12.

14. Mark Chaves, "All Creatures Great and Small: Megachurches in Context," *Review of Religious Research* 47, no. 4 (2006): 329–346; Scott Thumma and Dave Travis, *Beyond Megachurch Myths: What We Can Learn from America's Largest Churches* (San Francisco: Jossey-Bass, 2007).

15. For more on popular misunderstandings of megachurches, see Thumma and Travis, *Beyond Megachurch Myths,* 21–22.

16. Through their original empirical work on American megachurches, Scott Thumma and Dave Travis sort U.S. megachurches into four categories: (1) what they call "Old line/Program-Based," makes up 30 percent of U.S. megachurches and are located in downtowns of small and midsize cities. These "overgrown country churches" are ethnically homogenous, culturally, and theologically conservative, and have become "mega" through long and steady growth; (2) the "Seeker" megachurch. Making up 30 percent of all megachurches, this type is best known and most often associated with the megachurch movement. They are marked by innovative contemporary worship services and are generally found in the suburban fringe of large metropolitan areas; (3) the "Charismatic/Pastor-Focused" megachurch. Found in denser urban and older and newer suburban parts of large cities, these churches are typically Pentecostal or nondenominationally charismatic. They make up 25 percent of all U.S. megachurches; and (4) the "New Wave/Re-envisioned" megachurch. These churches are typically less than a decade old, target younger constituents, and have a more confrontational and activist style of outreach. They make up 15 percent of the megachurch population.

17. The most authoritative and comprehensive data on megachurches has been compiled by Scott Thumma at the Hartford Institute for Religion Research. A list of all known U.S. megachurches can be found at http://hirr.hartsem.edu/megachurch/database. html.

18. Donald E. Miller, *Reinventing American Protestantism: Christianity in the New Millennium* (Berkeley: University of California Press, 1997), 13.

19. Mark A. Noll, *American Evangelical Christianity: An Introduction* (Malden, MA: Blackwell Publishers, 2001), 10–11; Mark A. Noll, *The Rise of Evangelicalism: The Age of Edwards, Whitefield and the Wesleys* (Nottingham: IVP, 2004).

20. David W. Bebbington, *Evangelicalism in Modern Britain: A History From the 1730s to the 1980s* (Boston: Unwin Hyman, 1989), 1–17, quoted in Noll, *American Evangelical Christianity*, 13.

21. George Marsden, *Fundamentalism and American Culture* (New York: Oxford University Press, 2006); Donald Miller, *Reinventing American Protestantism*, 1–26; Christian Smith, *American Evangelicalism: Embattled and Thriving* (Chicago: University of Chicago Press, 1998); Randall Balmer, *Mine Eyes Have Seen the Glory: A Journey into the Evangelical Subculture in America* (New York: Oxford University Press, 2006); James M. Ault, *Spirit and Flesh: Life in a Fundamentalist Baptist Church* (New York: Alfred A. Knopf, 2004).

22. Robert Bruce Mullin and Russell E. Richey, "Denominations and Denominationalism: An American Morphology," *Reimagining Denominationalism: Interpretive Essays* (New York: Oxford University Press , 1994), 77; Kimon Howland Sargeant, *Seeker Churches: Promoting Traditional Religion in a Nontraditional Way* (New Brunswick: Rutgers University Press, 2000), 15–35; Smith, *American Evangelicalism*, 9–13; Donald Miller, *Reinventing American Protestantism*, 20–21.

23. Thumma and Travis, *Beyond Megachurch Myths*, 31–43.

24. These characteristics closely match some of the twelve characteristics of "new paradigm" churches that Donald E. Miller lists in *Reinventing American Protestantism*. While I agree with much of his analysis, my reading of the same movement differs from his in that (1) I see traditional evangelicalism to be an important part of these churches and not "too broad" to be meaningfully descriptive (cf. 2); (2) the "new paradigm" he describes seems to be much broader and more general than his sample suggests; and (3) charismatic "gifts of the spirit" do not appear to be central to post-denominational churches, even those with Pentecostal roots.

25. Loosely denominational churches "remain within existing denominations, but their worship and organizational style differ decidedly from those of the more institutionalized churches in their denominations. Indeed, some of these new paradigm churches disguise the fact that they even have a denominational affiliation." Donald Miller, *Reinventing American Protestantism*, 1.

26. This is by no means an indication that PDE churches actually reach the unchurched. It is more likely that they grow from transfer growth, that is, by drawing members from smaller, less innovative churches. On PDE evangelism see Rick Warren, *The Purpose Driven Church: Growth without Compromising Your Message and Mission* (Grand Rapids: Zondervan, 1995), 104–105; Sargeant, *Seeker Churches*, 75, 110. Sometimes referred to as the "circulation of the saints," this transfer growth is sometimes seen as harmful to nearby, smaller, and more traditional evangelical churches. But because the PDE churches are located mostly in fast-growing, high-turnover

areas, many of the transfers are churchgoers who have recently moved into the
area and do not yet have a local church. For the perceived effects of megachurches
on smaller, local congregations, see Nancy L. Eisland, "Contending with a Giant:
The Impact of a Megachurch on Exurban Religious Institutions," in *Contemporary
American Religion: An Ethnographic Reader*, ed. Penny Edgell Becker and Nancy L.
Eiesland (Walnut Creek, CA: AltaMira Press, 1997), 191–220; Thumma and Travis,
Beyond Megachurch Myths, 118–134. On transfer growth, see Nancy L. Eiesland, *A
Particular Place: Urban Restructuring and Religious Ecology in a Southern Exurb* (New
Brunswick: Rutgers University Press, 2000), 215; Scott Thumma and Jim Petersen,
"Goliaths in Our Midst: Megachurches in the ELCA," in *Lutherans Today: American
Lutheran Identity in the Twenty-First Century* (Grand Rapids: W. B. Eerdmans , 2003),
102–124; Mark Chaves, "All Creatures Great and Small," 329–346; Thumma and Tra-
vis, *Beyond Megachurch Myths*, 123–125.

27. Warren, *Purpose Driven Church*, 279–292; Donald Miller, *Reinventing American
Protestantism*, 12; Sargeant, *Seeker Churches*, 19; Richard Flory and Donald E. Miller,
Finding Faith: The Spiritual Quest of the Post-Boomer Generation (New Brunswick:
Rutgers University Press, 2008); Stephen Ellingson, *The Megachurch and the Main-
line: Remaking Religious Tradition in the Twenty-First Century* (Chicago: University of
Chicago Press, 2007), 67–70.

28. Donald Miller, *Reinventing American Protestantism*, 21–22; Sargeant, *Seeker Churches*,
119; Roof, *Spiritual Marketplace*, 39–40; Wuthnow, *After Heaven*, 142–167; Ellingson,
Megachurch and the Mainline, 78–143.

29. Balmer, *Mine Eyes Have Seen the Glory*, 332; Geof Surratt, Greg Ligon, and Warren
Bird, *The Multi-Site Church Revolution* (Grand Rapids: Zondervan, 2006).

30. Smith, *American Evangelicalism*, 10-11; Thumma and Travis, *Beyond Megachurch
Myths*, 91–117.

31. See chap. 3.

32. Robert Wuthnow, "Small Groups and Spirituality: Exploring the Connections," in *"I
Come Away Stronger": How Small Groups Are Shaping American Religion*, ed. Robert
Wuthnow (Grand Rapids: W. B. Eerdmans, 1994), 1–7; See also chap. 5 and the
appendix.

33. Warren, *Purpose Driven Church*, 190. Robert H. Schuller, *My Journey: From An Iowa
Farm to a Cathedral of Dreams* (New York: HarperCollins, 2001), 220.

34. Warren, *Purpose Driven Church*, 191–192.

35. Rick Warren, "Keynote Address," *Purpose Driven Network Summit* (Lake Forest,
California, 2008).

36. Warner, "Work in Progress," 1044–1093; Stark and Finke, *Acts of Faith*; Christian
Smith, "Introduction: Rethinking the Secularization of American Public Life," in
*The Secular Revolution: Power, Interests, and Conflict in the Secularization of American
Public Life*, ed. Christian Smith (Berkeley: University of California Press, 2003),
1–78; Talal Asad, *Formations of the Secular: Christianity, Islam, Modernity* (Stanford:
Stanford University Press, 2003); Saba Mahmood, "Secularism, Hermeneutics, and
Empire: The Politics of Islamic Reformation," *Public Culture* 18 no. 2 (2006): 323–347.

37. Steve Bruce, *God Is Dead: Secularization in the West* (Malden, MA: Blackwell, 2002);
José Casanova, *Public Religions in the Modern World* (Chicago: University of Chicago
Press, 1994); Mark Chaves, "Secularization As Declining Religious Authority,"
Social Forces 72, no. 3 (1994): 749–774; Paul Colomy, "Revisions and Progress in

Differentiation Theory," in *Differentiation Theory and Social Change: Comparative and Historical Perspectives,* ed. Jeffrey Alexander and Paul Colomy (New York: Columbia University Press, 1990), 465–495; Karel Dobbelaere, "Secularization: A Multi-Dimensional Concept," *Current Sociology* 29, no. 2 (1981): 3-153; Karel Dobbelaere, "Towards An Integrated Perspective of the Processes Related to the Descriptive Concept of Secularization," *Sociology of Religion* 60, no. 3 (1999): 229–247.

38. Here I allude to Henri Levebvre's tripartite distinction of social space as "social practice" ("perceived"), "representations of space" ("conceived"), and "representational space" ("lived"). Henri Lefebvre, *The Production of Space* (Malden, MA: Blackwell, 1991), 38–39. I elaborate on Lefebvre's contribution to spatial differentiation in chap. 2.

39. I rely heavily on Robert Fishman's masterful reconstruction of the "rise and fall of suburbia" here and in chap. 3. However, he uses the term "technoburb" to describe postsuburbia. Robert Fishman, *Bourgeois Utopias: The Rise and Fall of Suburbia* (New York: Basic Books, 1987), 182–207.

40. See Jeffrey C. Alexander, *The Meanings of Social Life: A Cultural Sociology* (New York: Oxford University Press, 2003); Mustafa Emirbayer, "The Alexander School of Cultural Sociology," *Thesis Eleven* 79, no. 1 (2004): 5–15; Jeffrey C. Alexander, Bernhard Giesen, and Jason L. Mast, *Social Performance: Symbolic Action, Cultural Pragmatics, and Ritual* (New York: Cambridge University Press, 2006); Jeffrey Alexander, "Performing Cultural Sociology: A Conversation with Jeffrey Alexander," *European Journal of Social Theory* 11, no. 4 (2008): 525–542.

41. Jeffrey C. Alexander, "Cultural Pragmatics: Social Performance Between Ritual and Strategy," *Sociological Theory* 22, no. 4 (2004): 548.

42. Karl Marx, "The Eighteenth Brumaire of Louis Bonaparte," in *Karl Marx: Selected Writings,* ed. Jon Elster (New York: Cambridge University Press, 1986), 277.

43. See Donald Miller, *Reinventing American Protestantism*; Flory and Miller, *Finding Faith*; Eileen Luhr, *Witnessing Suburbia: Conservatives and Christian Youth Culture* (Berkeley: University of California Press, 2009).

44. William P. Young, *The Shack* (Newbury Park, CA: Windblown Media, 2007)

45. Michael Quinn Patton, *Qualitative Research and Evaluation Methods* (Thousand Oaks, CA: Sage, 2002), 452–460; Paul J. Cloke, et al., *Practicing Human Geography* (Thousand Oaks, CA: Sage, 2004), chap. 10.

46. Lee and Sinitiere, *Holy Mavericks.*

NOTES TO CHAPTER 2

1. Smith, introduction" to Smith, *The Secular Revolution,* 5.

2. Paul Cloke, Sarah Johnsen, and Jon May, "Exploring Ethos? Discourses of 'Charity' in the Provision of Emergency Services for Homeless People," *Environment and Planning A* 37 (2005): 385–402; Paul Cloke, Sarah Johnsen, and Jon May, "Ethical Citizenship? Volunteers and the Ethics of Providing Services for Homeless People," *Geoforum* 38, no. 6 (2007): 1089-1101.

3. In geography, see Justin Beaumont, "Introduction: Faith-Based Organizations and Urban Social Issues," *Urban Studies* 45, no. 10 (2008): 2011–2017; Cloke, Johnson, and May, "Exploring Ethos?" and "Ethical Citizenship?"; Benedikt Korf, "Geography and Benedict XVI," *Area* 38, no. 3 (2006): 326–329; Nick Megoran, "Christianity and Political Geography: On Faith and Geopolitical Imagination," *Brandywine Review of*

Faith and International Affairs (Fall 2004): 40–46; and the three paper sessions titled "The Postsecular City" at the 2008 annual meeting of the Association of American Geographers. For examples outside of geography, see Peter van der Veer, *Imperial Encounters: Religion and Modernity in India and Britain* (Princeton: Princeton University Press, 2001); Asad, *Formations of the Secular*; Mahmood, "Secularism, Hermeneutics, and Empire," *Public Culture* 18, no. 2 (2006): 323–347.

4. Megoran, "Christianity and Political Geography," 45.

5. In geography, see Paul Cloke, "Inter-Connecting Geo-Ethics and Radical Faith-Based Praxis in the Post-Secular City," paper delivered at the Annual Meeting of the Association of American Geographers, Boston, MA (April 17, 2008). Outside of geography, see Mahmood, "Secularism, Hermeneutics and Empire."

6. Peter L. Berger, "The Desecularization of the World: A Global Overview," in *The Desecularization of the World: Resurgent Religion and World Politics,* ed. Peter L Berger (Grand Rapids: W. B. Eerdmans, 1999), 1–18; Martin Riesebrodt, "Theses on a Theory of Religion," *International Political Anthropology* 1, no. 1 (2008): 25–41; Christopher Pieper and Michael P. Young, "Religion and Post-Secular Politics," *Handbook of Politics* (2010): 349–365. In geography see, Reinhard Henkel, "Are Human Geographers Religiously Unmusical?" Geographies of Religion Working Paper Series, Newcastle University (2010).

7. Steve Bruce argues that "paradigm" is less tendentious than "theory" as way of describing the various models, theories, and empirical findings that are used in various formulations of what secularization is. I follow his lead here.

8. For the argument of secularization-as-ideology, see van der Veer, *Imperial Encounters*, 14–15; Asad, *Formations of the Secular*, 181–203; Mahmood, "Secularism, Hermeneutics and Empire," 335. For secularization-as-subtraction-story, see Taylor, *Secular Age*, 22. For secularization-as-embarrassing-leftover, see Stark and Finke, *Acts of Faith*, 58; Smith, *Secular Revolution*, 5.

9. David Harvey, *The Condition of Postmodernity* (Cambridge, MA: Blackwell, 1989), 205–207.

10. "Why, even in this time, the Swiss church refutes the Roman Church, the Lutheran opposes both. The Catholics oppose the Anabaptists; the Puritans oppose the superstitious, and the Abyssinians the Greeks, the Greeks the Latins, and in turn, all are refuted by all." Jean Bodin, *Colloquium of the Seven About Secrets of the Sublime* (Princeton: Princeton University Press, 2008 [1588]), 256.

11. Bruce, *God Is Dead*.

12. Peter L. Berger, *The Sacred Canopy: Elements of a Sociological Theory of Religion* (New York: Doubleday, 1967); Thomas Luckmann, *The Invisible Religion: The Problem of Religion in Modern Society* (New York: Macmillan, 1967); Bryan R. Wilson, *Contemporary Transformations of Religion* (New York: Oxford University Press, 1976); David Martin, *A General Theory of Secularization* (Oxford: Basil Blackwell, 1978); Karel Dobbelaere, "Secularization: A Multi-Dimensional Concept," *Current Sociology* 29, no. 2 (1981): 3–153; Roy Wallis and Steve Bruce, "Secularization: The Orthodox Model," in *Religion and Modernization,* ed. Steve Bruce (New York: Oxford University, 1992); Chaves, "Secularization As Declining Religious Authority," 749–774.

13. Berger, *Sacred Canopy*, 127–153.

14. Bruce, *God Is Dead*, 22–26; Pippa Norris and Ronald Inglehart, *Sacred and Secular: Religion and Politics Worldwide* (New York: Cambridge University Press, 2004).

15. Norris and Inglehart, *Sacred and Secular,* 106–110.

16. Stark and Finke, *Acts of Faith*, 79.

17. Ibid., 200.

18. Charles Taylor, *A Secular Age* (Cambridge, MA: Belknap Press of Harvard University Press, 2007), 431.

19. Megoran, "Christianity and Political Geography," 45; Roger W. Stump, *The Geography of Religion: Faith, Place and Space* (New York: Rowman and Littlefield, 2008), 369.

20. Lily Kong, "Religion and Spaces of Technology: Constructing and Contesting Nation, Transnation, and Place," *Environment and Planning A* 38, no. 5 (2006): 903–918; Michael Pacione, "The Geography of Religious Affiliation in Scotland," *Professional Geographer* 57, no. 2 (2005): 235–255; Oliver Valins, "Institutionalised Religion: Sacred Texts and Jewish Spatial Practice," *Geoforum* 31, no. 4 (2000): 575–586. For an older vintage, see David Edward Sopher, *Geography of Religions* (Englewood Cliffs, NJ: Prentice-Hall, 1967).

21. See Christopher Baker, "Religious Faith in the Exurban Community: A Case Study of Christian Faith-Communities in Milton Keynes," *City* 9, no. 1 (2005): 109–123; Brian Graham, "Contested Images of Place Among Protestants in Northern Ireland," *Political Geography* 17, no. 2 (1998): 129–144; Julian Holloway, "Enchanted Spaces: The Séance, Affect, and Geographies of Religion," *Annals of the Association of American Geographers* 96, no. 1 (2006): 182–187; Simon Naylor and James R. Ryan, "The Mosque in the Suburbs: Negotiating Religion and Ethnicity in South London," *Social and Cultural Geography* 3, no. 1 (2002): 39–59; Roger W. Stump, *Boundaries of Faith: Geographical Perspectives on Religious Fundamentalism* (New York: Rowman and Littlefield, 2000); Peter Vincent and Barney Warf, "Eruvim: Talmudic Places in a Postmodern World," *Transactions of the Institute of British Geographers* 27, no. 1 (2002): 30–51.

22. For examples of this emphasis on the local, see John Connell, "Hillsong: A Megachurch in the Sydney Suburbs," *Australian Geographer* 36, no. 3 (2005): 315–332; Claire Dwyer, "'Where Are You From?': Young British Muslim Women and the Making of Home," in *Postcolonial Geographies, London: Continuum,* ed. Alison Blunt and Cheryl McEwan (New York: Continuum, 2002), 184–199; Lily Kong, "In Search of Permanent Homes: Singapore's House Churches and the Politics of Space," *Urban Studies* 39 (2002): 1573–1586; Naylor and Ryan, "Mosque in the Suburbs"; Vincent and Wraf, "Eruvim."

23. Steve Bruce, "The Charismatic Movement and the Secularization Thesis," *Religion* 28, no. 3 (1998): 223–232; Bruce, *God Is Dead*, 30; Bruce, "Secularization and the Impotence of Individualized Religion," *Hedgehog Review* 8 (2006): 35–46. See also Dobbelaere, "Secularization: A Multi-Dimensional Concept," 15.

24. David Martin, *On Secularization: Towards a Revised General Theory* (Burlington, VT: Ashgate, 2005), 47–57.

25. John Agnew, "The Devaluation of Place in Social Science," in *The Power of Place: Bringing Together Geographical and Sociological Imaginations,* ed. John Agnew and James S. Duncan (Winchester, MA: Unwin Hyman, 1989); Entrikin, *Betweenness of Place*, 41.

26. Gibson Winter, *The Suburban Captivity of the Churches: An Analysis of Protestant Responsibility in the Expanding Metropolis* (New York: Doubleday, 1961), 103–104.

27. See Rick Warren, *The Purpose-Driven Life: What on Earth Am I Here For?* (Grand Rapids: Zondervan, 2002).

28. Darren Dochuk, "'Praying for a Wicked City'": Congregation, Community, and the Suburbanization of Fundamentalism," *Religion and American Culture* 13, no. 2 (2003): 167–203.

29. Taylor, *Secular Age*, 423–472.

30. Warren, *Purpose Driven Church*, 198.

31. Roger Finke, "An Unsecular America," in *Religion and Modernization: Sociologists and Historians Debate the Secularization Thesis,* ed. Steve Bruce. (New York: Oxford University Press, 1992), 154; Asad, *Formations of the Secular*, 182; Smith, *American Evangelicalism*, 89–120, 154.

32. Frances Fitzgerald, "Come One, Come All." *New Yorker*, December 3, 2007, 46; Flory and Miller, *Finding Faith*; Donald Miller, *Reinventing American Protestantism*; Gustav Niebuhr, "Where Religion Gets a Big Dose of Shopping-mall Culture," *New York Times*, April 16, 1995.

33. Pew Forum on Religion and Public Life, "U.S. Religious Landscape Survey." Washington, DC: Pew Research Center, April 23, 2008. Available at http://religions.pewforum.org/, last accessed April 4, 2010; Roger Finke and Rodney Stark, *Churching of America, 1776–2005*; Barry Kosmin and Ariela Keysar, *American Religious Identification Survey 2008* (Hartford, CT: Trinity College, 2009).

34. Bruce, "The Charismatic Movement," 224.

35. Casanova, *Public Religions in the Modern World.*

36. Casanova accepts this third proposition while rejecting the first two. This move separates him from the orthodox line of secularization theory that holds that differentiation leads to privatization (but not necessarily to religious decline).

37. This broad definition is culled from Jeffrey C. Alexander, "Differentiation Theory: Problems and Prospects," in Alexander and Colomy, *Differentiation Theory and Social Change*; Chaves, "Declining Religious Authority"; Dobbelaere, "Secularization: A Multi-Dimensional Concept," 11–12; Niklas Luhmann, *The Differentiation of Society* (New York: Columbia University Press, 1982).

38. Dobbelaere, "Secularization: A Multi-Dimensional Concept," 8–9; Berger, *Sacred Canopy*, 107.

39. Bruce, *God Is Dead*, 3.

40. Chaves, "Declining Religious Authority."

41. Dobbelaere, "Towards An Integrated Perspective," 231.

42. Martin, *On Secularization*, 17.

43. Berger, *Sacred Canopy*, 107.

44. Emile Durkheim, *The Division of Labor in Society* (New York: Free Press, 1964 [1894]), 169.

45. Finke and Stark, *Acts of Faith.*

46. Ibid., 200.

47. Smith, "Rethinking Secularization," 5.

48. Peter L. Berger, "An Interview with Peter Berger," *Hedgehog Review* 8 (2006): 152–153.

49. Asad, *Formations of the Secular,* 182.

50. Luhmann, *Differentiation of Society*; Richard Münch, "Differentiation, Rationalization, Interpenetration: The Emergence of Modern Society," in Alexander and Colomy, *Differentiation Theory and Social Change.*

51. Jurgen Habermas, "Religion in the Public Sphere," *European Journal of Philosophy* 14, no. 1 (2006): 1–25.

52. Bruce, *God Is Dead*, 21.

53. For a representative sample see the American conservative Christian advocacy group, the Family Research Council, and their position on "abstinence and sexual health" (http://www.frc.org/human-sexuality#abstinence, last retrieved on June 10, 2008).

54. Talal Asad, "The Trouble of Thinking: An Interview with Talal Asad" in *Powers of the Secular Modern: Tala Asad and His Interlocutors*, ed. David Scott and Charles Hirschkind (Stanford: Stanford University Press, 2006), 208.

55. Stark and Finke, *Acts of Faith*, 85.

56. David Martin, "Does the Advance of Science Mean Secularisation?" *Scottish Journal of Theology* 61, no. 1 (2008): 56. Social differentiation is largely conceived of developing in one of two ways. In its earliest formulation, differentiation was seen as the result of a quasi-natural evolutionary process. Here it is seen as the product of the autonomous internal logic of functional social spheres in the face of increasing social density and complexity. See S. N. Eisenstadt, "Social Change, Differentiation and Evolution," *American Sociological Review* 29, no. 3 (1964): 375–386; Talcott Parsons, *The Structure of Social Action* (New York: Free Press, 1968); Luhmann, *Differentiation of Society*; Münch, "Differentiation, Rationalization, Interpenetration," in Alexander and Colomy, *Differentiation Theory and Social Change*. More recently, differentiation has been formulated as the product of intentional action by various social groups with particular interests, as in Paul Colomy, "Revisions and Progress in Differentiation Theory," in Alexander and Colomy, *Differentiation Theory and Social Change*; Christian Smith, "Introduction: Rethinking the Secularization of American Public Life," in Smith, *Secular Revolution*.

57. Though, for Alexander, modern society's fragmentation is ameliorated by a multi-institutional "civil sphere" that coordinates solidarity. Jeffrey C. Alexander, *The Civil Sphere* (New York: Oxford University, 2006).

58. Karl Marx, "On the Jewish Question," in *The Marx-Engels Reader*, ed. Robert C. Tucker (New York: Norton, 1978 [1843]), 35.

59. Berger, *Sacred Canopy*, 132; Luckmann, *Invisible Religion*, 103–104.

60. Luckmann, *Invisible Religion*, 129.

61. Berger, *Sacred Canopy*, 134.

62. Casanova, *Public Religions in the Modern World*, 21.

63. There is also a significant body of work inspired by the "supply-side" approach of Rodney Stark and Roger Finke that argues that there is a strong positive correlation between advanced social differentiation (in terms of "religious market deregulation") and levels of religious belief and practice. See Stark and Finke, *Acts of Faith*; Rodney Stark and William Sims Bainbridge, *A Theory of Religion* (New York: Lang, 1987). Despite the fact that these findings have been called into question and seem doubtful, the reverse has not been shown to be any more valid. See Kevin D. Breault, "New Evidence on Religious Pluralism, Urbanism, and Religious Participation," *American Sociological Review* 54 (1989): 1048–1053; Steve Bruce, *Choice and Religion: A Critique of Rational Choice Theory* (New York: Oxford University Press, 1999); Mark Chaves and Philip S. Gorski, "Religious Pluralism and Religious Participation," *Annual Review of Sociology* 27, no. 1 (2001): 261–281; Daniel V. A. Olson, "Comment: Religious Pluralism in Contemporary U.S. Counties," *American Sociological Review* 63

(1998): 759–761; David Voas, Alasdair Crockett, and Daniel V. A. Olson, "Religious Pluralism and Participation: Why Previous Research Is Wrong," *American Sociological Review* 67, no. 2 (2002): 212–230.

64. Berger, *Sacred Canopy*, 127–135; Bruce, *God Is Dead*, 19–21; Luckmann, *Invisible Religion*, 77–106.

65. Robert N. Bellah et al., *Habits of the Heart: Individualism and Commitment in American Life* (Berkeley: University of California Press, 1985), 221.

66. Alexander, "Differentiation Theory"; Zygmunt Bauman, *The Individualized Society* (Malden, MA: Blackwell, 2001); Ulrich Beck and Elisabeth Beck-Gernsheim, *Individualization: Institutionalized Individualism, and Its Social and Political Consequences* (Thousand Oaks, CA: Sage, 2002); Luckmann, *Invisible Religion*; Albert W. Musschenga, "Introduction: The Many Faces of Individualism," in *The Many Faces of Individualism*, ed. Anton van Harskamp and Albert W. Musschenga (Sterling, VA: Peeters, 2001).

67. Alexander, "Differentiation Theory," 11–12; Paul Colomy, "Revisions and Progress in Differentiation Theory," in Alexander and Colomy, *Differentiation Theory and Social Change*, 488.

68. See especially Beck, *Individualization*, 23; Musschenga, introduction, in Harskamp and Musschenga, *Many Faces of Individualism*, 7.

69. Berger, "Desecularization of the World: A Global Overview," 3.

70. Berger, *Sacred Canopy*, 134.

71. Smith, *American Evangelicalism*, 144.

72. Dobbelaere, "Secularization: A Multi-Dimensional Concept," 11–12.

73. In public debates over issues like these, religious justification is rarely used. In the recent stem-cell debates in the United States, religious critics of stem-cell research have attempted to frame the issue as an ethical balancing act between two groups of human agents: those who might benefit from stem-cell research and those who are unborn embryos (for an example, see P. J. O'Rourke, "Stem Cell Sham," *Weekly Standard*, March 23, 2009, available at http://www.weeklystandard.com/Content/Public/Articles/000/000/016/269mfvp0.asp). As for religious monuments on U.S. government property, the arguments often revolve around civil rights, states' rights, and free speech with little religious justification (for an excellent analysis, see Nicolas Howe, "Thou Shalt Not Misinterpret: Landscape As Legal Performance," *Annals of the Association of American Geographers* 98, no. 2 (2008): 435–460).

74. Smith, *Secular Revolution*, 13.

75. For recent debates see Sallie A. Marston, John Paul Jones III, and Keith Woodward, "Human Geography Without Scale," *Transactions of the Institute of British Geographers* 30, no. 4 (2005): 416–432; Adam Moore, "Rethinking Scale as a Geographical Category: From Analysis to Practice," *Progress in Human Geography* 32, no. 2 (2007): 203–225.

76. Its founder, Bill Bright, did not originally envision his organization at a global scale, but the global scalar logic of Cold War narratives provided a platform for his scalar reframing. The organization today emphasizes that, despite its larger events and campaigns, it still focuses on "one-on-one" evangelism. See John G. Turner, *Bill Bright and Campus Crusade for Christ: The Renewal of Evangelicalism in Postwar America* (Chapel Hill: University of North Carolina Press, 2008). The most recent self-reported statistics can be found on the organization's website: http://campuscrusadeforchrist.com/about-us/facts-and-statistics.

77. For an excellent interpretation of Falwell's efforts see Sandra Friend Harding, *The Book of Jerry Falwell: Fundamentalist Language and Politics* (Princeton. NJ: Princeton University Press, 2000). His de-secularizing work in the 1970s and 1980s can be seen as a series of performances that rescripted the cultural, political and economic marginalization of local white working-class Americans.

78. Robert C. Liebman, "Mobilizing the Moral Majority," in *The New Christian Right: Mobilization and Legitimation,* ed. Robert C Liebman and Robert Wuthnow (Hawthorne, NY: Aldine Transaction, 1983), 58.

79. Dwyer, "'Where Are You From?'"; Holloway, "Enchanted Spaces"; Kong, "Negotiating Conceptions"; Kong, "In Search of Permanent Homes."

80. Paul Cloke, Sarah Johnsen, and Jon May, "Exploring Ethos? Discourses of 'Charity' in the Provision of Emergency Services for Homeless People," *Environment and Planning A* 37 (2005): 385–402; Hans Gerhardt, "Geopolitics, Ethics, and the Evangelicals' Commitment to Sudan," *Environment and Planning D: Society and Space* 26 (2008): 911–928.

81. Bruce, *God Is Dead,* 75–105; Bruce, "Secularization and the Impotence of Individualized Religion," *Hedgehog Review* 8 (2006): 35–46.

82. Kosmin and Keysar, *American Religious Identification Survey 2008*; Thumma and Travis, *Beyond Megachurch Myths.*

83. As the event unfolded in August 2008, a barrage of non-academic observers this event precisely in terms of conflictual desecularization. See DeWayne Wickham (2008), Frank Rich (2008), Kathleen Parker (2008), and Welton Gady (2008).

84. The sermon directly following the August forum was titled "The Kind of Leadership America Needs." However, the sermon was not about political leadership but rather personal leadership among one's friends and family. It was about how to live one's life with "integrity, humility, and generosity." It could not have been more apolitical. The sermon following the inaugural prayer focused on personal salvation and evangelizing to friends.

85. Kosmin and Keysar, *American Religious Identification Survey 2008,* 3–5; Pew Forum on Religion and Public Life, *U.S. Religious Landscape Survey.*

86. Thumma and Travis, *Beyond Megachurch Myths,* 118–134.

87. In 2008 Saddleback organized conferences on small groups, worship (i.e., music, lighting, and media), youth ministry (teen to college), children's ministry, substance abuse ministry, and pastor training. These conferences are held every year and regularly draw several thousand attendees. Exact attendance numbers are not made publicly available.

88. Alexander, "Differentiation Theory"; Luhmann, *Differentiation of Society*; Chaves, "Secularization as Declining Religious Authority."

89. See especially Paul Colomy, "Revisions and Progress in Differentiation Theory," in Alexander and Colomy, *Differentiation Theory and Social Change,* 465–495.

90. Excellent empirically grounded work from this perspective has been brought together by Christian Smith in his edited volume *The Secular Revolution* (2003). The overall argument is that social differentiation doesn't "just happen," but is led by institutional reformers with particular interests and grievances, and access to particular resources.

91. Colomy, "Revisions and Progress," 483.

92. Roger Friedland and Robert R. Alford, "Bringing Society Back In: Symbols, Practics, and Institutional Contradictions," in *The New Institutionalism in Organizational*

Analysis, ed. Walter W. Powell and Paul DiMaggio (Chicago: University of Chicago Press, 1991), 232, quoted in Chaves, "Secularization as Declining Religious Authority" 751; Luhmann, *Differentiation of Society*, 238.

93. Luhmann, *Differentiation of Society*, 238–239.

94. Niklas Luhmann, *Funktion Der Religion* (Frankfurt am Main: Suhrkamp, 1977), 242, quoted in Stephen Holmes and Charles Larmore, "Translator's Introduction," in Luhmann, *Differentiation of Society*, xiii–xxxvii.

95. Philippe Ariès, *Centuries of Childhood: A Social History of Family Life,* trans. Robert Baldick (New York: Vintage Books, 1962); Roger Chartier, ed., *History of Private Life: Passions of the Renaissance*, trans. Arthur Goldhammer (Cambridge, MA: Belknap Press of Harvard University, 1989); Witold Rybczynski, *Home: A Short History of An Idea* (New York: Viking, 1986).

96. Dobbelaere, "Secularization: A Multi-Dimensional Concept," 8–9.

97. Saddleback Church holds eight different types of services on the weekends, from "El Encuentro" (a Spanish-language service) to "Overdrive" (a service centered around alternative rock music and aesthetic). Between Saturday and Sunday services are held at six different times. This is in addition to the many other demographically targeted weeknight events such as worship-themed Monday Night Football.

98. Omar M. McRoberts, *Streets of Glory: Church and Community in a Black Urban Neighborhood* (Chicago: University of Chicago Press, 2003); Connell, "Hillsong"; George M. Thomas and Douglas S. Jardine, "Jesus and Self in Everyday Life: Individual Spirituality Through a Small Group in a Large Church," in Wuthnow, *"I Come Away Stronger"*, 275–299.

NOTES TO CHAPTER 3

1. Roger Finke and Laurence R. Iannaccone, "Supply-Side Explanations for Religious Change," *Annals of the American Academy of Political and Social Science* (1993): 27–39.

2. Lee and Sinitiere, *Holy Mavericks*. 15.

3. Stark and Finke, *Acts of Faith*, 36.

4. Ibid., 257.

5. Entrikin, *Betweenness of Place*; Jeffrey C. Alexander, *Action and Its Environments: Toward a New Synthesis* (New York: Columbia University Press, 1988).

6. H. Paul Douglass, *The Suburban Trend* (New York: Century, 1925); Darren Dochuk, "'Praying for a Wicked City': Congregation, Community, and the Suburbanization of Fundamentalism," *Religion and American Culture* 13, no. 2 (2003): 167–203.

7. Durkheim, *Elementary Forms of Religious Life*, 287.

8. Erving Goffman, *Interaction Ritual: Essays in Face-to-Face Behavior* (New York: Pantheon Books, 1967), 44.

9. For a cultural pragmatic appraisal of Durkheimian ritual see Jeffrey C. Alexander and Philip Smith, "Introduction: The New Durkheim," in *The Cambridge Companion to Durkheim,* ed. Jeffrey C. Alexander and Philip Smith (New York: Cambridge University Press, 2005), 25–30.

10. Alexander, "Cultural Pragmatics," 528.

11. Ibid., 529.

12. Ibid., 530–533.

13. Ibid., 531.

14. Ibid., 555–556.

15. Ibid., 557. Alexander also lists a third type of social power, hermeneutical power, that is, the power to render authoritative judgment. I hesitate to add it to this summary of his cultural pragmatics because it seems less a category of social power (in the sense that productive and distributive powers are) than a responsive yet independent performance of its own.

16. Bill Brown, "Thing Theory," *Critical Inquiry* 28, no. 1 (2001): 1–22; Tim Dant, "Material Civilization: Things and Society," *British Journal of Sociology* 57, no. 2 (2006): 289–308; Webb Keane, "Semiotics and the Social Analysis of Material Things," *Language and Communication* 23 (2003): 409–425; Carl Knappett, *Thinking Through Material Culture: An Interdisciplinary Perspective* (Philadelphia: University of Pennsylvania Press, 2005); Daniel Miller, *Material Culture and Mass Consumption* (New York: Blackwell, 1987); Daniel Miller, "Materiality: An Introduction," in *Materiality*, ed. Daniel Miller (Durham, NC: Duke University Press, 2005), 1–50.

17. Daniel Miller, *Material Culture*, 28.

18. For an account of the role that place and clothing objects play in the legitimacy of a presidential performance, see Bernie Becker, "Former Chief of Staff to Obama: Put Your Jacket On," *The Caucus*, The Politics and Government Blog of the *New York Times* (February 4, 2009) http://thecaucus.blogs.nytimes.com/2009/02/04/former-chief-of-staff-to-obama-put-your-jacket-on/.

19. Even Durkheim argues that sacred and profane need space and matter for their existence: "First, religious life and profane life cannot coexist in the same space. For religious life to flourish, a special place must be arranged from which profane life is excluded." Durkheim, *Elementary Forms*, 228–229.

20. Robert Wuthnow, *After Heaven*, 1–18; Wade Clark Roof, *Spiritual Marketplace*, 46–76; Sargeant, *Seeker Churches*; Jeffery L. Sheler, *Believers: A Journey into Evangelical America* (New York: Viking, 2006).

21. This notion of religious-organizational seeking is certainly not new. It is the heart of old-fashioned evangelism, of circuit-riding preachers and camp revivals. Postdenominational Evangelical congregations should certainly be seen as direct inheritors of this tradition. See Noll, *Rise of Evangelicalism*.

22. James Davison Hunter, *American Evangelicalism: Conservative Religion and the Quandary of Modernity* (New Brunswick, NJ: Rutgers University Press, 1983); Marsden, *Fundamentalism and American Culture*; Smith, *American Evangelicalism*; R. Stephen Warner, *New Wine in Old Wineskins: Evangelicals and Liberals in a Small-Town Church* (Berkeley: University of California Press, 1988).

23. For studies showing the advantage of locally sensitive and flexible congregations in a postdenominational context see Roof (1972; 1976); Roof and Hoge (1980); Warner (1988). The story of denominational decline is told most forcefully by Kelly (1972) and later by Stark and Finke (2005).

24. Douglass, *Suburban Trend*, 208.

25. William H. Whyte, *The Organization Man* (New York: Simon and Schuster, 1956), 365.

26. Rodney Stark and Roger Finke (*Churching of America, 1776–2005*) show how general observers of the American religious scene began arguing for interdenominational unification from the 1930s to the 1960s. Their conclusion, however, is that "the attempts at local unification efforts in order to replace denominationalism with

community churches in the rapidly growing suburbs never seemed to come into their own." They add a very important caveat: "With the exception of nondenominational fundamentalist churches, which often did very well" (226). What they meant when they argued that nondenominationalism failed is that a single unified Christian church never emerged. What they found was that churchgoers were split between the theologically conservative and liberal.

27. Berger, *Sacred Canopy*; Harvey Cox, *The Secular City: Secularization and Urbanization in Theological Perspective* (New York: Macmillan, 1965); Gibson Winter, *The Suburban Captivity of the Churches: An Analysis of Protestant Responsibility in the Expanding Metropolis* (New York: Doubleday, 1961).

28. Finke and Stark, *Churching of America, 1776–2005*; Dean M. Kelley, *Why Conservative Churches Are Growing: A Study in Sociology of Religion* (New York: Harper and Row, 1972).

29. Warren, *Purpose Driven Church*, 182. See C. Kirk Hadaway and Wade Clark Roof, "Those Who Stay Religious 'Nones' and Those Who Don't: A Research Note," *Journal for the Scientific Study of Religion*, 18 no. 2 (1979): 194–200; Kevin J. Christiano, "Church as a Family Surrogate: Another Look at Family Ties, Anomie, and Church Involvement," *Journal for the Scientific Study of Religion*, 25 no. 3 (1986): 339–354. for data supporting Warren's hypothesis.

30. Warren, *Purpose Driven Church*, 34.

31. Ibid., 182.

32. For overviews, see Ellingson, *Megachurch and the Mainline*; Finke and Stark, *Churching of America, 1776–2005*; Kelley, *Why Conservative Churches Are Growing*; Smith, *American Evangelicalism*. For data see Carl S. Dudley and David A. Roozen, *Faith Communities Today: A Report on Religion in the United States Today* (Hartford, CT: Hartford Institute for Religion Research, 2001); Kosmin and Keysar, *American Religious Identification Survey 2008* ; C. Kirk Hadaway, *Facts on Growth: A New Look at the Dynamics of Growth and Decline in American Congregations Based on the Faith Communities Today 2005 National Survey of Congregations* (Hartford, CT: Faith Communities Today and CCSP, 2006); "U.S. Religious Landscape Survey," Pew Forum on Religion and Public Life (2008), accessible at http://religions.pewforum.org/.

33. Thumma and Travis, *Beyond Megachurch Myths*; Chaves, "All Creatures Great and Small," 329–346.

34. Cf. David L. Goetz, *Death by Suburb: How to Keep the Suburbs From Killing Your Soul* (New York: HarperOne, 2007); Fitzgerald, "Come One, Come All," ; Albert Y. Hsu, *The Suburban Christian: Finding Spiritual Vitality in the Land of Plenty* (Downers Grove, IL: InterVarsity, 2006); Jonathan Mahler, "The Soul of the New Exurb," *New York Times*, March 27, 2005, 37–38, 50, 54, 57; Jeff Sharlet, "Soldiers of Christ: Inside America's Most Powerful Megachurch with Pastor Ted Haggard," *Harper's Magazine*, May 2005, 41–54; Caleb Stegall, "Grand Illusions: Too Many Suburban Christians Are in the World—and Also of It," review of *Death by Suburb* by David Goetz, *Christianity Today* 50, no. 7 (2006): 55–57.

35. This discussion of Clapham relies heavily on Fishman, *Bourgeois Utopias*, 54–61.

36. Noll, *Rise of Evangelicalism*, 236–240.

37. Catherine Hall, "Early Formation of Victorian Domestic Ideology," in *Fit Work for Women*, ed. Sandra Burman (New York: St. Martin's Press, 1979), 22.

38. William Wilberforce, *A Practical View of the Prevailing Religious System of Professed Christians, in the Higher and Middle Classes in This Country: Contrasted with Real Christianity* (New York: Crocker and Brewster, 1829), 222.

39. Ibid., 43.

40. Fishman, *Bourgeois Utopias*; Kenneth T. Jackson, *Crabgrass Frontier: The Suburbanization of the United States* (New York: Oxford University Press, 1985).

41. For classical social analyses see Whyte, *Organization Man* ; David Riesman, Nathan Glazer, and Reuel Denney, *The Lonely Crowd: A Study of the Changing American Character* (New Haven, CT: Yale University, 1961); Betty Friedan, *The Feminine Mystique* (New York: Norton, 1963); Lewis Mumford, *The City in History: Its Origins, Its Transformations, and Its Prospects* (New York: Harcourt, Brace and World, 1961). For classical cultural interpretations see John Keats, *The Crack in the Picture Window* (New York: Houghton Mifflin, 1957); Richard Yates, *Revolutionary Road* (New York: Little, Brown and Company, 1961); Malvina Reynolds, "Little Boxes," Schroder Music Co. (ASCAP), 1962.

42. Winter, *Suburban Captivity of the Churches*, 39–58; Peter L. Berger, *The Noise of Solemn Assemblies: Christian Commitment and the Religious Establishment in America* (Garden City, NY: Doubleday, 1961).

43. Winter, *Suburban Captivity of the Churches*, 15–38.

44. Frederick Alexander Shippey, *Protestantism in Suburban Life* (New York: Abingdon Press, 1964), 77.

45. David Brooks, *On Paradise Drive: How We Live Now (And Always Have) in the Future Tense* (New York: Simon and Schuster, 2004); Joel Garreau, *Edge City: Life on the New Frontier* (New York: Doubleday, 1991); Jackson, *Crabgrass Frontier*; Robert Lang and Jennifer LeFurgy, *Boomburbs: The Rise of America's Accidental Cities* (Washington, DC: Brookings Institution Press, 2007); Witold Rybczynski, *Last Harvest: How a Cornfield Became New Daleville: Real Estate Development in America From George Washington to the Builders of the Twenty-First Century, and Why We Live in Houses Anyway* (New York: Scribner, 2007).

46. Mark Gottdiener and George Kephart, "The Multinucleated Metropolitan Region: A Comparative Analysis," in *Postsuburban California: The Transformation of Orange County Since World War II,* ed. Spencer C. Olin, Mark Poster, and Rob Kling (Berkeley: University of California Press, 1991), 31–54.

47. For this succinct definition I draw on Robert Fishman's *Bourgeois Utopias* and Kenneth T. Jackson's *Crabgrass Frontier*. For Fishman, suburbia refers "only to a residential community beyond the core of a large city. Though physically separated from the urban core, the suburb nevertheless depends on it economically for the jobs that support its residents. It is also culturally dependent on the core for the major institutions of urban life: professional offices, department stores and other specialized shops, hospitals, theaters, and the like" (5) For Jackson, the modern American suburb is distinguished by (1) low density residential development, (2) high levels of homeownership, (3) a strong distinction between the periphery and center of a city, and (4) longer commuting times (6–10).

48. Fishman, *Bourgeois Utopias*, 185.

49. Paul L. Knox, *Metroburbia, USA* (New Brunswick, NJ: Rutgers University Press, 2008).

50. Arthur C. Nelson and Thomas W. Sanchez, "Exurban and Suburban Households: A Departure from Traditional Location Theory?" *Journal of Housing Research* 8, no. 2 (1997): 249–275; Nelson and Sanchez, "Debunking the Exurban Myth: A Comparison of Suburban Households," *Housing Policy Debate* 10, no. 3 (1999): 689–710.

51. Cf. Mark Gottdiener, *The Social Production of Urban Space* (Austin: University of Texas Press, 1985).

52. Alan J. Scott, *Geography and Economy: Three Lectures* (New York: Oxford University Press, 2006).

53. Durkheim, *Division of Labor in Society*, 46–48.

54. Ernest W. Burgess, "The Growth of the City," in *The City*, ed. Robert E. Park, Ernest W. Burgess, and Roderick D. McKenzie (Chicago: University of Chicago Press, 1925).

55. For the former see Michael Dear and Steven Flusty, "Postmodern Urbanism," *Annals of the Association of American Geographers* 88, no. 1 (1998): 52. For the latter, see Robert J. Sampson, "'After-School' Chicago: Space and the City," *Urban Geography* 29, no. 2 (2008): 128.

56. Robert E. Park, "The City: Suggestions for the Investigation of Human Behavior in the City Environment," *American Journal of Sociology* 20, no. 5 (1915): 608.

57. Louis Wirth, "Urbanism As a Way of Life," *American Journal of Sociology* 44, no. 1 (1938): 1–24.

58. Ibid., 16.

59. Herbert J. Gans, "Urbanism and Suburbanism As Ways of Life," in *Modernity: Critical Concepts,* vol. 2, ed. Malcolm Waters (New York: Routledge, 1999), 64–75.

60. For the former, see Gottdiener, *Production of Urban Space*; Allen J. Scott, *Global City-Regions: Trends, Theory, Policy* (New York: Oxford University Press, 2001). For the latter, see Mike Davis, *City of Quartz: Excavating the Future in Los Angeles* (New York: Verso, 1990); David Harvey, *Justice, Nature, and the Geography of Difference* (Oxford: Blackwell Publishers, 1996), 334–365; Edward W. Soja, *Postmetropolis: Critical Studies in Cities and Regions* (Cambridge, MA: Blackwell, 2000), 233–263; Richard A. Walker, "A Theory of Suburbanization: Capitalism and the Construction of Urban Space in the United States," in *Urbanization and Urban Planning in Capitalist Society,* ed. Michael Dear and Alan Scott (New York: Meuthen and Co., 1981), 383–430.

61. Mark Gottdiener, *Planned Sprawl: Private and Public Interests in Suburbia* (Beverly Hills: Sage Publications, 1977); Gottdiener, *Production of Urban Space*; Gottdiener, "Multinucleated Metropolitan Region."

62. Lefebvre, *Production of Space*, 206.

63. Ibid., 13–14.

64. Ibid., 290.

65. Walker, "A Theory of Suburbanization," in Dear and Scott, *Urbanization and Urban Planning in Capitalist Society,* 383.

66. Manuel Castells, "European Cities, the Informational Society and the Global Economy," *New Left Review* 204, no. 3–4 (1994): 30; Castells, *The Informational City: Information Technology, Economic Restructuring, and the Urban-Regional Process* (Malden, MA: Blackwell Publishers, 1989).

67. Steven Graham and Simon Marvin, *Splintering Urbanism* (New York: Routledge, 2001).

68. The use of "delocalization" here is different, though related, to the questionable conception of delocalization via globalization. Delocalization via socio-spatial differentiation

means that the relationship between a particular local place and social action has changed, not, as in the globalization argument, that local place has lost its particularity (see Ron Martin, "Geography: Making a Difference in a Globalizing World," *Transactions of the Institute of British Geographers*, 29 no. 2 (2004): 147–150.).

69. Bauman, *Individualized Society*; Beck and Beck-Gernsheim, *Individualization*; Musschenga, introduction, in *Many Faces of Individualism*.

70. Park, "The City," 608.

71. Fishman, *Bourgeois Utopias*, 182–207; Rob Kling, Spencer Olin, and Mark Poster, "The Emergence of Postsuburbia: An Introduction," in Olin, Poster, and Kling, *Postsuburban California*, 1–30; Robert Lang, *Edgeless Cities: Exploring the Elusive Metropolis* (Washington, DC: Brookings Institution Press, 2003); Soja, *Postmetropolis*, 233–263.

72. Jackson, *Crabgrass Frontier*, chap. 15; David Morley, *Home Territories: Media, Mobility, and Identity* (New York: Routledge, 2000); Setha Low, *Behind the Gates: Life, Security, and the Pursuit of Happiness in Fortress America* (New York: Routledge, 2003), chap. 4; Rybczynski, *Last Harvest*, chap. 15, 17.

73. John Archer, *Architecture and Suburbia: From English Villa to American Dream House, 1690–2000* (Minneapolis: University of Minnesota Press, 2005).

74. For the importance of agonism—the construction of conflict—to any effective and durable cultural performance, see Alexander, "Cultural Pragmatics," 552–553. For the specific cultural codes of early modern suburbia, see John Archer, "Ideology and Aspiration: Individualism, the Middle-Class, and the Genesis of the Anglo-American Suburb," *Journal of Urban History* 14, no. 2 (1988): 214–253; John Archer, "Colonial Suburbs in South Asia, 1700–1850, and the Spaces of Modernity," in *Visions of Suburbia* (New York: Routledge, 1997), 26–54.

75. Hall, "Victorian Domestic Ideology"; Noll, *Rise of Evangelicalism*, 266–173; Taylor, *Secular Age*, 377–419.

76. Fishman, *Bourgeois Utopias*, 54–63; Hall, "Victorian Domestic Ideology"; Noll, *Rise of Evangelicalism*, 236–240.

77. Christopher Tolley, *Domestic Biography: The Legacy of Evangelicalism in Four Nineteenth-Century Families* (New York: Oxford University Press, 1997).

78. Jon C. Teaford, *The Metropolitan Revolution: The Rise of Post-Urban America* (New York: Columbia University Press, 2006), 239–262.

79. Rybczynski, *Last Harvest*; Knox, *Metroburbia*.

80. Dolores Hayden, *A Field Guide to Sprawl* (New York: W. W. Norton, 2004).

81. David L. Goetz, *Death by Suburb: How to Keep the Suburbs From Killing Your Soul* (New York: HarperOne, 2007); Hsu, *Suburban Christian*; Mike Erre, *The Jesus of Suburbia: Have We Tamed the Son of God to Fit Our Lifestyle?* (Nashville, TN: Thomas Nelson Publishers, 2006); Eric Sandras, *Plastic Jesus: Exposing the Hollowness of Comfortable Christianity* (Colorado Springs, CO: NavPress, 2006).

NOTES TO CHAPTER 4

1. Warren, *Purpose-Driven Life*, 17.

2. For journalist accounts see Cathy Lynn Grossman, "This Evangelist Has a 'Purpose,'" *USA Today*, July 21, 2003, 1D; Rob Walker, "Godly Synergy: How a Religious Advice Book Is Filling More Pews . . . With More Book Buyers," *New York Times Magazine*, April 11, 2004, 24; Sonja Steptoe, "Rick Warren," *Time Magazine*, April 18, 2005, 108.

3. See Rebecca Osaigbovo, *It's Not About You, It's About God* (Downers Grove, IL: Inter-Varsity Press, 2004); Dave Ferguson, Jon Ferguson, and Eric Bramlett, *The Big Idea: Focus the Message, Multiply the Impact,* illustrated ed. (Grand Rapids: Zondervan, 2007); Jim Seybert, *Leadership Re:Vision* (Carol Stream, IL: Tyndale House Publishers, 2009).

4. Archer, *Architecture and Suburbia*, chap. 1, 7.

5. Fishman, *Bourgeois Utopias*, 182–207; Knox, *Metroburbia*, 76–78.

6. Robert Bruegmann, *Sprawl: A Compact History* (Chicago: University of Chicago, 2005); Anne Dupuis and David C. Thomas, "Home, Home Ownership, and the Search for Ontological Security," *Sociological Review* 46, no. 1 (1998): 24–47; Shelley Mallett, "Understanding Home: A Critical Review of the Literature," *Sociological Review* 52, no. 1 (2004): 62–89.

7. Warren, *Purpose Driven Church*, 131.

8. Flory and Miller, *Finding Faith*, 69–75; Thumma and Travis, *Beyond Megachurch Myths'*, 93.

9. Jeffery L. Sheler, *Prophet of Purpose: The Life of Rick Warren,* illustrated ed. (New York: Random House, 2009), 78–79.

10. Warren, *Purpose Driven Church*, 165.

11. Jerusalem, here, is a biblical reference by Warren to Acts 1:8, "But you will receive power when the Holy Spirit has come upon you; and you will be my witnesses in Jerusalem, Judea and Samaria, and to the ends of the earth." This verse is used as a cornerstone in the performance of local, regional, and global evangelism at Saddleback. See chap. 7 for more detail.

12. Rick Warren, "Mapping the Future! 2004 State of the Church Message" (weekend sermon), Saddleback Church, September 12, 2004.

13. Warren, *Purpose Driven Church*, 295.

14. Ibid., 300.

15. Ibid., 327.

16. Ibid., 134.

NOTES TO CHAPTER 5

1. Several non-vital facts have been changed in this account to protect the identity of this small group and its members.

2. Berger, *Sacred Canopy*, 133; Kelley, *Why Conservative Churches Are Growing*; Wuthnow, "Small Groups and Spirituality: Exploring the Connections," in *"I Come Away Stronger"*, 1–7; Stark and Finke, *Acts of Faith*, 145–157; Bruce, *God Is Dead*, 22–25.

3. Anne C. Loveland and Otis B. Wheeler, *From Meetinghouse to Megachurch: A Material and Cultural History* (Columbia: University of Missouri Press, 2003).

4. Darren Dochuk, "'Praying for a Wicked City'": Congregation, Community, and the Suburbanization of Fundamentalism," *Religion and American Culture* 13, no. 2 (2003): 167–203; Winter, *Suburban Captivity of the Churches*, 15–38; Fishman, *Bourgeois Utopias*, 51–72.

5. According to one Saddleback pastor, "There are so many different types of people with so many different needs that a typical church is just confused as to how to meet all these needs. What Saddleback does is create small churches within the larger church." Interestingly, this perceived diversity is not seen as specific to the urban environment of Saddleback, or as historically contingent. It is perceived as universal

and natural. Warren writes in the *Purpose Driven Church*, "Because human beings are so different, no single church can possibly reach everyone. That's why we need all kinds of churches" (156).

6. Berger, *Sacred Canopy*, 133, 134.

7. Flory and Miller, *Finding Faith*; Sally K. Gallagher, *Evangelical Identity and Gendered Family Life* (New Brunswick, NJ: Rutgers University Press, 2003); James Davison Hunter, *Evangelicalism: The Coming Generation* (Chicago: University of Chicago Press, 1987); Donald Miller, *Reinventing American Protestantism.*

8. See Howard Astin, *Body and Cell* (Littleton, CO: Monarch, 2002); Terry A. Bowland, *Make Disciples!: Reaching the Postmodern World for Christ* (Joplin, MO: College Press, 1999); Jimmy Long, *Emerging Hope: A Strategy for Reaching the Postmodern Generations* (Downers Grove, IL: InterVarsity Press, 2004).Greg Ogden, *Unfinished Business: Returning the Ministry to the People of God* (Grand Rapids: Zondervan, 2003); Frank Viola, *Reimagining Church: Pursuing the Dream of Organic Christianity* (Colorado Springs, CO: David C. Cook, 2008).

9. Martin E. Marty, *Protestantism in the United States: Righteous Empire* (New York: Scribners, 1986), 67–77; Amos R. Wells, *The Ideal Adult Class in the Sunday-School* (New York: Pilgrim Press, 1912).

10. Gladen, Saddleback's senior pastor for small groups, envisioned Sunday school working so well in the past because socio-spatial life revolved around a single, central church campus: "In the fifties and sixties when Sunday school was flourishing, you didn't have any of that [different events and spaces competing for attention]. Everything was shut down on Sunday. When you're looking at marketing—when you have the market cornered on the day when everything is shut down, you're going to flourish and you're going to have it because you have the market cornered. Well, once culture moved away from church, or church values, then the church had to readapt—some of them did, some of them didn't."

11. Wells, *Ideal Adult Class*, 10.

12. "Come all ye faithful," *Economist* (November 3, 2007), 6–11.

13. Joel Comiskey, "Cell-Based Ministry: A Positive Factor for Church Growth in Latin America" (PhD diss., Fuller Theological Seminary, Pasadena, CA, 1997).

14. Ibid., 60–71.

15. Ibid.

16. Fishman, *Bourgeois Utopias*, 54–63; Hall, "Early Formation of Victorian Domestic Ideology," in Burman, *Fit Work for Women*, 15–32.

17. William Wilberforce, *A Practical View of the Prevailing Religious System of Professed Christians, in the Higher and Middle Classes in This Country: Contrasted with Real Christianity* (New York: Crocker and Brewster, 1829), 43.

18. Edward Shorter, *The Making of the Modern Family* (New York: Basic Books, 1977), 255–268.

19. Ariès, *Centuries of Childhood*; Krishan Kumar, "Home: Promise, and Predicament of Private Life," in *Public and Private in Thought and Practice: Perspectives on a Grand Dichotomy* (Chicago: University of Chicago Press, 1997), 204–236; Colleen McDannell, *The Christian Home in Victorian America, 1840–1900* (Bloomington: Indiana University Press, 1986); Rybczynski, *Home: A Short History of An Idea.*

20. D. Benjamin Barros, "Home As a Legal Concept," *Santa Clara Law Review* 46, no. 1 (2006): 255–306; Justin Wilford, "Out of Rubble: Natural Disaster and the Materiality

of the House," *Environment and Planning D: Society and Space* 26, no. 4 (2008): 647–662.

21. Catharine Esther Beecher and Harriet Beecher Stowe, *The American Woman's Home* (New Brunswick: Rutgers University Press, 2002 [1869]).

22. Steve Bruce, *The Rise and Fall of the New Christian Right: Conservative Protestant Politics in America, 1978–1988* (New York: Oxford University Press, 1988); Harding, *Book of Jerry Falwell*; Lisa McGirr, *Suburban Warriors: The Origins of the New American Right* (Princeton, NJ: Princeton University Press, 2001).

23. Harding, *Book of Jerry Falwell*, chap. 6.

24. Warren, *Purpose Driven Church*, 182.

25. Ibid., 122.

26. Bill Hybels and Lynn Hybels, *Rediscovering the Church: The Story and the Vision of Willow Creek Community Church* (Grand Rapids: Zondervan, 1997), 8.

27. Interview with Steve Gladen, May 13, 2008.

28. For more on the individualization of worship at Saddleback, see chap. 4.

29. All of Saddleback's strategies can be located within the broader church-growth movement. Indeed, Warren's first major book, *The Purpose Driven Church*, is one of its landmark texts. For more on the contemporary church-growth movement see, Steve Brouwer, Paul Gifford, and Susan D. Rose, *Exporting the American Gospel: Global Christian Fundamentalism* (New York: Routledge, 1996), chap. 3; Mara Einstein, *Brands of Faith* (New York: Routledge, 2008); Erling Jorstad, *Popular Religion in America: The Evangelical Voice* (Westport, CT: Greenwood Press, 1993); Gary L. McIntosh, ed., *Evaluating the Church Growth Movement: Five Views* (Grand Rapids: Zondervan, 2004). For a paradigmatic example of the movement see Donald A. McGavran and C. Peter Wagner, *Understanding Church Growth* (Grand Rapids: W. B. Eerdmans, 1990).

30. Andy Stanley, North Point Community Church, "Foyer to Kitchen." Available at http://www.northpoint.org/adults/index/C54 (last accessed April 15, 2009).

31. See chap. 3 and also M. P. Baumgartner, *The Moral Order of a Suburb* (New York: Oxford University Press, 1988); Archer, *Architecture and Suburbia*, chap. 1.

32. Steve Gladen, *"Wired": 2008 Saddleback Small Group Conference Handbook* (Lake Forest, CA: Saddleback Valley Community Church, 2008), 20.

33. Ibid, 18–20.

34. Ibid., 18.

35. Pseudonyms are used to protect the subjects' identity and maintain privacy.

36. Stark and Finke, *Acts of Faith*, 155–159.

37. For a classic statement on how differentiation leads to both diversity and uniformity, see Louis Wirth, "Urbanism As a Way of Life," 15.

38. Berger, *Sacred Canopy*, chap. 6.

39. Chaves, "Secularization As Declining Religious Authority," 749–774.

NOTES TO CHAPTER 6

1. I could not detect common binary distinctions regarding Saddleback members' geographic location within the United States. The distinctions jumped scales between the urban region and the globe, implying that Saddleback members saw their suburban geographical identity as homologous with their national geographic identity. In other words, south Orange County, in effect, *is* the United States, for these postsuburbanites.

2. Cf. William E. Connolly, "The Evangelical-Capitalist Resonance Machine," *Political Theory* 33, no. 6 (2005): 869–886; Connolly, "The Christo-Capitalist Assemblage," *Theory, Culture and Society* 24, no. 7/8 (2007): 303–305.

3. Gallagher, *Evangelical Identity*; Marsden, *Fundamentalism and American Culture*, 239–243; Harding, *Book of Jerry Falwell*, 153–181.

4. David Neff, "Global Is the New Local: Princeton's Robert Wuthnow Says American Congregations Are More International Than Ever," *Christianity Today*, June 3, 2009, available online at http://www.ctlibrary.com/ct/2009/june/14.38.html (last accessed April 15, 2010).

5. Robert Wuthnow and Stephen Offutt, "Transnational Religious Connections," *Sociology of Religion* 69, no. 2 (2008): 218.

6. Ibid.

7. Such numbers belie the mixed feelings within American evangelicalism about short-term missions. While there is no shortage of enthusiastic praise for the STMs by evangelicals, they are just as often derided as "Christian tourism." See, e.g., J. J. Hanciles, "Beyond Christendom: African Migration and Transformations in Global Christianity," *Studies in world Christianity* 10, no. 1 (2004): 93–113; Christopher L. Heuertz, *Simple Spirituality: Learning to See God in a Broken World* (Downers Grove, IL: InterVarsity Press, 2008), 86; Craig Ott and Harold A. Netland, *Globalizing Theology: Belief and Practice in An Era of World Christianity* (Grand Rapids: Baker Academic, 2006.), 159.

8. This quote and the following quotes from Warren in this section (unless noted otherwise) are taken from a personal transcription of audio recording at the Purpose Driven Network Summit, May 22–24, 2008, at the Saddleback Church Campus, Lake Forest, California.

9. Marsden, *Fundamentalism and American Culture*, 85–93.

10. Rick Warren, "Global P.E.A.C.E. Announcement," sermon delivered at Saddleback Church, Lake Forest, CA (November 9, 2003).

11. Rick Warren, quoted in Timothy C. Morgan, "Purpose Driven in Rwanda." *Christianity Today*, September 23, 2005, available online at http://www.christianitytoday.com/ct/2005/october/17.32.html (last accessed April 15, 2010).

12. David van Biema, "The Global Ambition of Rick Warren," *Time Magazine*, August 18, 2008, 36.

13. Alan Wolfe, "A Purpose-driven Nation?" *Wall Street Journal*, August 26, 2005, W13.

14. Krista Tippett, "The New Evangelical Leaders, pt. 2: Rick and Kay Warren," *Speaking of Faith* (American Public Media) December 6, 2007, available online at http://speakingoffaith.publicradio.org/programs/warren/particulars.shtml (last accessed April 15, 2010).

15. Rick Warren, "Myths of the Modern Mega-Church," (a panel session sponsored by the *Pew Forum on Religion and Public Life*, Key West, FL, May 25, 2005) available online at http://pewforum.org/Christian/Evangelical-Protestant-Churches/Myths-of-the-Modern-Megachurch.aspx (last accessed April 15, 2010).

16. To "witness," in modern evangelical parlance, means to attempt to convert nonbelievers by telling one's personal religious narrative. In other words, it means to literally bear witness to non-Christians to the perceived effects of Christianity in one's life. See Randall Herbert Balmer, *Encyclopedia of Evangelicalism* (Waco, TX: Baylor University Press, 2004), 207.

17. John Rawls, *A Theory of Justice* (Cambridge, MA: Harvard University Press, 1971), 64–65.

18. For classic cultural representations see Richard Yates, *Revolutionary Road* (New York: Little, Brown and Company, 1961); Sloan Wilson, *The Man in the Gray Flannel Suit* (Cambridge, MA: Bentley, 1955). For aesthetic design rationales see Archer, *Architecture and Suburbia*. For empirical studies see Matthew D. Lassiter, *The Silent Majority: Suburban Politics in the Sunbelt South* (Princeton, NJ: Princeton University Press, 2006); Luhr, *Witnessing Suburbia*; McGirr, *Suburban Warriors*.

19. Bellah et al., *Habits of the Heart*, 32–54.

20. Cf. Jean Elshtain, "In Common Together: Unity, Diversity and Civic Virtue," in *Toward a Global Civil Society,* ed. Michael Walzer (New York: Berghahn Books, 1995), 77–98; Taylor, *Secular Age*, 473.

21. Bellah et al., *Habits of the Heart*, 32–39; Charles Taylor, *Sources of the Self: The Making of the Modern Identity* (New York: Cambridge University Press, 1992), chap. 21.

22. Warren, *Purpose Driven Church*, 370, 375.

23. This separation of method and goal is connected to an older Protestant tradition of a "Personal" vs. "General Calling." The well-known seventeenth-century Puritan clergyman, Cotton Mather, put it this way: "Every Christian hath a GENERAL CALLING; which is to Serve the Lord Jesus Christ, and Save his own Soul . . . But then, every Christian hath also a PERSONAL CALLING; or a certain *Particular Employment,* by which his *Usefulness,* in his Neighborhood, is distinguished . . . A Christian at his *Two Callings,* is a man in a Boat, Rowing for Heaven" (quoted in Micki McGee, *Self-Help, Inc.: Makeover Culture in American Life* (New York: Oxford University Press, 2005), 26–27, capitals and italics in original).

24. See also C. B. Macpherson, "Pluralism, Individualism, and Participation," *Economic and Industrial Democracy* 1 (1980): 25.

25. McGee, *Self-Help, Inc.*

26. Ulrich Beck, *Risk Society: Towards a New Modernity* (Thousand Oaks, CA: Sage, 1992), 135.

27. Archer, *Architecture and Suburbia*, 203.

28. Anthony Giddens, *Modernity and Self-Identity: Self and Society in the Late Modern Age* (Stanford: Stanford University Press, 1991), 172.

NOTES TO CHAPTER 7

1. For more on the discursive role of pollution in cultural binary codes, see Alexander, *Meanings of Social Life*, 6–9.

2. Saddleback Civil Forum on the Presidency, CNN transcript, italics added.

3. Miller, *Reinventing American Protestantism*, 171–172; Smith, *American Evangelicalism*, 45.

4. See Jeffrey K. Hadden and Charles E. Swann, *Prime Time Preachers: The Rising Power of Televangelism* (New York: Addison-Wesley, 1981); Justin Wilford, "Televangelical Publics: Secularized Publicity and Privacy in the Trinity Broadcasting Network," *Cultural Geographies* 16, no. 4 (2009): 505–524.

5. Saddleback has produced several events using the title "Civil Forum," the first being the Civil Forum on Holocaust Survivors. Since the Civil Forum on the Presidency there have been fora on "Leadership" (a friendly interview with George W. Bush in November 2008, months before he left office), "Reconciliation"

(with Rwandan president Paul Kagame), "Peace in a Globalized Economy" (with former British prime minister Tony Blair), "Global Health," and "Orphans and Adoption."

6. Connolly, "The Evangelical-Capitalist Resonance Machine," 869–886; Nigel Thrift, "Intensities of Feeling: Towards a Spatial Politics of Affect," *Geografiska Annaler* 86, no. 1 (2004): 57–78. Cf. Clive Barnett, "Political Affects in Public Space: Normative Blind-Spots in Non-Representational Ontologies," *Transactions of the Institute of British Geographers* 33, no. 2 (2008): 186–200.

7. All non-referenced quotes in this section are taken from a personal transcription of the Saddleback Civil Forum on the Holocaust, April 14, 2008.

8. One woman said she saw herself as spiritual but not religious, and another man was openly hostile to the notion of God.

9. CNN Election Center, July 25, 2008.

10. "Presumed Presidential Nominees McCain and Obama to Make First Joint Appearance on August 16 at Saddleback Church," press release by A. Larry Ross Communications, July 21, 2008.

11. This statement was repeated verbatim in interviews leading up to the event, at the weekly Saddleback Church staff meeting days before the event, at the beginning of the event, and then in nearly every press interview after the event.

12. For an overview of the main narrators of this story see Marsden, *Fundamentalism and American Culture,* and Harding, *Book of Jerry Falwell.* For classic statements see Jerry Falwell, *Listen, America!* (New York: Doubleday Books, 1981); Francis Schaefer, *How Then Should We Live?: The Rise and Decline of Western Thought and Culture* (Wheaton, IL: Crossway Books, 1983). See also James Dobson's Focus on the Family in analyses by Dan Gilgoff, *The Jesus Machine: How James Dobson, Focus on the Family, and Evangelical America Are Winning the Culture War* (New York: St. Martin's Press, 2007); Paul Apostolidis, *Stations of the Cross: Adorno and Christian Right Radio* (Durham, NC: Duke University, 2000).

13. Jean L. Cohen and Andrew Arato, *Civil Society and Political Theory* (Cambridge, MA: MIT Press, 1992); Craig J. Calhoun, *Habermas and the Public Sphere* (Cambridge, MA: MIT Press, 1992).

14. Rick Warren, "The most important election," email correspondence, October 30, 2004: available online at http://holycoast.blogspot.com/2004/10/letter-from-rick-warren-pastor-of.html (last accessed April 15, 2010).

15. See chap. 3, for the role scripts play in the enactment of cultural performances. I use "background script" in the same way that Jeffrey Alexander uses "script" in his cultural pragmatics. They are middle-range articulations between deep binary cultural codes and the fully articulated texts of performances. See also Alexander, "Cultural Pragmatics," 527–573; Alexander, *Meanings of Social Life*; Jeffrey C. Alexander and Jason L. Mast, "Symbolic Action in Theory and Practice: The Cultural Pragmatics of Symbolic Action," in Alexander, Giesen, and Mast, *Social Performance.*

16. "Evangelicals in Politics," *Talk of the Nation* (National Public Radio). November 9, 2004.

17. *The Newshour with Jim Lehrer,* November 3, 2004.

18. "Evangelicals in Politics," *Talk of the Nation* (National Public Radio), November 9, 2009.

19. *Larry King Live,* November 22, 2004.

20. Rick Warren, "Myths of the Modern Mega-Church," (a panel session sponsored by the *Pew Forum on Religion and Public Life*, Key West, FL, May 25, 2005) available online at http://pewforum.org/Christian/Evangelical-Protestant-Churches/Myths-of-the-Modern-Megachurch.aspx (last accessed April 15, 2010).

21. Wendy Kaminer, "Rick Warren: America's Pastor," *Nation* 281, no. 7 (2005): 30.

22. Brian MacQuarrie, "Pastor Rivets Many without Politics." *Boston Globe*, October 11, 2005, A1.

23. Hannah Rosin, "What's Up with the Christian Right?" *Slate.com*, November 3, 2006, available online at http://www.slate.com/id/2152890/ (last accessed April 15, 2010).

24. "Saddleback Church Civil Forum Inappropriate Campaign Event," press release for Atheists United, August 16, 2008, available online at http://www.atheistsunited.org/home/press-releases/51-saddleback-church-civil-forum-inapropriate-campaign-event (last accessed April 15, 2005); Barry W. Lynn, "Voters have heard enough about the presidential candidates and religion," blog post for Americans United for the Separation of Church and State, August 15, 2008, accessed online at http://www.au.org/site/News2?abbr=pr&page=NewsArticle&id=10005&security=1002&news_iv_ctrl=2882 (link no longer active).

25. DeWayne Wickham, "Next President Need not be the Vicar of Saddleback," *USA Today*, August 19, 2008: 13A; Frank Rich, "Last Call for Change We Can Believe In," *New York Times*, August 24, 2008: WK9.

26. For a sample see the blogs at *Homo Economicus*: http://homoeconomicusnet.word-press.com/2008/08/19/religion-is-private-yet-politically-expedient/
American Free Thought: http://www.americanfreethought.com/wordpress/2008/08/25/podcast-24-saddleback-forum/
The Nation: http://www.thenation.com/doc/20080901/oltman
Mother Jones: http://www.motherjones.com/mojoblog/archives/2008/08/9274_obama_mccain_christian_evangelicals_saddleback.html
People for the American Way: http://www.rightwingwatch.org/2008/08/warren_wows_the.html

27. Kathleen Parker, "Pastor Rick's Test: The Candidates Submit, and a Principle Suffers." *Washington Post*, August 20, 2008: A15.

28. Michelle Malkin, "The Pointless Rick Warren Presidential Forum," Michelle Malkin (blog), August 12, 2010, available online at http://michellemalkin.com/2008/08/12/the-pointless-rick-warren-presidential-forum/ (last accessed April 15, 2010).

29. Welton Gady, "One step forward, two steps back," *Progressive Revival* (Beliefnet.com blog), available online at http://blog.beliefnet.com/progressiverevival/2008/08/one-step-forward-two-steps-bac.html (last accessed April 15, 2010).

30. "Religion in the 2008 Presidential Campaign," *The Diane Rehm Show*, August 19, 2008, available at http://wamu.org/programs/dr/08/08/19.php#21029 (last accessed April 15, 2010).

31. The "cone of silence" controversy arose days after the event when it was discovered that McCain was not in seclusion, barred from media, or unable to hear or receive communication about the live event. Before the event Warren said that neither candidate would know what questions would be asked; the candidate who goes last, McCain in this case, would be in a "cone of silence," so he wouldn't have an unfair advantage of hearing the questions and his opponent's answers. While Obama was live on stage with Warren, it was reported that McCain was in a motorcade to the

event and also in an unsupervised room in the back of the auditorium. Although McCain almost certainly would have been able to receive communication about the questions and answers through cell phones or other handheld devices, Warren defended McCain for weeks after the event, saying that it was "impossible" for McCain to have received communication about the event.

32. Warren, *Purpose Driven Church*, 131.

33. This is not true of most evangelical pastors, or most Protestant pastors, because they can be easily dismissed by church boards of directors. Warren, famously, does not draw a salary from the church and gives 90 percent of his income from book sales and other activities to the church. This makes him the church's largest single source of income. Besides this the organizational structure of Saddleback is intentionally designed as a loose-knit patriarchy with Warren in unquestioned authority.

34. R. Stephen Warner, "Religion in the 'Burbs'" (interviewed by A. Tennet), *Christianity Today* 47, no. 7 (2003): 35.

35. Warren, "Myths of the Modern Megachurch."

36. Warren, *Purpose Driven Church*, 192.

37. Small groups at Saddleback are cells of roughly six to twelve members who meet regularly in one of the member's homes. They are considered to be "the backbone of everything else Saddleback does," according to Steve Gladen, the pastor of small groups at Saddleback. They are seen as a "way to make a big church small" and "close the back door of the church" by creating intimate communities of members. A weekly small group meeting typically consists of discussing personal issues of group members, prayer, and a short bible study or use of prepared small group materials. Saddleback claims to have more members attending small groups each week than the weekend service.

38. See Christian Smith's *American Evangelicalism* (188–190) for a very incisive account of the radical individualistic politics of American evangelicals. This individualist politics is part of the "personal influence strategy of social change," which holds that all socio-political change must come from individuals' acceptance of Christian salvation. This view leads to a deep pessimism in the usefulness of state politics and systemic change.

39. The original title of the sermon, announced in the July 21 press release was "Making Up Your Mind: Questions to Consider before the Election." Eerily similar to phrasing in the 2004 "non-negotiable issues" letter, this would have interested the few who remembered back that far. In that letter, just before listing the non-negotiable issues, Warren writes, "Here are five questions to ask when considering who to vote for in this election."

40. An argument could be made that the integrity portion of the sermon was a subtle endorsement of McCain over Obama because of the charges circulating at the time of Obama and his wife harboring secret political and religious commitments that they eschew in public settings. Such charges were part and parcel of the Jeremiah Wright and William Ayers stories and the secret-Muslim rumors as well. The other qualities of humility and generosity did not relate as clearly to contemporary mediatic narratives about the candidates.

41. Gottdiener, *Social Production of Urban Space*; Kling, Olin, and Poster, "The Emergence of Postsuburbia:" in *Postsuburban California*, 1–30; Knox, *Metroburbia*.

42. Graham and Marvin, *Splintering Urbanism*.

43. Olin, Poster, and Kling, eds., *Postsuburban California*. See also, McGirr, *Suburban Warriors*.
44. Debra Gold Hansen and Mary P. Ryan, "Public Ceremony in a Private Culture: Orange County Celebrates the Fourth of July," in Olin, Poster, and Kling, *Postsuburban California*, 165–190; Olin, "Intraclass Conflict and the Politics of a Fragmented Region," in Olin, Poster, and Kling, *Postsuburban California*, 223–254.
45. Archer, *Architecture and Suburbia*; Fishman, *Bourgeois Utopias*; Jackson, *Crabgrass Frontier*; Knox, *Metroburbia*; Low, *Behind the Gate*; Rybczynski, *Home: A Short History of An Idea*).
46. Brooks, *On Paradise Drive*.
47. Edward J. Blakely and Mary Gail Snyder, *Fortress America: Gated Communities in the United States* (Washington, DC: Brookings Institution Press, 1999).
48. Rick Warren and Dan Gilgoff. "Rick Warren on his Saddleback summit with McCain and Obama," Beliefnet.com, available online at http://www.beliefnet.com/News/Politics/2008/08/Rick-Warren-On-His-Saddleback-Summit-With-Mccain-And-Obama.aspx (last accessed April 15, 2010).
49. The award has since been given to Rwandan president Paul Kagame and former British prime minister Tony Blair, each at their own civil fora. The award "is given on behalf of the Global PEACE Coalition for outstanding contribution toward alleviating the five global giants recognized by the Coalition." See chap. 6 for a history and explanation of Saddleback's "P.E.A.C.E. Plan."
50. L. Ian MacDonald, "The U.S. Religious Forum Would Not Have Happened Here; The Separation of Church and State Is More Notional Than Real in the U.S." *Gazetter* (Montreal), August 20, 2008, A21.
51. Joel Carpenter, "Now What? Revivalist Christianity and Global South Politics," *Christianity Today*, March/April (2009), available online at http://www.booksandculture.com/articles/2009/marapr/16.34.html (last accessed April 15, 2010); Robert Wuthnow, *Boundless Faith: The Global Outreach of American Churches* (Berkeley: University of California Press, 2009).
52. However, Warren posts the transcript and audio of each sermon online the week after it is delivered so that other pastors can download and use them in their own services. I discovered several instances of pastors delivering Warren's postforum sermon, "The Type of Leader America Needs," in the weeks before the 2008 presidential election. See Coldspring Methodist Church in Coldspring, Texas (available at http://www.coldspringmethodist.org/uploads/11-02-08_Sermon.mp3), NorthPointe Church in Adairsville, Georgia (available at http://www.northpointechurch.com/11_02_08), and Hillside Church in Antioch, California (available at http://www.hillsidecares.org/sitebuildercontent/sitebuilderfiles/TheKindOfLeadershipAmericaNeeds.mp3) for two examples.

NOTES TO CHAPTER 8

1. Smith, *American Evangelicalism*; Robert Wuthnow, *After Heaven*; Bruce, *God Is Dead*, chap. 11.
2. See Catherine Bell, *Ritual: Perspectives and Dimensions* (New York: Oxford University Press, 1997) for the argument that "ritual as practice" is more apt than "ritual" because the latter recapitulates the Protestant critique of Catholicism, as well as reinforcing several problematic assumptions in ritual theory.

3. For the way ritual "focuses attention" see Jonathan Z. Smith, *To Take Place: Toward Theory in Ritual* (Chicago: University of Chicago Press, 1987), 104; for the way ritual creates environments and actors see Bell, *Ritual*, 81.

4. William E. Connolly, *Neuropolitics: Thinking, Culture, Speed* (Minneapolis: University of Minnesota Press, 2002); Connolly, "The Evangelical-Capitalist Resonance Machine," *Political Theory* 33, no. 6 (2005): 869–886; Connolly, *Capitalism and Christianity, American Style* (Durham, NC: Duke University Press, 2008); Wendy Brown, "American Nightmare: Neoliberalism, Neoconservatism, and De-Democratization," *Political Theory* 34, no. 6 (2006): 690–714; Linda Kintz, "Finding the Strength to Surrender: Marriage, Market Theocracy and the Spirit of America," *Theory, Culture and Society* 24, no. 4 (2007): 111–130.

5. van Biema, "The Global Ambition of Rick Warren," 36–42.

6. His emailed video in which he asks congregants to support Proposition 8 was sent a little more than one week before the election (October 23, 2008). It was one topic among four others, and a little over 300 words in a message of nearly 3,000 words. He claims in the message that he was prompted to speak out about it because he kept being asked what his church's stance on the issue was. In a message sent out two months later he said that he believes gay couples should have all the same rights and benefits of marriage but "I think gays should use another term for their consenting adult relationships and partnerships." More than five months later he told Larry King, "I am not an anti-gay or anti-gay marriage activist. I never have been, never will be. During the whole Proposition 8 thing, I never once went to a meeting, never once issued a statement, never—never once even gave an endorsement in the two years Prop 8 was going." ("Larry King Live," *CNN*, April 6, 2009).

7. Connolly, "The Christo-Capitalist Assemblage," 304.

BIBLIOGRAPHY

A. Larry Ross Communications: News Release. "Presumed Presidential Nominees McCain and Obama to Make First Joint Appearance on August 16 at Saddleback Church." July 21, 2008.

Agnew, John. "The Devaluation of Place in Social Science." In *The Power of Place: Bringing Together Geographical and Sociological Imaginations*, edited by John Agnew and James S. Duncan. Winchester, MA: Unwin Hyman, 1989.

Alexander, Jeffrey C. *Action and Its Environments: Toward a New Synthesis*. New York: Columbia University, 1988.

———. *The Civil Sphere*. New York: Oxford University, 2006.

———. "Differentiation Theory: Problems and Prospects." In *Differentiation Theory and Social Change: Comparative and Historical Perspectives*, edited by Jeffrey C. Alexander and Paul B. Colomy. New York: Columbia University Press, 1990.

———. *The Meanings of Social Life: A Cultural Sociology*. New York: Oxford University Press, 2003.

———. "Performing Cultural Sociology: A Conversation with Jeffrey Alexander." *European Journal of Social Theory* 11, no. 4 (2008): 525–542.

Alexander, Jeffrey C., and Jason L. Mast. "Symbolic Action in Theory and Practice: The Cultural Pragmatics of Symbolic Action." In *Social Performance: Symbolic Action, Cultural Pragmatics, and Ritual*, edited by Jeffrey C. Alexander, Bernhard Giesen, and Jason L. Mast. New York: Cambridge University Press, 2006.

Alexander, Jeffrey C., and Philip Smith, eds. *The Cambridge Companion to Durkheim*. New York: Cambridge University Press, 2005.

Apostolidis, Paul. *Stations of the Cross: Adorno and Christian Right Radio*. Durham, NC: Duke University, 2000.

Arato, Andrew, and Jean Cohen. "Civil Society and Social Theory." *Thesis Eleven* 21, no. 1 (1988).

Archer, John. *Architecture and Suburbia: From English Villa to American Dream House, 1690–2000*. Minneapolis: University of Minnesota Press, 2005.

———. "Colonial Suburbs in South Asia, 1700–1850, and the Spaces of Modernity." In *Visions of Suburbia*, edited by Roger Silverstone. New York: Routledge, 1997.

———. "Ideology and Aspiration: Individualism, the Middle-Class, and the Genesis of the Anglo-American Suburb." *Journal of Urban History* 14, no. 2 (1988): 214–253.

Ariès, Philippe. *Centuries of Childhood: A Social History of Family Life*. Translated by Robert Baldick. New York: Vintage Books, 1962.

Asad, Talal. *Formations of the Secular: Christianity, Islam, Modernity*. Stanford: Stanford University Press, 2003.

———. "The Trouble of Thinking: An Interview with Talal Asad." In *Powers of the Secular Modern: Tala Asad and His Interlocutors*, edited by David Scott and Charles Hirschkind. Stanford: Stanford University Press, 2006.

Astin, Howard. *Body and Cell*. Littleton, CO: Monarch, 2002.

Atheists United. "Saddleback Church Civil Forum Inappropriate Campaign Event." August 16, 2008. http://www.atheistsunited.org/home/press-releases/51-saddleback-church-civil-forum-inapropriate-campaign-event.

Ault, James M. *Spirit and Flesh: Life in a Fundamentalist Baptist Church*. New York: Alfred
A. Knopf, 2004.

Baker, Christopher. "Religious Faith in the Exurban Community: A Case Study of Christian
Faith-Communities in Milton Keynes." *City* 9, no. 1 (2005): 109–123.

———. "Seeking Hope in the Indifferent City—Faith-Based Contributions to Spaces of
Production and Meaning-Making in the Postsecular City." Paper presented at the annual
meeting of the Association of American Geographers. Boston, MA, April 17, 2008.

Balmer, Randall Herbert. *Encyclopedia of Evangelicalism*. Waco, TX: Baylor University Press,
2004.

———. *Mine Eyes Have Seen the Glory: A Journey Into the Evangelical Subculture in America*.
New York: Oxford University Press, 2006.

Barnett, Clive. "Political Affects in Public Space: Normative Blind-Spots in Non-Representational Ontologies." *Transactions of the Institute of British Geographers* 33, no. 2 (2008):
186–200.

Barros, D. Benjamin. "Home As a Legal Concept." *Santa Clara Law Review* 46, no. 1 (2006):
255–306.

Bauman, Zygmunt. *The Individualized Society*. Malden, MA: Blackwell, 2001.

Baumgartner, M. P. *The Moral Order of a Suburb*. New York: Oxford University Press, 1988.

Beaumont, Justin. "Introduction: Faith-Based Organizations and Urban Social Issues."
Urban Studies 45, no. 10 (2008): 2011–2017.

———. "Postsecular Urbanism and Social Justice." Paper presented at the annual meeting of
the Association of American Geographers. Boston, MA, April 17, 2008.

Bebbington, D. W. *Evangelicalism in Modern Britain: A History from the 1730S to the 1980s*.
Boston: Unwin Hyman, 1989.

Beck, Ulrich. *Risk Society: Towards a New Modernity*. Thousand Oaks, CA: Sage, 1992.

Beck, Ulrich, and Elisabeth Beck-Gernsheim. *Individualization: Institutionalized Individualism, and Its Social and Political Consequences*. Thousand Oaks, CA: Sage, 2002.

Beecher, Catharine Esther, and Harriet Beecher Stowe. *The American Woman's Home*. New
Brunswick, NJ: Rutgers University Press, 2002.

Bell, Catherine. *Ritual: Perspectives and Dimensions*. New York: Oxford University Press, 1997.

Bellah, Robert N., Richard Madsen, William M. Sullivan, Ann Swidler, and Steven M.
Tipton. *Habits of the Heart: Individualism and Commitment in American Life*. Berkeley:
University of California Press, 1985.

Benhabib, Seyla. "Democratic Iterations: The Local, the National, and the Global." In *Another
Cosmopolitanism*, edited by Robert Post. New York: Oxford University Press, 2006.

Berger , Peter L. "The Desecularization of the World: A Global Overview." In *The Desecularization of the World: Resurgent Religion and World Politics*, edited by Peter L Berger.
Grand Rapids: W. B. Eerdmans, 1999.

———. "An Interview with Peter Berger." *Hedgehog Review* 8 (2006): 152–162.

———. *The Noise of Solemn Assemblies: Christian Commitment and the Religious Establishment in America*. Garden City: Doubleday, 1961.

———. *The Sacred Canopy: Elements of a Sociological Theory of Religion*. New York: Doubleday, 1967.

Berube, Alan, Bruce Katz, and Robert E. Lang. *Redefining Urban and Suburban America:
Evidence From Census 2000*. Washington, DC: Brookings Institution Press, 2006.

Beuka, Robert. *Suburbianation: Reading Suburban Landscape in Twentieth-Century American Fiction and Film*. New York: Palgrave Macmillan, 2004.

Blakely, Edward J., and Mary Gail Snyder. *Fortress America: Gated Communities in the United States*. Washington, DC: Brookings Institution Press, 1999.

Bodin, Jean. *Colloquium of the Seven About Secrets of the Sublime*. Princeton: Princeton University Press, 1975.

Bowland, Terry A. *Make Disciples!: Reaching the Postmodern World for Christ*. Joplin, MO: College Press, 1999.

Brace, Catherine, Adrian R. Bailey, and David C. Harvey. "Religion, Place and Space: A Framework for Investigating Historical Geographies of Religious Identities and Communities." *Progress in Human Geography* 30, no. 1 (2006).

Breault, Kevin D. "New Evidence on Religious Pluralism, Urbanism, and Religious Participation." *American Sociological Review* 54 (1989): 1048–1053.

Brooks, David. *On Paradise Drive: How We Live Now (And Always Have) in the Future Tense*. New York: Simon and Schuster, 2004.

Brouwer, Steve, Paul Gifford, and Susan D. Rose. *Exporting the American Gospel: Global Christian Fundamentalism*. New York: Routledge, 1996.

Brown, Bill. "Thing Theory." *Critical Inquiry* 28, no. 1 (2001): 1–22.

Bruce, Steve. "The Charismatic Movement and the Secularization Thesis." *Religion* 28, no. 3 (1998): 223–232.

———. *Choice and Religion: A Critique of Rational Choice Theory*. New York: Oxford University Press, 1999.

———. *God Is Dead: Secularization in the West*. Malden, MA: Blackwell, 2002.

———. "Secularization and the Impotence of Individualized Religion." *Hedgehog Review* 8 (2006): 35–46.

Bruegmann, Robert. *Sprawl: A Compact History*. Chicago: University of Chicago, 2005.

Burgess, Ernest W. "The Growth of the City." In *The City*, edited by Robert E. Park, Ernest W. Burgess, and Roderick D. McKenzie. Chicago: University of Chicago Press, 1925.

Calhoun, Craig J. *Habermas and the Public Sphere*. Cambridge, MA: MIT Press, 1992.

Carpenter, Joel. "Now What? Revivalist Christianity and Global South Politics." *Christianity Today*, March/April, 2009.

Casanova, José. *Public Religions in the Modern World*. Chicago: University of Chicago Press, 1994.

Castells, Manuel. "European Cities, the Informational Society and the Global Economy." *New Left Review* 204, no. 3–4 (1994): 18–32.

———. *The Informational City: Information Technology, Economic Restructuring, and the Urban-Regional Process*. Malden, MA: Blackwell Publishers, 1989.

Chaves, Mark. "All Creatures Great and Small: Megachurches in Context." *Review of Religious Research* 47, no. 4 (2006): 329–346.

———. "Secularization As Declining Religious Authority." *Social Forces* 72, no. 3 (1994): 749–774.

Chaves, Mark, and Philip S. Gorski. "Religious Pluralism and Religious Participation." *Annual Review of Sociology* 27, no. 1 (2001): 261–281.

Chartier, Roger, ed. *History of Private Life: Passions of the Renaissance*. Translated by Arthur Goldhammer. Cambridge, MA: Belknap Press of Harvard University, 1989.

Chidester, David, and Edward Tabor Linenthal. Introduction to *American Sacred Space*, edited by David Chidester and Edward T. Linenthal. Bloomington: Indiana University Press, 1995.

Christiano, Kevin J. "Church As a Family Surrogate: Another Look at Family Ties, Anomie, and Church Involvement." *Journal for the Scientific Study of Religion* 25, no. 3 (1986): 339–354.

Cloke, Paul J. "Inter-Connecting Geo-Ethics and Radical Faith-Based Praxis in the Post-
Secular City." Paper presented at the annual meeting of the Association of American
Geographers. Boston, MA, April 17, 2008.

———. *Practicing Human Geography*. Thousand Oaks, CA: Sage, 2004.

Cloke, Paul, Sarah Johnsen, and Jon May. "Ethical Citizenship? Volunteers and the Ethics of
Providing Services for Homeless People." *Geoforum* 38, no. 6 (2007): 1089–1101.

———. "Exploring Ethos? Discourses of 'Charity' in the Provision of Emergency Services for
Homeless People." *Environment and Planning A* 37 (2005): 385–402.

CNN Election Center. "Politics of Faith: Interview with Pastor Rick Warren." July 25, 2008.

CNN Live Event. "Saddleback Presidential Candidates Forum." August 17, 2008.

Cohen, Jean L., and Andrew Arato. *Civil Society and Political Theory.* Cambridge, MA: MIT
Press, 1992.

Colomy, Paul. "Revisions and Progress in Differentiation Theory." In *Differentiation Theory
and Social Change: Comparative and Historical Perspectives*, edited by Jeffrey Alexander
and Paul Colomy. New York: Columbia University Press, 1990.

Comiskey, Joel. "Cell-based Ministry: A Positive Factor for Church Growth in Latin
America." PhD diss., Fuller Theological Seminary, Pasadena, CA, 1997.

Connell, John. "Hillsong: A Megachurch in the Sydney Suburbs." *Australian Geographer* 36,
no. 3 (2005): 315–332.

Connolly, William E. "The Christo-Capitalist Assemblage." *Theory, Culture and Society* 24,
no. 7/8 (2007): 303–305.

———. "The Evangelical-Capitalist Resonance Machine." *Political Theory* 33, no. 6 (2005):
869–886.

Cox, Harvey. *The Secular City: Secularization and Urbanization in Theological Perspective.*
New York: Macmillan, 1965.

Cresswell, Tim. *Place: A Short Introduction.* Malden, MA: Wiley-Blackwell, 2004.

Cronon, William. "Introduction: In Search of Nature." In *Uncommon Ground: Toward Reinventing Nature*, edited by William Cronon. New York: W. W. Norton, 1996.

Cross, Gary. "The Suburban Weekend: Perspectives on a Vanishing Twentieth-Century
Dream." In *Visions of Suburbia*, edited by Roger Silverstone. London: Routledge, 1997.

Dant, Tim. "Material Civilization: Things and Society," *British Journal of Sociology* 57, no. 2
(2006): 289–308.

Davis, Mike. *City of Quartz: Excavating the Future in Los Angeles.* New York: Verso, 1990.

Dear, Michael, and Steven Flusty. "Postmodern Urbanism." *Annals of the Association of
American Geographers* 88, no. 1 (1998): 50–72.

Diane Rehm Show. "Religion in the 2008 Presidential Campaign." August 19, 2008.

Dittmer, Jason, and Tristan Strum, eds. *Mapping the End Times: American Evangelical Geopolitics and Apocalyptic Visions.* Aldershot: Ashgate, 2010.

Dobbelaere, Karel. "Secularization: A Multi-Dimensional Concept." *Current Sociology* 29,
no. 2 (1981): 3–153.

———. "Towards An Integrated Perspective of the Processes Related to the Descriptive
Concept of Secularization." *Sociology of Religion* 60, no. 3 (1999): 229–247.

Dochuk, Darren. "'Praying for a Wicked City': Congregation, Community, and the Suburbanization of Fundamentalism." *Religion and American Culture* 13, no. 2 (2003): 167–203.

Douglass, H. Paul. *The Suburban Trend.* London: Century, 1925.

Dudley, Carl S., and David A. Roozen. *Faith Communities Today: A Report on Religion in the
United States Today.* Hartford, CT: Hartford Institute for Religion Research, 2001.

Duncan, James S., and Nancy G. Duncan. "Deep Suburban Irony: The Perils of Democracy in Westchester County, New York." In *Visions of Suburbia*, edited by Roger Silverstone. New York: Routledge, 1997.

Durkheim, Émile. *The Division of Labor in Society*. New York: Free Press, 1964.

———. *The Elementary Forms of Religious Life*. Translated by Carol Cosman. New York: Oxford University Press, 2001.

Dwyer, Claire. "'Where Are You From?': Young British Muslim Women and the Making of Home." In *Postcolonial Geographies, London: Continuum*, edited by Alison Blunt and Cheryl McEwan. New York: Continuum, 2002.

Eiesland, Nancy L. "Contending with a Giant: The Impact of a Megachurch on Exurban Religious Institutions." In *Contemporary American Religion: An Ethnographic Reader*, edited by Penny Edgell Becker and Nancy L Eiesland. Walnut Creek, CA: AltaMira Press, 1997.

———. *A Particular Place: Urban Restructuring and Religious Ecology in a Southern Exurb*. New Brunswick, NJ: Rutgers University Press, 2000.

Einstein, Mara. *Brands of Faith*. New York: Routledge, 2008.

Eisenstadt, S. N. "Social Change, Differentiation and Evolution." *American Sociological Review* 29, no. 3 (1964): 375–386.

Eliade, Mircea. *The Sacred and the Profane: The Nature of Religion*. New York: Harcourt, Brace and World, 1959.

Ellingson, Stephen. *The Megachurch and the Mainline: Remaking Religious Tradition in the Twenty-First Century*. Chicago: University of Chicago Press, 2007.

———. "The Rise of the Megachurch and Changes in Religious Culture: Review Article." *Sociology Compass* 3, no. 1 (2009): 16–30.

Elshtain, Jean. "In Common Together: Unity, Diversity, and Civic Virtue." In *Toward a Global Civil Society*. 2nd ed., edited by Michael Walzer. New York: Berghahn Books, 1995.

Emirbayer, Mustafa. "The Alexander School of Cultural Sociology." *Thesis Eleven* 79, no. 1 (2004): 5.

Entrikin, J. Nicholas. *The Betweenness of Place: Towards a Geography of Modernity*. Baltimore: Johns Hopkins University Press, 1991.

Falwell, Jerry. *Listen, America!* New York: Doubleday Books, 1981.

Ferguson, Dave, Jon Ferguson, and Eric Bramlett. *The Big Idea: Focus the Message, Multiply the Impact*. Grand Rapids: Zondervan, 2007.

Finke, Roger. "An Unsecular America." In *Religion and Modernization: Sociologists and Historians Debate the Secularization Thesis*, edited by Steve Bruce. New York: Oxford University Press, 1992.

Finke, Roger, and Rodney Stark. *The Churching of America, 1776–2005: Winners and Losers in Our Religious Economy*. New Brunswick, NJ: Rutgers University Press, 2005.

Fishman, Robert. *Bourgeois Utopias: The Rise and Fall of Suburbia*. New York: Basic Books, 1987.

Fitzgerald, Frances. "Come One, Come All." *New Yorker*, December 3, 2007.

Flory, Richard, and Donald E. Miller. *Finding Faith: The Spiritual Quest of the Post-Boomer Generation*. New Brunswick, NJ: Rutgers University Press, 2008.

Frank, David John, and John W. Meyer. "The Profusion of Individual Roles and Identities in the Postwar Period." *Sociological Theory* 20, no. 1 (2002): 86–105.

Friedan, Betty. *The Feminine Mystique*. New York: Norton, 1963.

Friedland, Roger, and Robert R. Alford. "Bringing Society Back In: Symbols, Practics, and Institutional Contradictions." In *The New Institutionalism in Organizational Analysis*, edited by Walter W. Powell and Paul DiMaggio. Chicago: University of Chicago Press, 1991.

Gady, Welton. "One Step Forward, Two Steps Back." *Beliefnet.com*. http://blog.beliefnet. com/progressiverevival/2008/08/one-step-forward-two-steps-bac.html.

Gallagher, Sally K. *Evangelical Identity and Gendered Family Life*. New Brunswick, NJ: Rutgers University Press, 2003.

Gans, Herbert J. "Urbanism and Suburbanism As Ways of Life." In *Modernity: Critical Concepts*. vol. 2, , edited by Malcolm Waters. New York: Routledge, 1999.

Garreau, Joel. *Edge City: Life on the New Frontier*. New York: Doubleday, 1991.

Gerhardt, Hannes. "Geopolitics, Ethics, and the Evangelicals' Commitment to Sudan." *Environment and Planning D: Society and Space* 26 (2008): 911–928.

Giddens, Anthony. *Modernity and Self-Identity: Self and Society in the Late Modern Age*. Reprint, Stanford: Stanford University Press, 1991.

Gilgoff, Dan. *The Jesus Machine: How James Dobson, Focus on the Family, and Evangelical America Are Winning the Culture War*. New York: St. Martin's Press, 2007.

Goetz, David L. *Death by Suburb: How to Keep the Suburbs from Killing Your Soul*. New York: HarperOne, 2007.

Goffman, Erving. *Interaction Ritual: Essays in Face-to-Face Behavior*. New Brunswick, NJ: Aldine Transaction, 2005 [1964].

Gokariksel, Banu, and Katharyne Mitchell. "Veiling, Secularism, and the Neoliberal Subject: National Narratives and Supranational Desires in Turkey and France." *Global Networks* 5, no. 2 (2005): 147–165.

Gottdiener, Mark. *Planned Sprawl: Private and Public Interests in Suburbia*. Beverly Hills, CA: Sage, 1977.

———. *The Social Production of Urban Space*. Austin: University of Texas Press, 1985.

Gottdiener, Mark, and George Kephart. "The Multinucleated Metropolitan Region: A Comparative Analysis." In *Postsuburban California: The Transformation of Orange County Since World War II*, edited by Spencer C. Olin, Mark Poster and Rob Kling. Berkeley: University of California Press, 1991.

Gourgouris, Stathis. "Detranscendentalizing the Secular." *Public Culture* 20, no. 3 (2008): 437.

Gökarıksel, Banu. "Beyond the Officially Sacred: Religion, Secularism, and the Body in the Production of Subjectivity." *Social and Cultural Geography* 10, no. 6 (2009).

Graham, Brian. "Contested Images of Place among Protestants in Northern Ireland." *Political Geography* 17, no. 2 (1998): 129–144.

Graham, Steven, and Simon Marvin. *Splintering Urbanism*. New York: Routledge, 2001.

Gross, Neil. "The Detraditionalization of Intimacy Reconsidered." *Sociological Theory* 23, no. 3 (2005): 286–311.

Grossman, Cathy Lynn. "Almost All Denominations Losing Ground, Survey Finds: Faith Is Shifting, Drifting or Vanishing Outright." *USA Today*, March 9, 2009, 1A.

———. "This Evangelist Has a 'Purpose.'" *USA Today*, July 21, 2003, 1D.

Hadaway, C. Kirk. *Facts on Growth: A New Look at the Dynamics of Growth and Decline in American Congregations Based on the Faith Communities Today 2005 National Survey of Congregations*. Hartford, CT: Faith Communities Today and CCSP, 2006.

Hadaway, C. Kirk, and Wade Clark Roof. "Those Who Stay Religious 'Nones' and Those Who Don't: A Research Note." *Journal for the Scientific Study of Religion* 18, no. 2 (1979): 194–200.

Hadden, Jeffrey K., and Charles E. Swann. *Prime Time Preachers: The Rising Power of Televangelism*. New York: Addison-Wesley, 1981.

Hall, Catherine. "Early Formation of Victorian Domestic Ideology." In *Fit Work for Women*, edited by Sandra Burman. New York: St. Martin's Press, 1979.

Hanciles, J. J. "Beyond Christendom: African Migration and Transformations in Global Christianity." *Studies in World Christianity* 10, no. 1 (2004): 93–113.

Hancock, Claire. "Spatialities of the Secular: Geographies of the Veil in France and Turkey." *European Journal of Women's Studies* 15, no. 3 (2008): .

Hansen, Debra Gold, and Mary P. Ryan. "Public Ceremony in a Private Culture: Orange County Celebrates the Fourth of July." In *Postsuburban California: The Transformation of Orange County Since World War II*, edited by Spencer C Olin, Mark Poster, and Rob Kling. Berkeley: University of California Press, 1991.

Harding, Sandra Friend. *The Book of Jerry Falwell: Fundamentalist Language and Politics*. Princeton: Princeton University Press, 2000.

Harvey, David. *Justice, Nature, and the Geography of Difference*. Oxford: Blackwell Publishers, 1996.

Hayden, Dolores. *A Field Guide to Sprawl* . Photography by Jim Wark. New York: W. W. Norton, 2004.

Helfand, Duke. "More People Say They Have No Religion." *Los Angeles Times*, March 10, 2009, A13.

Heuertz, Christopher L. *Simple Spirituality: Learning to See God in a Broken World*. Downers Grove, IL: InterVarsity Press, 2008.

Holloway, Julian. "Enchanted Spaces: The Séance, Affect, and Geographies of Religion." *Annals of the Association of American Geographers* 96, no. 1 (2006).

Holmes, Stephen, and Charles Larmore. "Translator's Introduction." In *The Differentiation of Society by Niklas Luhmann*. New York: Columbia University Press, 1982.

Howe, Nicolas. "Secular Iconoclasm: Purifying, Privatizing, and Profaning Public Faith." *Social and Cultural Geography* 10, no. 6 (2009): 639–656 .

———. "Thou Shalt Not Misinterpret: Landscape As Legal Performance." *Annals of the Association of American Geographers* 98, no. 2 (2008): 435–460.

Hsu, Albert Y. *The Suburban Christian: Finding Spiritual Vitality in the Land of Plenty*. Downers Grove, IL: InterVarsity, 2006.

Hunter, James Davison. *American Evangelicalism: Conservative Religion and the Quandary of Modernity*. New Brunswick, NJ: Rutgers University Press, 1983.

———. *Evangelicalism: The Coming Generation*. Chicago: University of Chicago Press, 1987.

Hybels, Bill, and Lynn Hybels. *Rediscovering the Church: The Story and the Vision of Willow Creek Community Church*. Grand Rapids: Zondervan, 1997.

Jackson, Kenneth T. *Crabgrass Frontier: The Suburbanization of the United States*. New York: Oxford University Press, 1985.

Jessop, Bob, Neil Brenner, and Martin Jones. "Theorizing Sociospatial Relations." *Environment and Planning D: Society and Space* 26, no. 4 (2008): 389–401.

Jones, Katherine T. "Scale As Epistemology." *Political Geography* 17, no. 1 (1998): 25–28.

Jorstad, Erling. *Popular Religion in America: The Evangelical Voice* . Westport, CT: Greenwood Press, 1993.

Kaminer, Wendy. "Rick Warren: America's Pastor." *Nation* 281, no. 7 (2005): 28.

Karlgaard, Rich. "Purpose Driven," *Forbes.com*. February 16, 2004 http://www.forbes.com/forbes/2004/0216/039.html.

Keats, John. *The Crack in the Picture Window.* New York: Houghton Mifflin, 1957.

Keane, Webb. "Semiotics and the Social Analysis of Material Things." *Language and Communication* 23 (2003): 409–425.

Kelley, Dean M. *Why Conservative Churches Are Growing: A Study in Sociology of Religion.* New York: Harper and Row, 1972.

Kling, Rob, Spencer C. Olin, and Mark Poster. "The Emergence of Postsuburbia: An Introduction." In *Postsuburban California: The Transformation of Orange County Since World War II,* edited by Spencer C. Olin, Mark Poster and Rob Kling. Berkeley: University of California Press, 1991.

Knappett, Carl. *Thinking through Material Culture: An Interdisciplinary Perspective.* Philadelphia: University of Pennsylvania Press, 2005.

Knippenberg, Hans. "The Political Geography of Religion: Historical State-Church Relations in Europe and Recent Challenges." *GeoJournal* 67, no. 4 (2006).

Knox, Paul L. *Metroburbia, USA.* New Brunswick, NJ: Rutgers University Press, 2008.

Kong, Lily. "Geography and Religion: Trends and Prospects." *Progress in Human Geography* 14, no. 3 (1990): 355–371.

———. "In Search of Permanent Homes: Singapore's House Churches and the Politics of Space." *Urban Studies* 39 (2002): 1573–1586.

———. "Mapping New Geographies of Religion: Politics and Poetics in Modernity." *Progress in Human Geography* 25, no. 2 (2001): 211–233.

———. "Negotiating Conceptions of 'Sacred Space': A Case Study of Religious Buildings in Singapore." *Transactions of the Institute of British Geographers* 18, no. 3 (1993): 342–358.

———. "Religion and Spaces of Technology: Constructing and Contesting Nation, Transnation, and Place." *Environment and Planning A* 38, no. 5 (2006): 903–918.

Korf, Benedikt. "Geography and Benedict XVI." *Area* 38, no. 3 (2006): 326–329.

Kosmin, Barry A., Egon Mayer, and Ariela Keysar. *American Religious Identification Survey.* New York: City University of New York Press, 2001.

Kosmin, Barry, and Ariela Keysar. *American Religious Identification Survey 2008.* Harford, CT: Trinity College, 2009.

Kumar, Krishan. "Home: Promise and Predicament of Private Life." In *Public and Private in Thought and Practice: Perspectives on a Grand Dichotomy.* Chicago: University of Chicago Press, 1997.

Lang, Robert. *Edgeless Cities: Exploring the Elusive Metropolis.* Washington, DC: Brookings Institution Press, 2003.

Lang, Robert, and Jennifer LeFurgy. *Boomburbs: The Rise of America's Accidental Cities.* Washington, DC: Brookings Institution Press, 2007.

Larry King Live. "Interview with Rick Warren." November 22, 2004.

Lassiter, Matthew D. *The Silent Majority: Suburban Politics in the Sunbelt South.* Princeton: Princeton University Press, 2006.

Lee, Shayne, and Phillip Luke Sinitiere. *Holy Mavericks: Evangelical Innovators and the Spiritual Marketplace.* New York: New York University Press, 2009.

Lefebvre, Henri. *The Production of Space.* Malden, MA: Blackwell, 1991.

———. "Space: Social Product and Use Value." In *Critical Sociology: European Perspectives.* New York: Irvington Publishers, 1979.

———. *The Urban Revolution.* Minneapolis: University of Minnesota Press, 2003.

Leitner, Helga, and Byron Miller. "Scale and the Limitations of Ontological Debate: A Commentary on Marston, Jones and Woodward." *Transactions of the Institute of British Geographers* 32, no. 1 (2007): 116–125.

Leitner, Helga, Eric Sheppard, and Kristin M. Sziarto. "The Spatialities of Contentious Politics." *Transactions of the Institute of British Geographers* 33, no. 2 (2008): 157–172.

Liebman, Robert C. "Mobilizing the Moral Majority." In *The New Christian Right: Mobilization and Legitimation,* edited by Robert C. Liebman and Robert Wuthnow. Hawthorne, NY: Aldine Transaction, 1983.

Long, Jimmy. *Emerging Hope: A Strategy for Reaching the Postmodern Generations*. Downers Grove, IL: InterVarsity Press, 2004.

Loveland, Anne C., and Otis B. Wheeler. *From Meetinghouse to Megachurch: A Material and Cultural History.* Columbia: University of Missouri Press, 2003.

Low, Setha. *Behind the Gates: Life, Security, and the Pursuit of Happiness in Fortress America.* Routledge: New York, 2003.

Luckmann, Thomas. *The Invisible Religion: The Problem of Religion in Modern Society.* New York: Macmillan, 1967.

Luhmann, Niklas. *The Differentiation of Society.* New York: Columbia University Press, 1982.

———. *Funktion Der Religion.* Frankfurt am Main: Suhrkamp, 1977.

———. "The Paradox of System Differentiation and the Evolution of Society." In *Differentiation Theory and Social Change: Comparative and Historical Perspectives,* edited by Jeffrey Alexander and Paul Colomy. New York: Columbia University Press, 1990.

Luhr, Eileen. *Witnessing Suburbia: Conservatives and Christian Youth Culture.* Berkeley: University of California Press, 2009.

MacDonald, L. Ian. "The U.S. Religious Forum Would Not Have Happened Here: The Separation of Church and State Is More Notional Than Real In the U.S." *Gazetter* (Montreal), August 20, 2008.

Macpherson, C. B. "Pluralism, Individualism, and Participation." *Economic and Industrial Democracy* 1 (1980): .

MacQuarrie, Brian. "Pastor Rivets Many without Politics." *Boston Globe*, October 11, 2005, A1.

Mahler, Jonathan. "The Soul of the New Exurb." *New York Times*, March 27, 2005, 37–38, 50, 54, 57.

Mahmood, Saba. "Is Critique Secular? A Symposium at UC Berkeley." *Public Culture* 20, no. 3 (2008): 447.

———. "Secular Imperatives?" *Public Culture* 20, no. 3 (2008): 461.

———. "Secularism, Hermeneutics, and Empire: The Politics of Islamic Reformation." *Public Culture* 18, no. 2 (2006): 323–347.

Malkin, Michelle. "The Pointless Rick Warren Presidential Forum." http://michellemalkin.com/2008/08/12/the-pointless-rick-warren-presidential-forum/.

Marsden, George M. *Fundamentalism and American Culture.* New York: Oxford University Press, 2006.

Marston, Sallie A., John Paul Jones, and Keith Woodward. "Human Geography Without Scale." *Transactions of the Institute of British Geographers* 30, no. 4 (2005).

Martin, David. "Does the Advance of Science Mean Secularisation?" *Scottish Journal of Theology* 61, no. 1 (2008): 51–63.

———. *A General Theory of Secularization.* Oxford: Basil Blackwell, 1978.

————. *On Secularization: Towards a Revised General Theory.* Burlington, VT: Ashgate, 2005.

Martin, Ron. "Editorial: Geography: Making a Difference in a Globalizing World." *Transactions of the Institute of British Geographers* 29, no. 2 (2004): 147–150.

Marty, Martin E. *Protestantism in the United States: Righteous Empire.* New York: Scribners, 1986.

Marx, Karl. "On the Jewish Question." In *The Marx-Engels Reader,* 2nd ed., edited by Robert C. Tucker. New York: Norton, 1978.

McDannell, Colleen. *The Christian Home in Victorian America, 1840–1900.* Bloomington: Indiana University Press, 1986.

McGavran, Donald A., and C. Peter Wagner. *Understanding Church Growth* . Grand Rapids: W. B. Eerdmans, 1990.

McGee, Micki. *Self-Help, Inc.: Makeover Culture in American Life.* New York: Oxford University Press, 2005.

McGirr, Lisa. *Suburban Warriors: The Origins of the New American Right.* Princeton: Princeton University Press, 2001.

McIntosh, Gary L., ed. *Evaluating the Church Growth Movement: Five Views,* edited by Gary L. McIntosh. Grand Rapids: Zondervan, 2004.

McRoberts, Omar M. *Streets of Glory: Church and Community in a Black Urban Neighborhood.* Chicago: University Of Chicago Press, 2003.

Meacham, Jon. "The End of Christian America." *Newsweek,* April 13, 2009.

Megoran, Nick. "Christianity and Political Geography: On Faith and Geopolitical Imagination." *Brandywine Review of Faith and International Affairs,* Fall (2004): 40–46.

Miller, Daniel. "Materiality: An Introduction." In *Materiality,* edited by Daniel Miller. Durham: Duke University Press, 2005.

————. *Material Culture and Mass Consumption.* New York: Blackwell, 1987.

Miller, Donald E. *Reinventing American Protestantism: Christianity in the New Millennium.* Berkeley: University of California Press, 1997.

Moore, Adam. "Rethinking Scale as a Geographical Category: From Analysis to Practice." *Progress in Human Geography,* 32, no. 2 (2007): 203–225.

Morgan, Timothy C. "Purpose Driven in Rwanda." *Christianity Today,* September 23, 2005.

Mullin, Robert Bruce, and Russell E. Richey. "Denominations and Denominationalism: An American Morphology." In *Reimagining Denominationalism: Interpretive Essays,* edited by Robert Bruce Mullin and Russell E. Richey. New York: Oxford University , 1994.

Mumford, Lewis. *The City in History: Its Origins, Its Transformations, and Its Prospects.* New York: Harcourt, Brace and World, 1961.

Musschenga, Albert W. "Introduction: The Many Faces of Individualism." In *The Many Faces of Individualism,* edited by Anton van Harskamp and Albert W. Musschenga. Sterling, VA: Peeters, 2001.

Münch, Richard. "Differentiation, Rationalization, Interpenetration: The Emergence of Modern Society." In *Differentiation Theory and Social Change: Comparative and Historical Perspectives,* edited by Jeffrey C. Alexander and Paul B. Colomy. New York: Columbia University Press, 1990.

Naylor, Simon, and James R Ryan. "The Mosque in the Suburbs: Negotiating Religion and Ethnicity in South London." *Social and Cultural Geography* 3, no. 1 (2002): 39–59.

Neff, David. "Global Is the New Local: Princeton's Robert Wuthnow Says American Congregations Are More International Than Ever." *Christianity Today,* June 3, 2009.

Nelson, Arthur C., and Thomas W. Sanchez. "Debunking the Exurban Myth: A Comparison of Suburban Households." *Housing Policy Debate* 10, no. 3 (1999): 689–710.

———. "Exurban and Suburban Households: A Departure From Traditional Location Theory?" *Journal of Housing Research* 8, no. 2 (1997): 249–275.

New Zealand Herald. "Losing faith in modern America." May 7, 2008, A1.

Newshour with Jim Lehrer. November 3, 2004.

Niebuhr, Gustav. "Where religion gets a big dose of shopping-mall culture." *New York Times,* April 16, 1995.

Nightline: ABC News. "Faith matters: a purpose driven strife," March 7, 2007

Noll, Mark A. *American Evangelical Christianity: An Introduction.* Malden, MA: Blackwell Publishers, 2001.

———. *The Rise of Evangelicalism: The Age of Edwards, Whitefield and the Wesleys.* Downers Grove, IL: InterVarsity Press, 2004.

Norris, Pippa, and Ronald Inglehart. *Sacred and Secular: Religion and Politics Worldwide.* New York: Cambridge University Press, 2004.

O'Rourke, P. J. "Stem Cell Sham." *Weekly Standard,* March 23, 2009.

Ogden, Greg. *Unfinished Business: Returning the Ministry to the People of God .* Grand Rapids: Zondervan, 2003.

Olin, Spencer C. "Intraclass Conflict and the Politics of a Fragmented Region." In *Postsuburban California: The Transformation of Orange County Since World War II,* edited by Spencer C. Olin, Mark Poster, and Rob Kling. Berkeley: University of California Press, 1991.

Olson, Daniel V.A. "Comment: Religious Pluralism in Contemporary U.S. Counties." *American Sociological Review* 63 (1998): 759–761.

Osaigbovo, Rebecca. *It's Not About You, It's About God.* Downers Grove, IL: InterVarsity Press, 2004.

Ott, Craig, and Harold A. Netland. *Globalizing Theology: Belief and Practice in An Era of World Christianity.* Grand Rapids: Baker Academic, 2006.

Pacione, Michael. "The Geography of Religious Affiliation in Scotland." *Professional Geographer* 57, no. 2 (2005): .

Park, Robert E. "The City: Suggestions for the Investigation of Human Behavior in the City Environment." *American Journal of Sociology* 20, no. 5 (1915): 577–612.

Parker, Kathleen. "Pastor Rick's test: the candidates submit, and a principle suffers." *Washington Post,* August 20, 2008.

Parsons, Talcott. *The Structure of Social Action.* New York: Free Press, 1968.

Pate, Ronald. "The Transformation of the Megachurch for the Common Good: De-Privatizing Personhood and Socializing Church Mission." In *Annual Meeting of the Association of American Geographers.* Boston, MA, April 17, 2008.

Patton, Michael Quinn, and Michael Quinn. *Qualitative Research and Evaluation Methods,* 3. Thousand Oaks, CA: Sage, 2002.

Peach, Ceri. "Social Geography: New Religions and Ethnoburbs—Contrasts with Cultural Geography." *Progress in Human Geography* 26, no. 2 (2002): 252–260.

Pew Forum on Religion and Public Life. "U.S. Religious Landscape Survey." Washington, DC: Pew Research Center, April 23, 2008. http://religions.pewforum.org/pdf/report-religious-landscape-study-full.pdf.

Proctor, James. "Introduction: Theorizing and Studying Religion." *Annals of the Association of American Geographers* 96, no. 1 (2006): 165–168.

Rawls, John. *A Theory of Justice*. Cambridge, MA: Harvard University Press, 1971.

Reynolds, Malvina. *Little Boxes*. Schroder Music Co. (ASCAP), 1962.

Rich, Frank. "Last Call for Change We Can Believe In." *New York Times*, August 24, 2008.

Riesman, David, Nathan Glazer, and Reuel Denney. *The Lonely Crowd*. New Haven: Yale University, 1961.

Roof, Wade Clark. "The Local-Cosmopolitan Orientation and Traditional Religious Commitment." *Sociological Analysis* 33, no. Spring (1972): 1–15.

———. *Spiritual Marketplace: Baby Boomers and the Remaking of American Religion*. Princeton: Princeton University Press, 1999.

———. "Traditional Religion in Contemporary Society: A Theory of Local-Cosmopolitan Plausibility." *American Sociological Review* 41, no. 2 (1976): 195–208.

Roof, Wade Clark, and Dean R. Hoge. "Church Involvement in America: Social Factors Affecting Membership and Participation." *Review of Religious Research* 21, no. 4 (1980): 405–426.

Rosin, Hannah. "What's Up with the Christian Right?" *Slate.Com*, November 3, 2006.

Rybczynski, Witold. *Home: A Short History of An Idea*. New York: Viking, 1986.

———. *Last Harvest: How a Cornfield Became New Daleville: Real Estate Development in America From George Washington to the Builders of the Twenty-First Century, and Why We Live in Houses Anyway*. New York: Scribner, 2007.

Sampson, Robert J. "'After-School' Chicago: Space and the City." *Urban Geography* 29, no. 2 (2008): 127–137.

Sargeant, Kimon Howland. *Seeker Churches: Promoting Traditional Religion in a Nontraditional Way*. New Brunswick: Rutgers University Press, 2000.

Schaeffer, Francis. *How Then Should We Live?: The Rise and Decline of Western Thought and Culture*. Wheaton, IL: Crossway Books, 1983.

Schuller, Robert H. *My Journey: From An Iowa Farm to a Cathedral of Dreams*. New York: HarperCollins, 2001.

Scott, Alan J. *Geography and Economy: Three Lectures*. New York: Oxford University Press, 2006.

———. *Global City-Regions: Trends, Theory, Policy*. New York: Oxford University Press, 2001.

Scott, Joan Wallach. *Parité!: Sexual Equality and the Crisis of French Universalism*. Chicago: University of Chicago Press, 2005.

Seybert, Jim. *Leadership Re:Vision*. Carol Stream, IL: Tyndale House Publishers, 2009.

Sharlet, Jeff. "Soldiers of Christ: Inside America's Most Powerful Megachurch with Pastor Ted Haggard." *Harper's Magazine*, May 2005.

Sheler, Jeffery L. *Believers: A Journey Into Evangelical America*. New York: Viking, 2006.

Shiner, Larry. "The Concept of Secularization in Empirical Research." *Journal for the Scientific Study of Religion* 6, no. 2 (1967): 207–220.

Shippey, Frederick Alexander. *Protestantism in Suburban Life*. New York: Abingdon Press, 1964.

Shorter, Edward. *The Making of the Modern Family*. New York: Basic Books, 1977.

Sies, Mary Corbin. "Toward a Performance Theory of the Suburban Ideal, 1877–1917." *Perspectives in Vernacular Architecture* 4 (1991): 197–207.

Smith, Christian. *American Evangelicalism: Embattled and Thriving*. Chicago: University of Chicago Press, 1998.

———. "Introduction: Rethinking the Secularization of American Public Life." In *The Secular Revolution: Power, Interests, and Conflict in the Secularization of American Public Life*, edited by Christian Smith. Berkeley: University of California Press, 2003.

Smith, Jonathan Z. *To Take Place: Toward Theory in Ritual*. Chicago: University of Chicago Press, 1987.

Soja, Edward W. *Postmetropolis: Critical Studies in Cities and Regions*. Cambridge, MA: Blackwell, 2000.

Sopher, David E. *Geography of Religions*. Englewood Cliffs, NJ: Prentice-Hall, 1967.

Stark, Rodney, and Roger Finke. *Acts of Faith: Explaining the Human Side of Religion*. Berkeley: University of California Press, 2000.

Stark, Rodney, and William Sims Bainbridge. *A Theory of Religion*. New York: Lang, 1987.

Stegall, Caleb. "Grand Illusions: Too Many Suburban Christians Are in the World—And Also of It. (Book Review)." *Christianity Today* 50, no. 7 (2006): 55–57.

Stump, Roger W. *Boundaries of Faith: Geographical Perspectives on Religious Fundamentalism*. New York: Rowman and Littlefield Publishers, 2000.

———. *The Geography of Religion: Faith, Place and Space*. New York: Rowman and Littlefield, 2008.

Surratt, Geof, Greg Ligon, and Warren Bird. *The Multi-Site Church Revolution*. Grand Rapids: Zondervan, 2006.

Talk of the Nation (National Public Radio). "Evangelicals in Politics." November 9, 2004.

Taves, Ann. "The Camp Meeting and the Paradoxes of Evangelical Protestant Ritual." In *Teaching Ritual*, edited by Catherine Bell. New York: Oxford University Press, 2007.

Taylor, Charles. *A Secular Age*. Cambridge, MA: Belknap Press of Harvard University, 2007.

———. *Sources of the Self: The Making of the Modern Identity*. New York: Cambridge University Press, 1992.

Thomas, George M., and Douglas S. Jardine. "Jesus and Self in Everyday Life: Individual Spirituality Through a Small Group in a Large Church." In *"I Come Away Stronger": How Small Groups Are Shaping American Religion*, edited by Robert Wuthnow. Grand Rapids: W. B. Eerdmans, 1994.

Thrift, Nigel. "Intensities of Feeling: Towards a Spatial Politics of Affect." *Geografiska Annaler* 86, no. 1 (2004): 57–58.

Thumma, Scott, and Warren Bird. "Megachurch Database." http://hirr.hartsem.edu/megachurch/database.html.(last accessed on November 12, 2011)

Thumma, Scott, and Dave Travis. *Beyond Megachurch Myths: What We Can Learn From America's Largest Churches*. San Francisco: Jossey-Bass, 2007.

Thumma, Scott, and Jim Petersen. "Goliaths in Our Midst: Megachurches in the ELCA." In *Lutherans Today: American Lutheran Identity in the Twenty-First Century*. Grand Rapids: W. B. Eerdmans, 2003.

Tippett, Krista. "The New Evangelical Leaders, pt 2: Rick and Kay Warren." *Speaking of Faith (American Public Media)*. December 6, 2007. http://speakingoffaith.publicradio.org/programs/warren/particulars.shtml.

de Tocqueville, Alexis. *Democracy in America*. New York: Bantam Books, 2000.

Tolley, Christopher. *Domestic Biography: The Legacy of Evangelicalism in Four Nineteenth-Century Families*. New York: Oxford University Press, 1997.

Urry, John. "The 'System' of Automobility." *Theory Culture Society* 21, no. 4–5 (2004). Valins, Oliver. "Institutionalised Religion: Sacred Texts and Jewish Spatial Practice." *Geoforum* 31, no. 4 (2000): 575–586.

van Biema, David. "The Global Ambition of Rick Warren." *Time*, August 18, 2008.

Veer, Peter van der. *Imperial Encounters: Religion and Modernity in India and Britain.* Princeton: Princeton University Press, 2001.

Vincent, Peter, and Barney Warf. "Eruvim: Talmudic Places in a Postmodern World." *Transactions of the Institute of British Geographers* 27, no. 1 (2002): 30–51.

Viola, Frank. *Reimagining Church: Pursuing the Dream of Organic Christianity* . Colorado Springs, CO: David C. Cook, 2008.

Voas, David, Alasdair Crockett, and Daniel V.A. Olson. "Religious Pluralism and Participation: Why Previous Research Is Wrong." *American Sociological Review* 67, no. 2 (2002): 212–230.

Walker, Richard A. "A Theory of Suburbanization: Capitalism and the Construction of Urban Space in the United States." In *Urbanization and Urban Planning in Capitalist Society,* edited by Michael Dear and Alan Scott. New York: Meuthen and Co., 1981.

Walker, Rob. "Godly Synergy: How a Religious Advice Book Is Filling More Pews . . . With More Book Buyers." *New York Times Magazine*, April 11, 2004.

Wallis, Roy, and Steve Bruce. "Secularization: The Orthodox Model." In *Religion and Modernization,* edited by Steve Bruce. New York: Oxford University, 1992.

Warner, Michael. "Speech and space." http://blogs.ssrc.org/tif/2009/11/27/speech-and-space/.

Warner, R. Stephen. "Enlisting Smelser's Theory of Ambivalence to Maintain Progress in Sociology of Religion's New Paradigm." In *Self, Social Structure, and Beliefs: Explorations in Sociology,* edited by Jeffrey C Alexander, Gary T Marx and Christine L Williams. Berkeley: University of California Press, 2004.

———. *New Wine in Old Wineskins: Evangelicals and Liberals in a Small-Town Church.* Berkeley: University of California Press, 1988.

———. "Religion in the 'Burbs'" (interviewed by A. Tennet), *Christianity Today* 47, no. 7 (2003): 34–35.

———. "Work in Progress Toward a New Paradigm for the Sociological Study of Religion in the United States." *American Journal of Sociology* 98, no. 5 (1993): 1044–1093.

Warren, Rick. "5 Non-Negotiables." October 30, 2004.

———. "Myths of the Modern Mega-Church." *Pew Forum on Religion and Public Life.* May 25, 2005. http://pewforum.org/Christian/Evangelical-Protestant-Churches/Myths-of-the-Modern-Megachurch.aspx.

———. *The Purpose Driven Church: Growth Without Compromising Your Message and Mission.* Grand Rapids: Zondervan, 1995.

———. *The Purpose-Driven Life: What on Earth Am I Here For?* Grand Rapids: Zondervan, 2002.

Warren, Rick, and Dan Gilgoff. "Rick Warren on his Saddleback summit with McCain and Obama." http://www.beliefnet.com/News/Politics/2008/08/Rick-Warren-On-His-Saddleback-Summit-With-Mccain-And-Obama.aspx.

Wells, Amos R. *The Ideal Adult Class in the Sunday-School.* New York: Pilgrim Press, 1912.

Whyte, William H. *The Organization Man.* New York: Simon and Schuster, 1956.

Wickham, DeWayne. "Next President Need Not Be the Vicar of Saddleback." *USA Today*, August 19, 2008, 13A.

Wilberforce, William. *A Practical View of the Prevailing Religious System of Professed Christians, in the Higher and Middle Classes in This Country: Contrasted with Real Christianity.* New York: Crocker and Brewster, 1829.

Wilford, Justin. "Out of Rubble: Natural Disaster and the Materiality of the House." *Environment and Planning D: Society and Space* 26, no. 4 (2008): 647–662.

———. "Televangelical Publics: Secularized Publicity and Privacy in the Trinity Broadcasting Network." *Cultural Geographies* 16, no. 4 (2009): 505–524.

Wilson, Bryan R. *Contemporary Transformations of Religion.* New York: Oxford University Press, 1976.

Wilson, Sloan. *The Man in the Gray Flannel Suit.* Cambridge, MA: Bentley, 1955.

Winter, Gibson. *The Suburban Captivity of the Churches: An Analysis of Protestant Responsibility in the Expanding Metropolis.* New York: Doubleday, 1961.

Wirth, Louis. "Urbanism As a Way of Life." *American Journal of Sociology* 44, no. 1 (1938): 1–24.

Wolfe, Alan. "A Purpose-driven Nation?" *Wall Street Journal,* August 26, 2005, W13.

Wood, James. "God in the Quad." *New Yorker,* August 31, 2009.

Wood, Richard L. *Faith in Action: Religion, Race, and Democratic Organizing in America.* Chicago: University of Chicago Press, 2002.

Woodward, Keith, John Paul Jones III, and Sallie A. Marston. "Downsizing Wal-Mart: A Reply to Prytherch." *Urban Geography* 29, no. 1 (2008): 78–84.

Wuthnow, Robert. *After Heaven: Spirituality in America Since the 1950s.* Berkeley: University of California Press, 1998.

———. *Boundless Faith: The Global Outreach of American Churches* . Berkeley: University of California Press, 2009.

Wuthnow, Robert, and Stephen Offutt. "Transnational Religious Connections." *Sociology of Religion* 69, no. 2 (2008): 209–232.

Yates, Richard. *Revolutionary Road.* New York: Little, Brown and Company, 1961.

INDEX

"5 Circles of Commitment," 13, 15, 19, 72, 80, 90–91, 148

abortion, 142, 143, 146
Alexander, Jeffrey, 4, 14, 31, 40, 45, 48–49, 68, 163

baptism, 1–2, 164–166
Berger, Peter L.: as a critic of secularization, 34; and "plausibility structures," 24, 91–92, 112–113, 163; and the "sacred canopy," 28–29, 34, 37–38, 163; and secularization theory, 27, 28–29, 92; and secular privatization, 32; and suburban churches, 59
Bright, Bill, and Campus Crusade for Christ International, 36, 182n76
Bruce, Steve, 25, 27–28, 30, 33, 38
Bush, George W., 142, 144, 158–159

Calvary Chapel, 7–8, 97
Campus Crusade for Christ International, 36–37
Chicago school of urban sociology, 61–63, 65–66, 91
Civil Forum on the Presidency: and Barack Obama, 39, 140, 157, 185n18; 197n40; and Civil Forum on Holocaust Survivors, 137–140; and civil society, 141–148, 156–158; and desecularization, 136–137; history of, 135–137; and secularization, 39
Clapham Saints, 56–60, 68–69, 95
cultural performance: cultural binaries, 48–49; cultural pragmatic theory of, 45–50; and de-fusion, 6, 13–14, 45–46, 166–168; and fusion, 48–49, 163, 166–168; and social differentiation, 45–46; spatiality

of, 50, 166–168
cultural pragmatics. *See* cultural performance

divorce, 73, 85, 108, 133, 168
Dobbelaere, Karl, 28, 35
Dobson, James, 142
domestic life: postdenominational evangelical, 103, 115–116, 124, 127–128, 163–164, 166–167; early modern suburban, 57, 60, 69, 95–96; and Saddleback's P.E.A.C.E. Program, 132; specialized spaces of, 46
Durkheim, Émile, 29, 47–48, 62, 172n6, 185n19

Evangelicalism: history, 8–9, 47, 56–60; culture of, 68–70
evangelism, 9, 47, 88, 108, 116, 122, 127, 175n26; 182n76; 185n21; and Civil Forum on the Presidency, 143, 148, 153–156, 159–161; and P.E.A.C.E. Project, 120–121, 190n11
exurbia. *See* postsuburbia

Falwell, Jerry, 7, 19, 37, 96, 115, 135, 141, 183n77
family. *See* domestic life
Fellowship of the Woodlands, 5
Fishman, Robert, 57–58, 60–61, 66–67, 97
Five Global Giants, 117–121, 128, 198n49
Five Purposes, 105–107

globalization, 114–115
Giddens, Anthony, 129
Goffman, Erving, 47–48

ABOUT THE AUTHOR

Justin G. Wilford is Visiting Lecturer in the Department of Geography at the University of California, Los Angeles, and Research Associate at the Center for Religion and Civic Culture at the University of Southern California.